T0189991

Computer Communications and Networks

Series editors
Prof. Jacek Rak
Gdansk University of Technology
Faculty of Electronics, Telecommunications and Informatics
Department of Computer Communications
Gdansk, Poland

Prof. A.J. Sammes
Cyber Security Centre
Faculty of Technology
De Montfort University
Leicester, UK

The **Computer Communications and Networks** series is a range of textbooks, monographs and handbooks. It sets out to provide students, researchers, and non-specialists alike with a sure grounding in current knowledge, together with comprehensible access to the latest developments in computer communications and networking.

Emphasis is placed on clear and explanatory styles that support a tutorial approach, so that even the most complex of topics is presented in a lucid and intelligible manner.

More information about this series at http://www.springer.com/series/4198

Zaigham Mahmood

Editor

Connected Environments for the Internet of Things

Challenges and Solutions

 Springer

Editor
Zaigham Mahmood
Debesis Education UK
University of Derby
Derby, UK

Shijiazhuang Tiedao University
Shijiazhuang Shi, China

ISSN 1617-7975   ISSN 2197-8433   (electronic)
Computer Communications and Networks
ISBN 978-3-319-88887-3   ISBN 978-3-319-70102-8   (eBook)
https://doi.org/10.1007/978-3-319-70102-8

Printed on acid-free paper

This Springer imprint is published by Springer Nature
The registered company is Springer International Publishing AG
The registered company address is: Gewerbestrasse 11, 6330 Cham, Switzerland

Dedication

My tenth publication was dedicated to my
parents. This twentieth book is also in memory
of my parents *Ghazi Ghulam Hussain
Bahadur* and *Mukhtar Begum* who spent the
prime of their life in fighting for the freedom
and independence of their motherland. At a
very young age, my father joined a paramilitary
organization with the mission to engage in
peaceful struggle to free the country from
foreign occupation. Although the struggle for
independence started many decades before
and various political parties participated in
many diverse ways towards it, there is one
event that stands out – it took place on 19
March 1940.

On this day, the organization my father
belonged to decided to stage a much more
decisive countrywide peaceful protest. The
government, fearing the shutdown of the
country, had already banned the gatherings,
but, on this day, supporters and the general
public were out in such huge numbers that the
army patrolling the streets received orders to
shoot to kill. Live bullets were fired: many

thousands were killed or injured and many more taken as political prisoners. That day, my father was leading a group of 313 men – totally unarmed – marching on the streets to oppose the ban on political activities. According to newspaper reports, more than 200 of this group were killed and many dozens injured; majority of the remaining were captured and tried in the courts. There were 13 freedom fighters who were sentenced to *political imprisonment for life* – my father was one of the 13. His organization honoured these brave men with the titles of *Ghazi* (survivor in the fight between right and wrong) and *Bahadur* (valiant).

This brutality by foreign occupiers and the massacre of the unarmed public on 19 March 1940 proved such a turning point in the struggle for independence that only 4 days later, on 23 March 1940, an all-party confederation passed a unanimous resolution demanding the *formation of an independent state*. Soon after, a declaration was signed to transfer power to the leading political parties. However, the process took another 7 years, and eventually the country achieved independence on 14 August 1947. On this day, all freedom fighters were released; my father also returned home *Ghazi* and victorious. My mother, a young girl at the time, was no less courageous in her struggles: she fully supported her husband's mission and raised a young daughter totally independently while my father was away.

Now that the independence was gained and the mission accomplished, my father devoted his time to engaging in the study of Oriental languages and theology, bringing up his family and serving the community as a social activist. *Achieve excellence … Make a difference*: my parents would constantly remind us. Looking back at their life now, I am proud to say that they were certainly most excellent in what they achieved and undoubtedly made a huge difference for the entire nation to remember. They are my heroes and inspiration in my life.

Zaigham Mahmood
14 August 2017

Preface

Overview

Internet of Things (IoT) is a dynamic global network of self-configuring smart objects that are embedded with connectivity protocols to enable collection and exchange of data with other similar objects. It suggests a vision of a connected world where smart devices, intelligent objects and web-based systems are autonomously linked via the Internet. This is now the vision of the *Internet of the Future* that has the potential to revolutionize pervasive computing. The underlying technologies and processes include distributed computing, big data analytics, artificial intelligence, machine learning, signal processing and communication protocols.

This vision of the connected world is already transforming our daily lives. With the employment of relevant technologies, IoT can result in living in self-governing smart cities, driving autonomous cars in the *Internet of Vehicles* scenario on smart roads and using smart devices of diverse varieties for human comfort and ease. IoT is also transforming the business sector where the growth potential is expected to be exponential. It is predicted that there will be 20 to 50 billion connected objects by the year 2020.

Notwithstanding the benefits that connected digital world brings, success of the IoT paradigm is dependent on the network architectures, system capabilities, communication protocols and ubiquitous computing technologies to support the effective and reliable physical and cyber interconnections. Since IOT presents a heterogeneous environment where devices from various vendors follow different communication protocols and utilize diverse technologies, varying data formats and processing mechanisms hinder the smooth interoperability between connected devices. Lack of ubiquitous interoperability between devices is therefore a major concern. Since seamless connectivity and interoperability are prerequisites in multi-network heterogeneous distributed environments, achieving reliable and resilient connectivity is vitally important. Also, the increasing sophistication of *objects* is beginning to impact on regulatory compliance which, in turn, raises additional issues with respect to service availability, reliability, security and device communication. A major challenge that the IoT ecosystem must also overcome is the risks resulting from legal issues and performance problems caused by the mass deployment of inefficient, insecure and/or defective devices within the IoT. So, benefits of the IoT paradigm are numerous; issues and limitations are also many.

With this background, there is an urgent need for properly integrated solutions taking into account data and device security, signalling and device detection, device and data management, communication protocols and platforms, network bandwidth and topology, seamless connectivity and interoperability and worldwide regulations and legal compliance.

In this context, this book, *Connected Environments for the IoT: Challenges and Solutions*, aims to capture the state of the art on the current advances in the connectivity of diverse devices in a distributed computing environment. Majority of contributions in this volume focus on various aspects of device connectivity including communication, security, privacy, interoperability, networking, access control and authentication. Thirty-two researchers and practitioners of international repute have presented latest research developments, frameworks and methodologies, current trends, state-of-the-art reports, case studies and suggestions for further understanding, development and enhancement of the IoT vision.

Objectives

The aim of this volume is to present and discuss the state of the art in terms of frameworks, methodologies, challenges and solutions for connected environments. The core objectives include:

- Capturing the state-of-the-art research and practice with respect to the issues and limitation of connected environments
- Presenting case studies illustrating challenges, best practices and practical solutions
- Discussing corporate analysis and a balanced view of benefits and inherent limitations
- Developing a complete reference for students, researchers and practitioners of distributed computing
- Identifying further research directions and technologies in this area

Organization

There are 13 chapters in *Connected Environments for the IoT: Challenges and Solutions*. These are organized in three parts, as follows:

- **Part I**: *Challenges and Solutions*. This section has a focus on issues, limitations and solutions relating to connectivity of IoT devices. There are five chapters. In the first contribution, the emphasis is on security of IoT-enabled smart services in relation to enterprise information systems. The second chapter also discusses the security and privacy relating to connected environments but in general terms. The third contribution presents challenges pertaining to the management of big data in the context of IoT environments. The next chapter in the section suggests solutions to the issues and barriers inherent in the IoT paradigm through the use of cloud computing technologies. The last contribution discusses the service-level interoperability problems and solutions relating to the IoT environment.

- **Part II**: *Methods and Frameworks*. This part of the book comprises four chapters that focus on frameworks and latest methodologies. The first chapter presents a mobile IoT simulator called MobIoTSim to evaluate the behaviour of IoT systems and to develop IoT-based cloud applications. The next contribution presents a novel approach to manage hyper-connectivity in IoT through connectors that are equipped with variability capability; the approach is illustrated with a case study. The third contribution illustrates the use of the Essence Framework to model software development methods and proposes a practice library for the development of IoT-based systems. The fourth chapter presents a vision of specific smart city domains to benefit from integration of buildings information with live data.
- **Part III**: *Advances and Latest Research*. There are four chapters in this section that focus on future and ongoing research. The first chapter proposes an asymmetric schema-matching mechanism to illustrate the impact of coupling, adaptability and changeability on interoperability of devices. The second contribution explores the challenges of automatic provenance capture at the middleware level in various different contexts including the MapReduce framework. The next chapter in the section has a focus on emerging network topologies and communication technologies presenting the relevant inherent issues, possible solutions and future directions. The final contribution proposes the adoption of Data Distribution Service as a middleware platform for IoT systems and distributed computing environments.

Target Audiences

The current volume is a reference text aimed at supporting a number of potential audiences, including the following:

- *Communication engineers* and *network security specialists* who wish to adopt the newer approaches to ensure the security of data and devices for seamless connectivity
- *Students and lecturers* who have an interest in further enhancing the knowledge of technologies, mechanisms and frameworks relevant to the IoT environment from a distributed computing perspective

- *Researchers* in this field who require up-to-date knowledge of the current practices, mechanisms, frameworks and limitations relevant to the IoT vision to further enhance the connectivity between heterogeneous devices

Derby, UK   Zaigham Mahmood
Hebei, China

Acknowledgements

I acknowledge the help and support of the following colleagues during the review, development and editing phases of this text:

- Prof. Zhengxu Zhao, Shijiazhuang Tiedao University, Hebei, China
- Dr. Alfredo Cuzzocrea, University of Trieste, Trieste, Italy
- Dr. Emre Erturk, Eastern Institute of Technology, New Zealand
- Prof. Jing He, Kennesaw State University, Kennesaw, GA, USA
- Josip Lorincz, FESB-Split, University of Split, Croatia
- Aleksandar Milić, University of Belgrade, Serbia
- Prof. Sulata Mitra, Indian Institute of Engineering Science and Technology, Shibpur, India
- Dr. S. Parthasarathy, Thiagarajar College of Engineering, Tamil Nadu, India
- Daniel Pop, Institute e-Austria Timisoara, West University of Timisoara, Romania
- Dr. Pethuru Raj, IBM Cloud Center of Excellence, Bangalore, India
- Dr. Muthu Ramachandran, Leeds Beckett University, Leeds, UK
- Dr. Lucio Agostinho Rocha, State University of Campinas, Brazil
- Dr. Saqib Saeed, University of Dammam, Saudi Arabia
- Prof. Claudio Sartori, University of Bologna, Bologna, Italy
- Dr. Mahmood Shah, University of Central Lancashire, Preston, UK
- Dr. Fareeha Zafar, GC University, Lahore, Pakistan

I would also like to thank the contributors to this book: 32 authors and co-authors, from academia as well as industry from around the world, who collectively submitted 13 chapters. Without their efforts in developing quality contributions, conforming to the guidelines and meeting often the strict deadlines, this text would not have been possible.

Grateful thanks are also due to the members of my family – Rehana, Zoya, Imran, Hanya, Arif and Ozair – for their continued support and encouragement.

Every good wish, also, for the youngest in our family: Eyaad Imran Rashid Khan and Zayb-un-Nisa Khan.

Debesis Education, Derby, UK   Zaigham Mahmood
Shijiazhuang Tiedao University, Hebei, China
14 August 2017

Other Springer Books by Zaigham Mahmood

Data Science and Big Data Computing: Frameworks and Methodologies
This reference text has a focus on data science and provides practical guidance on big data analytics. Expert perspectives are provided by an authoritative collection of 36 researchers and practitioners, discussing latest developments and emerging trends, presenting frameworks and innovative methodologies and suggesting best practices for efficient and effective data analytics. ISBN: 978-3-319-31859-2

Connectivity Frameworks for Smart Devices: The Internet of Things from a Distributed Computing Perspective
This is an authoritative reference that focuses on the latest developments on the Internet of Things. It presents state of the art on the current advances in the connectivity of diverse devices and focuses on the communication, security, privacy, access control and authentication aspects of the device connectivity in distributed environments. ISBN: 978-3-319-33122-5

Software Project Management for Distributed Computing: Life-Cycle Methods for Developing Scalable and Reliable Tools
This unique volume explores cutting-edge management approaches to developing complex software that is efficient, scalable, sustainable and suitable for distributed environments. Emphasis is on the use of the latest software technologies and frameworks for life-cycle methods, including design, implementation and testing stages of software development. ISBN: 978-3319-543246

Cloud Computing: Methods and Practical Approaches
The benefits associated with cloud computing are enormous; yet the dynamic, virtualized and multi-tenant nature of the cloud environment presents many challenges. To help tackle these, this volume provides illuminating viewpoints and case studies to present current research and best practices on approaches and technologies for the emerging cloud paradigm. ISBN: 978-1-4471-5106-7

Cloud Computing: Challenges, Limitations and R&D Solutions
This reference text reviews the challenging issues that present barriers to greater implementation of the cloud computing paradigm, together with the latest research

into developing potential solutions. This book presents case studies and analysis of the implications of the cloud paradigm, from a diverse selection of researchers and practitioners of international repute. ISBN: 978-3-319-10529-1

Continued Rise of the Cloud: Advances and Trends in Cloud Computing

This reference volume presents latest research and trends in cloud-related technologies, infrastructure and architecture. Contributed by expert researchers and practitioners in the field, this book presents discussions on current advances and practical approaches including guidance and case studies on the provision of cloud-based services and frameworks. ISBN: 978-1-4471-6451-7

Software Engineering Frameworks for the Cloud Computing Paradigm

This is an authoritative reference that presents the latest research on software development approaches suitable for distributed computing environments. Contributed by researchers and practitioners of international repute, the book offers practical guidance on enterprise-wide software deployment in the cloud environment. Case studies are also presented. ISBN: 978-1-4471-5030-5

Cloud Computing for Enterprise Architectures

This reference text, aimed at system architects and business managers, examines the cloud paradigm from the perspective of enterprise architectures. It introduces fundamental concepts, discusses principles and explores frameworks for the adoption of cloud computing. The book explores the inherent challenges and presents future directions for further research. ISBN: 978-1-4471-2235-7

Requirements Engineering for Service and Cloud Computing

This text aims to present and discuss the state of the art in terms of methodologies, trends and future directions for requirements engineering for the service and cloud computing paradigm. Majority of the contributions in the book focus on requirements elicitation, requirements specifications, requirements classification and requirements validation and evaluation. ISBN: 978-3319513096

User Centric E-Government: Challenges and Opportunities

This text presents a citizens-focused approach to the development and implementation of electronic government. The focus is twofold: discussion on challenges of service availability and e-service operability on diverse smart devices, as well as on opportunities for the provision of open, responsive and transparent functioning of world governments. ISBN: 978-3319594415

Contents

Contributors

Rishav Agarwal Indian Institute of Technology, Guwahati, Assam, India

Darko Andročec Department of Information Systems Development, Faculty of Organization and Informatics, University of Zagreb, Varaždin, Croatia

P. Beaulah Soundarabai Department of Computer Science, Christ University, Bangalore, India

Turgay Çelik OPSGENIE, Ankara, Turkey

Anu Mary Chacko National Institute of Technology Calicut, Kozhikode, Kerala, India

Pethuru Raj Chelliah Reliance Jio Cloud, Bangalore, India

Alfredo Cuzzocrea University of Trieste and ICAR-CNR, Trieste, Italy

Abhishek Das Tripura University (A Central University), Agartala, India

José Carlos Martins Delgado Instituto Superior Técnico, Universidade de Lisboa, Porto Salvo, Portugal

Ali H. Dogru Department of Computer Engineering, Middle East Technical University, Ankara, Turkey

Marta Fidrich Software Engineering Department, University of Szeged, Szeged, Hungary

Bogdan Ghilic-Micu Department of Economic Informatics and Cybernetics, The Bucharest University of Economic Studies, Bucharest, Romania

Görkem Giray Independent Researcher, Izmir, Turkey

Markus Helfert Lero – The Irish Software Research Centre, School of Computing, Dublin City University, Dublin, Ireland

Jaswinder Kaur Curtin University, Perth, Australia

Muhammed Cagri Kaya Department of Computer Engineering, Middle East Technical University, Ankara, Turkey

Attila Kertesz Software Engineering Department, University of Szeged, Szeged, Hungary

Ömer Köksal Information Technology Group, Wageningen University, Wageningen, The Netherlands

S.D. Madhu Kumar National Institute of Technology Calicut, Kozhikode, Kerala, India

Marinela Mircea Department of Economic Informatics and Cybernetics, The Bucharest University of Economic Studies, Bucharest, Romania

Tamas Pflanzner Software Engineering Department, University of Szeged, Szeged, Hungary

Vidyasagar Potdar Curtin University, Perth, Australia

Zohreh Pourzolfaghar Lero – The Irish Software Research Centre, School of Computing, Dublin City University, Dublin, Ireland

Mahdi Saeedi Nikoo Department of Computer Engineering, Middle East Technical University, Ankara, Turkey

Marian Stoica Department of Economic Informatics and Cybernetics, The Bucharest University of Economic Studies, Bucharest, Romania

Parthasarathy Sudhaman Department of Computer Applications, Thiagarajar College of Engineering, Madurai, Tamil Nadu, India

Selma Suloglu Sosoft Information Technologies, Ankara, Turkey

Bedir Tekinerdogan Information Technology Group, Wageningen University, Wageningen, The Netherlands

Chandrakumar Thangavel Department of Computer Applications, Thiagarajar College of Engineering, Madurai, Tamil Nadu, India

Eray Tüzün Technology and Academy Directorate, Havelsan, Ankara, Turkey

V. Vijayaraghavan Infosys Limited, Bangalore, India

Pornpit Wongthongtham Curtin University, Perth, Australia

About the Editor

Prof. Dr. Zaigham Mahmood Professor Mahmood is a published author of 21 books, 6 of which are dedicated to electronic government and the other 15 focus on the subjects of cloud computing, data science, big data, Internet of Things, smart cities, project management and software engineering, including the textbook *Cloud Computing: Concepts, Technology & Architecture* which is also published in Korean and Chinese languages. Additionally, he is developing two new books to appear later in 2018. He has also published more than 100 articles and book chapters and organized numerous conference tracks and workshops.

Professor Mahmood is the editor-in-chief of the *Journal of E-Government Studies and Best Practices* as well as the series editor-in-chief of the IGI book series on *E-Government and Digital Divide.* He is a senior technology consultant at Debesis Education in the UK and a professor at Shijiazhuang Tiedao University in Hebei, China. He further holds positions as foreign professor at NUST and IIU in Islamabad, Pakistan. He has served as a reader (associated professor) at the University of Derby, UK, and professor extraordinaire at the North-West University, Potchefstroom, South Africa. Professor Mahmood is also a certified cloud computing instructor and a regular speaker at international conferences devoted to cloud computing and e-government. His specialized areas of research include distributed computing, project management and e-government.

Part I
Challenges and Solutions

Chapter 1
Security Challenges in the IoT Paradigm for Enterprise Information Systems

Chandrakumar Thangavel and Parthasarathy Sudhaman

Abstract A complex system has a large number of design variables, and decision-making requires real-time data collected from machines, processes, and diverse business environments. In this context, enterprise information systems (EISs) are used to support data acquisition, data analytics, communication, and related decision-making activities. Therefore, information technology infrastructure for data acquisition and sharing affects the performance of an EIS greatly. Our objective in the present work is to investigate the impact of security in the Internet of Things (IoT) paradigm for enterprise information systems. The breakthrough potential of the IoT conjures up immense possibilities for delivering value through new business models across industries, products, and service offerings. However, making IoT technologies reliable and secure is the key to realizing the potential of this breakthrough concept. Ensuring security and privacy of the IoT offerings is therefore a major concern for users and businesses. This chapter explores the potential of IoT-enabled smart services in EISs. It identifies security and privacy concerns for a variety of scenarios and discusses ways to address these concerns effectively.

1.1 Introduction

Internet of Things (IoT) is characterized by heterogeneous technologies, which concur to the provisioning of innovative services in various application domains [1]. Nowadays, the concept of IoT is multidimensional. It embraces many different technologies, services, and standards, and it is widely perceived as the angular stone of the ICT market in the next 10 years or so, at least [2–4]. The IoT is an extension of the Internet [5]. It gives an immediate access to information about physical objects and leads to innovative services with high efficiency and productivity [6]. Of course, this high level of heterogeneity, coupled with the wide scale and variety of

C. Thangavel (✉) • P. Sudhaman
Department of Computer Applications, Thiagarajar College of Engineering,
Madurai, Tamil Nadu, India
e-mail: t.chandrakumar@gmail.com

© Springer International Publishing AG 2017
Z. Mahmood (ed.), *Connected Environments for the Internet of Things*,
Computer Communications and Networks,
https://doi.org/10.1007/978-3-319-70102-8_1

IoT systems, is expected to magnify security threats of the current Internet, which is being increasingly used to allow interaction between humans, machines, and robots, in any combination [1]. The Internet of Things is an emerging global Internet-based information architecture facilitating the exchange of goods and services in global supply chain networks [7].

With reference to security, data anonymity, confidentiality, and integrity need to be guaranteed, as well as the authentication and authorization mechanisms in order to prevent unauthorized users (i.e., humans and devices) to access the systems. Whereas concerning the privacy requirement, both data protection and users' personal information confidentiality have to be ensured, since devices may manage sensitive information (e.g., user habits) [8] [9]. Finally, trust is a fundamental issue since the IoT environment is characterized by different devices which have to process and handle the data in compliance with user needs and rights [10] [11].

The Internet of Things, an emerging global Internet-based technical architecture facilitating the exchange of goods and services in global supply chain networks has an impact on the security and privacy of the involved stakeholders. Measures ensuring the architecture's resilience to attacks, data authentication, access control, and client privacy need to be established [7]. A recent study by the McKinsey Global Institute estimates that the IoT will have a potential economic impact of \$3.9tn–\$11.1tn per year by 2025 across nine settings – homes, offices, factories, retail environments, worksites, human health, outside environments, cities, and vehicles [12]. According to a recent survey by the SANS Institute covering organizations of all sizes, 66% of respondents are either currently involved in or are planning to implement IoT applications involving consumer devices, such as smartphones, smart watches, and other wearables. Smart buildings systems are increasingly being implemented as operations management systems get connected to networks. The IoT holds much promise for the energy, utilities, medical devices, and transport sectors, which will see the highest levels of adoption in the near term, according to SANS, as well as smart buildings. Unquestionably, the main strength of the IoT idea is the high impact it will have on several aspects of everyday life and behavior of potential users.

From the point of view of a private user, the most obvious effects of the IoT introduction are visible in both working and domestic fields. In this context, assisted living, e-health, and enhanced learning are only a few examples of possible application scenarios in which the new paradigm will play a leading role in the near future [13]. The wide adoption of computer numerical control (CNC) and industrial robots made flexible manufacturing systems (FMSs) feasible; the technologies for computer-aided design (CAD), computer-aided manufacturing (CAM), and computer-aided processing planning (CAPP) made computer-integrated manufacturing (CIM) practical. In developing their EISs, more and more enterprises rely on the professional providers of IT software service to replace or advance their conventional systems [14]. Primary functions of an EIS are (1) to acquire static and dynamic data from objects, (2) to analyze data based on computer models, and (3) to plan and control a system and optimize system performances using the processed data. The implementation of a manufacturing system paradigm relies heavily on available IT [15].

In the rest of this chapter, we first outline the concepts and technical background of the IoT and the IoT infrastructure for enterprises. We then discuss the varied IoT application areas in Sect. 1.2 and IoT security issues and challenges in Sect. 1.3. In Sect. 1.4, we provide a discussion on solving the IoT security challenges in enterprise information systems. Finally, Sect. 1.5 presents a brief summary.

1.2   The Internet of Things: An Overview

1.2.1   Concept and Technical Background

The Internet of Things (IoT) is an emerging global Internet-based information architecture facilitating the exchange of goods and services in global supply chain networks [12]. For example, the lack of certain goods would automatically be reported to the provider which in turn immediately causes electronic or physical delivery. The basic idea of this concept is the pervasive presence around us of a variety of things or objects – such as radio-frequency identification (RFID) tags, sensors, actuators, mobile phones, etc. – which, through unique addressing schemes, are able to interact with each other and cooperate with their neighbors to reach common goals [13]. From a technical point of view, the architecture is based on data communication tools, primarily the RFID-tagged items (radio-frequency identification) [16]. The IoT [17] has the purpose of providing an IT infrastructure facilitating the exchanges of "things" in a secure and reliable manner. A survey conducted by Atzori [18] gives a picture of the current state of the art on the IoT. More specifically:

- It provides the readers with a description of the different visions of the Internet of Things paradigm coming from different scientific communities.
- It reviews the enabling technologies and illustrates which are the major benefits of spread of this paradigm in everyday life.
- It offers an analysis of the major research issues the scientific community still has to face.

The Internet of Things (IoT) provides new functionalities to improve the quality of life and enables technological advances in critical areas. These include personalized healthcare, emergency response, traffic management, smart manufacturing, defense, home security, and smart energy distribution and utilization. New digital business models utilize the power of information to replace traditional products with innovative solutions and services leveraging IoT devices. Gartner's "Hype Cycle for Emerging Technologies, 2015" [19] shows that the IoT is at the "peak of inflated expectations"[2] and on the cusp of a multiyear, multifold growth. In 2020, 25 billion connected "things" will be in use [20]. This growth prospect is fueled by continuous reduction in the cost of computing power and the adoption of IPv6 technology.

In communication technologies, the transition from IPv4 to IPv6 technology promises unprecedented opportunity to interconnect existing as well as new services in utilities, healthcare, education, and other businesses over the Internet, due to the availability of more than two billion unique IP addresses. This is an important aspect to realize the "smart life" dream where cities will be provisioned with real-time data analytics and decision support systems. However, IoT-enabled smart services are not yet fully secure, and this is a key challenge. There are notable privacy concerns around data gathered from user-owned devices as well as the surrounding environment or other devices [21].

1.2.2 IoT Infrastructure for Enterprises

The aforementioned discussion has shown that IoT is aligned well with the architecture of a manufacturing enterprise. An enterprise model consists of a set of modular components and their interactions. Correspondingly, each system component in an EIS needs an information unit to make decisions on the component's behaviors based on the acquired data. Moreover, data acquisition, communication, and decision-making are essential functions for each module. Based on the axiomatic theory, the IoT is able to provide vital solutions to planning, scheduling, and controlling of manufacturing systems at all levels [15].

The features of next-generation enterprise are now discussed to evaluate if an IoT-based EIS is capable of meeting these challenging requirements.

Decentralized Decision-Making
Domains and levels of manufacturing activities are increasing and becoming diversified. Hierarchical architecture is used to the most efficient enterprise architecture for system integration. However, system complexity can be increased exponentially with the system scale and dynamics. A centralized system may lead to a significant time delay and inflexibility to respond changes promptly. Therefore, distributed and decentralized architecture would be effective means to deal with system complexity and dynamics.

Flat and Dynamic Organization
Prompt responses to uncertainties require distributed and decentralized enterprise architecture. In such a way, acquired data can be directly used for decision-making in real time. As far as the interactions among system components are concerned, it forms the challenges to distribute the information to associated components, in particular under a centralized structure. The data are collected and sent to the center database, and then it is sent to an object when the system receives the request from this object. However, a centralized model has its challenges in dealing with massive data and the heterogeneity of environment.

- **Massive data**: From the perspective of data management, information systems for next-generation manufacturing enterprises are facing two situations: (1) the cost for decision-making unit is likely increasing with system complexity and the need of fast responsiveness, and (2) it causes resources redundant to maintain data locally and the wastes of time and resources for communications when the data are shared by other decision-making units.

- **Heterogeneous environment**: Increased and diversified manufacturing resources have increased the heterogeneous nature of a manufacturing environment. The variety exists at the aspects of personalized products, geographical distribution, cultures, suppliers, regulations, optional operations, and standards.
- **Agility and adaptability for real-time changes**: Manufacturing enterprises are functioned to meet customers' needs, including functionalities, quantity, quantity, delivery time, and changes. The enterprises must be capable of dealing with changes at reasonable time and making products available as early as possible to catch the market niche. Without such a capability, the profit margin will be reduced significantly.
- **Reconfigurable capabilities**: To increase system flexibility, the structures of hardware and software systems are not static anymore. A system at a certain time can be decomposed into subsystems, and these subsystems can be reconfigured as manufacturing resources for other tasks. Extra system components are required to support hardware and software system configurations. System configurability or modularization decides the interoperability, which is extremely important in the globalized market.

1.2.3   IoT Application Areas

An important area that significantly benefits from the IoT is healthcare. Connected healthcare offers immense possibilities including remote monitoring of patients with critical ailments such as diabetes, cardiac issues, and kidney malfunction. This enables healthcare organizations and governments to capture and analyze population health data to identify potential health hazards at an early stage and take pre-emptive actions. In the future, smart retail solutions will provide cashless buying options, eliminating the need for point of sales (POS) counters. User preference data collected by IoT sensors attached to display zones and dressing areas at retail outlets can be utilized by retailers to track fast-moving items. Retailers can also use this data to replace less preferred items with popular items, driving faster, and increased sales. IoT will also promote smart agriculture, characterized by temperature control of warehouses, dashboard-based monitoring of inventory, and predictive analysis of usage and stock replenishment. Furthermore, factories can become more energy efficient by leveraging IoT-enabled manufacturing to analyze the usage and performance data gathered from sensors attached to machines. Data gathered on plant floors is analyzed to provide just-in-time information to floor managers, increasing supply chain efficiency and reducing material wastage and power utilization. Figure 1.1 shows what people search for on Google, what people talk about on Twitter, and what people write about on LinkedIn. The highest score received a

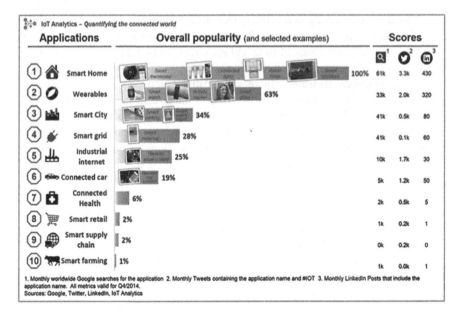

Fig. 1.1 The Internet of Things application ranking

rating of 100%; the other Internet of Things applications were ranked with a percentage that represents the relation to the highest score (relative ranking).

IoT-Enabled Smart Cities

With more and more people moving to cities and continuous growth in urban population, providing basic services to the increasing number of citizens is becoming a huge challenge for city councils. To meet the needs of the growing population, cities are expanding exponentially and stretching the operational limits of various services. In such a scenario, cities driven by IoT-enabled smart services can significantly improve the standard of living. By leveraging the IoT, a connected environment of interdependent systems can be built, enhancing all aspects of city life. This can be achieved by embedding IoT technologies in all types of physical objects and artifacts ranging from clothes, home appliances, and automobiles to street lighting systems, transport systems, public utilities, and even the human body. In a smart city, the IoT-enabled digital fabric of interdependent systems will be dynamic in nature, with instantaneous data gathering and near real-time analytics. This will help city councils strategize necessary actions and ensure effective governance based on continuous analysis of the huge volume of data collected from subsystems. The insights thus gained can help manage energy efficiency of buildings, map social data for crime prevention, monitor flood or drought situations, and drive public consultation and trend analysis. Other areas of application include infrastructure development across housing, education, transport, medical services, employment, and so on [22].

Smart Healthcare Systems
IoT-enabled healthcare services enable remote monitoring of patients with diabetes, kidney malfunction, heart problems, and more. This is possible through direct, round-the-clock data exchange between devices like pacemakers and glucose monitors implanted in patients' bodies and health monitoring systems in hospitals. Now, in the event of these devices being breached or the data obtained from them being unauthenticated, patients' lives are at risk.

Smart Billing and Payment Systems
In a retail outlet, IoT sensors are used to tally the purchases in a customer's cart. This means customers do not need to stand in the queue for checkout and billing, with sensors sending the data to a cloud-based billing and payment systems. Customers can pay the bill through a payment app on their smartphones.

Smart Home Security Systems
IoT-enabled home security solutions and temperature control systems use sensors to collect and share data from multiple edge devices. If an attacker gains access to these smart systems through malicious means, the underlying functional logic of control systems is vulnerable to misuse, compromising the physical security of residents.

Proximity Marketing
IoT has led to the advent of proximity marketing using Bluetooth-enabled beacons. Billboards embedded with beacons that include IoT sensors [23] identify interested customers in their vicinity. By activating an app on customer smartphones, relevant data is gathered by sensors and sent to the cloud for analytical processing. Based on the information and insights gathered, personalized marketing content is sent back. For example, Apple leverages iBeacons [24] to allow smartphones, tablets, and other devices to perform actions like determining the location of a person with an iOS device and providing information about nearby retail outlets, coffee shops, or multiplexes, and Facebook [25] makes recommendations on places to visit, things to do, and so on.

Smart Vending Machines
Smart vending machines allow customers to choose products from the display; during which, customer details are obtained through their smartphones by a near-field communication (NFC) smartphone payment system fitted to the vending machine. Merchants can use this data to improve stock replenishment, perform health checks on vending machines, and identify popular products.

1.3   Security Challenges in the IoT

The Internet of Things (IoT) is already starting to give rise to real-world applications, from connected homes and cars to health monitoring and smart utility meters. The Internet of Things (IoT) is finally here in 2017, and companies like Google and

Amazon are rushing to get out and become the main company to become the hub of this revolutionary concept. There have been multiple predictions over the years which declare that there will be at least tens of billions connected devices by 2020. The fundamental security weakness of the Internet of Things is that it increases the number of devices behind your network's firewall. In the development of any IoT application, security and testing frameworks play an important role.

IoT Infrastructure for Enterprises

An enterprise model consists of a set of modular components and their interactions. Correspondingly, each system component in an ES needs an information unit to make decisions on the component's behaviors based on the acquired data. Moreover, data acquisition, communication, and decision-making are essential functions for each module. Figure 1.2 illustrates the relations between the components in a manufacturing enterprise and the architecture of IoT. Based on the axiomatic theory, the IoT is able to provide vital solutions to planning, scheduling, and controlling of manufacturing systems at all levels. The manufacturing industries are hardly on our "first rodeo" in regard to how to properly address many of the security issues surrounding the use of Ethernet networks and IP-based protocols in manufacturing networks and applications. Ethernet-based automation systems work was starting in the 1980s, and since then, multiple industrial network protocols have evolved to run over standard Internet Protocol (IP) and UDP communications stacks – Modbus TCP/IP, PROFINET, EtherNet/IP CIP, FOUNDATION HSE, etc. Communications

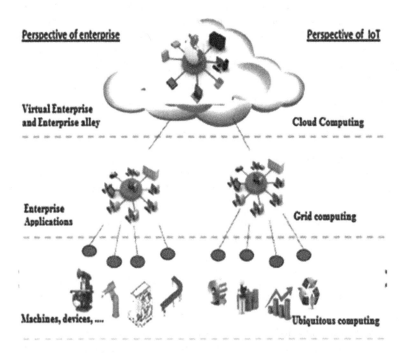

Fig. 1.2 IoT for manufacturing enterprise

between controllers/PLCs and workstation/server applications have evolved from slow serial ports to using high-speed Ethernet networks that commonly run the aforementioned protocols and OPC/OPC UA. Manufacturing Operations Management (MOM) applications like MES (Manufacturing Execution Systems), EMI (Enterprise Manufacturing Intelligence), APM (Asset Performance Management), and others are all typically networked via standard Ethernet networks to automation systems and enterprise business systems for information integration purposes.

All of this pervasive Ethernet/IP networking has resulted in many best practices that have been established for different security aspects such as network and virtual LAN segmentation, firewalls and selective port openings, user and application authentication, intrusion detection, antivirus, malware, security patching, and application software roles and privileges..

The Internet of Things offers countless new opportunities. The definition of IoT security is similar to that of mobile security which includes the protection of personal and business information that is stored, collected, and transmitted from devices connected to the Internet [26]. In recent years, cyber threats have grown exponentially in both quantity and volume [27]. Security breaches and cyber heists are happening all around us, and the authors of research papers do not expect that to change. This can and should be frightening to both the companies and the users. There are significant emerging security issues in IoT applications, networks, and devices/equipment, which could have major impacts on many industries and products [28]. Our personal lives are rapidly becoming more convenient, more mobile, and more digital. While the IoT holds much promise, many security issues have been uncovered. Owing to the wide range of sectors involved and their impact on everyday life, such security issues can have serious consequences, causing damage and disruption to operations or, in some scenarios, even loss of life. In a smart building – where systems ranging from HVAC (heating, ventilation, and air conditioning), lighting, and door access controls to video surveillance and elevators are all interconnected – a security threat that is exploited to disrupt power or lighting could cause loss of life if it were something like a hospital. In office buildings, a door access control that is hacked could provide an intruder with unauthorized access. Issues with the IoT devices are far from hypothetical: one example of a threat is the Stuxnet worm, which has been seen to be able to disrupt industrial control systems, causing extensive damage. A range of security risks have been uncovered in the devices themselves that make up the IoT. OWASP has identified the top 10 such issues involved with IoT devices [29]:

- Insecure web interfaces
- Insufficient authorization/authentication
- Insecure network services
- Lack of transport encryption
- Privacy concerns
- Insecure cloud interface
- Insecure mobile interface

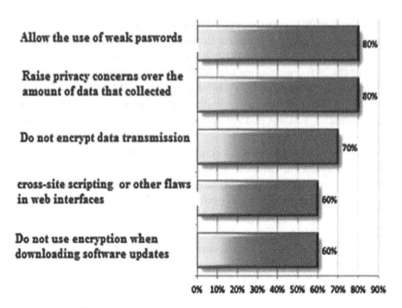

Fig. 1.3 Device-level IoT security vulnerabilities

- Insufficient security configurability
- Insecure software
- Poor physical security

This is echoed by recent research undertaken by HP Fortify, the findings of which are shown in Fig. 1.3. Overall, it found that 70% of the most commonly used IoT devices contain security vulnerabilities and there is an average of 25 security concerns per device.

Although the IoT offers tremendous opportunities for smart services across sectors, it is not completely secure or risk-free. In fact, the landscape becomes complex due to the vast network of IoT devices and interconnected systems that are required to realize the numerous benefits of smart services. The scale and complexity of IoT-enabled services make the implementation of traditional security techniques fairly complex. There are unique access control challenges (specifically for wireless sensor devices that can store energy for just about a few weeks to a month) and memory limitations (permissible upper limits being a few kilobytes) that restrict the communication and processing capabilities of these devices to run complex encryption algorithms. These issues are further compounded by the distributed nature of the IoT device network, which is vital to create a system that provides context aware services. In addition, non-trusted entities can physically or remotely intercept and manipulate data captured by IoT sensor nodes. Data transmission from sensors and gateway devices can be passively monitored in the absence of robust encryption, and malicious nodes can be embedded in wireless sensor networks to interfere with neighboring nodes. Privacy is another pressing concern. Personally identifiable information (PII) can be gathered from gateway devices without consent and can be used to conduct unscrupulous activities.

Looking at the IoT security through a more technical lens, the issues can be analyzed by utilizing preexisting IT security frameworks and expanding them to include IoT. Other more technical approaches take aim at what security procedures and techniques should be implemented when developing these devices. First, a secure boot must be performed each time the device is turned on or activated. This is most likely done through proper cryptography methods. Next, proper authentication is essential through the use of strong passwords (at minimum) or better yet the use of X.509, an encryption authenticator, or Kerberos, another method of properly verifying the user [30]. Once the device and the user have been authenticated, secure communication must occur by the transmission of the data through secure encryption channels (SSH or SSL) [30]. When done right, encryption can be extremely secure; however, there are many older forms of encryption that are less secure but popular to implement because of their simplicity. Finally, protection against cyber-attacks and intrusion detection mechanisms must also be done through the use of firewalls that limit communication to only known, trusted hosts (IBM, 2015) and, additionally, embedding a device designed to detect and report invalid log-in attempts and other malicious activities [30]. Last, but not least, the US Federal Trade Commission (FTC) notes that only basic, static security approaches cannot adequately secure an IoT device. It recommends that all devices be designed with continuous security procedure updates in mind, as security problems and solutions are always evolving [31]. So what are some of the new security challenges that get presented with billions of new smart devices being interconnected in the world of the IoT? To start with, smart industrial devices run much smaller footprints of computing power and operating systems. They may be installed once, and the software in them may never be updated or patched. This presents new technical challenges, as the devices will need to be highly secure by design and impervious to virus or denial of service attacks.

If IoT devices are to meet their full intelligence potential, then they will have the ability to be self-communicating between each other and with other computing devices, controllers, and software applications. It sounds good that anything can communicate to anything or anyone on an "as-needed" basis, but the reality is that this needs to be properly managed for practical and security reasons.

IoT devices may or may not participate in larger/centralized security domains (e.g., Active Directory) in order to operate; therefore, the concept of multiple distributed security domains will likely emerge for groupings of IoT devices and be another new security management consideration.

1.4   Solving the Security Challenges of Enterprise Architectures

IoT devices will need to intercommunicate with existing controllers, automation and manufacturing information networks, and applications. Therefore, existing security policies and approaches will need to be adapted to embrace these new IoT security challenges. In what follows, we propose the ways, mapped to five key dimensions, to address security concerns in an IoT setup:

- **Secure booting** – the authenticity and integrity of software on a device should be verified via a digital signature attached to the software image and verified by the device to ensure that it has been authorized to run on that device and that there are no runtime threats or malicious exploits present. Only then will it be allowed to load.
- **Access control** – mandatory or role-based access controls should be built into the operating system. If compromise of any component is detected, access to other parts of the system should be minimized as much as possible. This will help to minimize the effectiveness of any breach of security.
- **Device authentication** – a device should authenticate itself at the point at which it is plugged into the network, prior to receiving or transmitting data. Machine authentication only allows a device to access a network based on credentials that are stored in a secure storage area.
- **Firewalling and IPS** – each device needs to have a firewall or deep packet inspection capability for controlling traffic, but this requires that protocols are needed to identify malicious payloads hiding on non-IT protocols. And these protocols need to be industry specific since, for example, smart energy grids have their own set of protocols governing how devices talk to each other.
- **Updates and patches** – the ability to deliver software updates and patches to thousands of devices in a way that conserves limited bandwidth and intermittent connectivity of embedded devices, while ensuring that there is no possibility of functional safety being compromised, is a necessity

It is unlikely that security will become an overarching requirement in the design process any time soon. There are also standards that need to be developed before this happens, and it is also likely that some form of regulation or specific industry pressure will be required in order to force manufacturers to place the necessary emphasis on security. Organizations should look to limit what is allowed in the workplace, considering the risks versus the benefits, and look at how systems are interconnected and therefore how risks such as malware infections can be spread.

Organizations also need to find a way to enforce data protection policies on all devices in use and to control what data people can access. Identity and access rights should be tightly managed in order that all devices and connections are authenticated and authorized, and controls should be placed on what information can be viewed and how it is communicated and stored. All data held on devices or in transit should be encrypted to safeguard it from unauthorized access or loss. In terms of devices that are lost or stolen, device management tools that extend to remote data wipe should be considered, especially for consumer devices that are personally owned. For devices used for business operations, systems will need to be used to link physical and network security together to enable a total view of incidents, enabling management to make decisions regarding the threat posed and how it can be controlled. This requires that all IoT devices are managed the same way as other equipments connected to the Internet and the network. All activity should be closely and continuously monitored to look for anomalies from normal baseline behavior, and organizations should ensure that all devices are correctly configured and are operating properly.

Manufacturing is woven into economy and society. For example, manufacturing took 12% of gross domestic product (GDP) and 11% of workforce in the Unites States in 2011 [32]. Moreover, the significance of manufacturing is far beyond the scope these numbers represent. For example, the manufacturing sector in the United States used to take 19% of GDP and 30% of workforce in the 1950s [33]; however, this percentage has been shrinking continually for several decades. The advance of manufacturing technologies relates closely to information technologies (ITs). Since design and operation of a manufacturing system needs numerous types of decision-making at all of its levels and domains of business activities, prompt and effective decisions not only depend on reasoning techniques, but also on the quality and quantity of data [34]. Every major shifting of manufacturing paradigm has been supported by the advancement of IT. For example, the widely adoption of computer numerical control (CNC) and industrial robots made flexible manufacturing systems (FMSs) feasible; the technologies for computer-aided design (CAD), computer-aided manufacturing (CAM), and computer-aided processing planning (CAPP) made computer-integrated manufacturing (CIM) practical. In developing their ESs, more and more enterprises rely on the professional providers of IT software service to replace or advance their conventional systems [14]. Therefore, it makes sense to examine the evolution of the IT infrastructure and evaluate its impact on the evolution of manufacturing paradigms, when a new IT becomes influential.

1.5 Conclusion

The continual increase of the IoT devices and services requires customized security and privacy levels to be guaranteed. The broad overview provided in this chapter raises many open issues and sheds some light on research directions in the IoT security field. Moreover, a unified vision regarding the insurance of security and privacy requirements in such a heterogeneous environment, involving different technologies and communication standards, is still missing. Suitable solutions need to be designed and deployed, which are independent from the exploited platform, and able to guarantee confidentiality, access control, and privacy for users and "things," trustworthiness among devices and users, compliance with defined security, and privacy policies. Current manufacturing environment has been extensively discussed to identify key requirements of EISs of modern enterprises. It is found that the emerging IoT infrastructure can support information systems of next-generation manufacturing enterprises effectively. More specifically, anytime, anywhere, anything, data acquisition systems are more than appropriate to be applied in collecting and sharing data among manufacturing resources. However, the application of IoT in EISs is at its infant stage; more researches are in demand in the areas such as modularized and semantic integration, standardization, and the development of enabling technologies for safe, reliable, and effective communication and decision-making. The Internet of Things is a promising technological advancement that can offer several benefits to the society at large. However, businesses and city councils across the globe need to work collectively to build secure and reliable IoT technologies and eliminate undesired side effects. To realize the true potential of this technology, security and privacy concerns need to be effectively addressed. In addition to self-regulation, a structured and well-defined cyber security and privacy policy must be developed with efficient collaboration between governments and enterprises. It is also key to ensure that IoT-specific legislation and industry standard protocols do not stifle innovation. This will allow individuals and communities to reap the advantages of the IoT and build a smarter world that offers intelligent solutions for big and small challenges across all walks of life. So the manufacturing industries can continue to accelerate their business success by leveraging these exciting new technologies.

References

1. Sicari S, Rizzardi A, Grieco LA, Coen-Porisini A (2015) Security, privacy and trust in internet of things: the road ahead. Comput Netw 76:146–164
2. Emmerson B, Win-Win Mag J (2010) M2M: the internet of 50 billion devices. Huawei (4):19–22
3. Boswarthick D, Elloumi O, Hersent O (2012) M2M communications: a systems approach, 1st edn. Wiley Publishing, Hoboken
4. Hersent O, Boswarthick D, Elloumi O (2012) The internet of things: key applications and protocols, 2nd edn. Wiley Publishing, Chichester
5. Fleisch E (2010) What is the internet of things: an economics perspective, Auto-ID labs white paper, WP-BIZAPP-053
6. Bandyopadhyay D, Sen J (2011) Internet of things: Applications and challenges in technology and standardization. Wirel Pers Commun 58:49–59
7. Weber RH (2010) Internet of things–new security and privacy challenges. Comput Law Secur Rev 26(1):23–30
8. Feng H, Fu W (2010) Study of recent development about privacy and security of the internet of things. In: 2010 international conference on Web Information Systems and Mining (WISM), Sanya, pp 91–95
9. Roman R, Zhou J, Lopez J (2013) On the features and challenges of security and privacy in distributed internet of things. Comput Netw 57(10):2266–2279
10. Anderson J, Rainie L (2014) The internet of things will thrive by 2025. PewResearch Internet Project. www.pewinternet.org/2014/05/14/internet-of-things/
11. Bandyopadhyay S, Sengupta M, Maiti S, Dutta S (2011) A survey of middleware for internet of things. In: Third international conferences, WiMo 2011 and CoNeCo 2011, Ankara, pp 288–296

12. Manyika J, Chui M, Bisson P, Woetzel J, Dobbs R, Bughin J, Aharon D. Unlocking the potential of the internet of things. McKinsey Global Institute. Accessed June 2015
13. Giusto D, Iera A, Morabito G, Atzori L (eds) (2010) The internet of things. Springer. ISBN: 978-1-4419-1673-0
14. Li Q, Wang ZY, Li WH, Li J, Wang C, Du RY (2013) Applications integration in a hybrid cloud computing environment: Modelling and platform. Enterp Inf Syst 7(3):237–271
15. Bi Z, Da Xu L, Wang C (2014) Internet of things for enterprise systems of modern manufacturing. IEEE Trans Ind Inform 10(2):1537–1546
16. RFID is a technology used to identify, track and locate assets; the universal, unique identification of individual items through the EPC is encoded in an inexpensive RFID tag
17. The term "IoT" has been "invented" by Kevin Ashton in a presentation in 1998 (see Gerald Santucci, Paper for the International Conference on Future Trends of the Internet, From Internet of Data to Internet of Things, at p. 2 Available at: ftp://ftp.cordis.europa.eu/pub/fp7/ict/docs/enet/20090128-speech-iot-conference-lux_en.pdf
18. Atzori L, Iera A, Morabito G (2010) The internet of things: a survey. Comput Netw 54(15):2787–2805
19. Gartner (2015) Hype cycle for emerging technologies, 2015. http://www.gartner.com/document/3100227?ref=lib. Accessed 30 July 2015
20. Gartner (2014) Gartner says 4.9 billion connected "Things" will be in use in 2015. http://www.gartner.com/newsroom/id/2905717. Accessed 8 July 2015
21. Chaudhuri A (2015) Address security and privacy concerns to fully tap into IoT's potential. http://www.tcs.com/offerings/it_infrastructure/Pages/default.aspx
22. Government of India (2015) Smart Cities Mission: Ministry of Urban Development: Government of India, June 2015. http://smartcities.gov.in/writereaddata/SmartCityGuidelines.pdf https://www.gov.uk/government/uploads/system/uploads/attachment_data. Accessed 21 July 2015
23. Cloud Security Alliance (2015) Security guidance for early adopters of the Internet of Things (IoT). https://downloads.cloudsecurityalliance.org/whitepapers/Security_Guidance_for_Early_Adopters_of_the_Internet_of_Things.pdf. Accessed 18 June 2015
24. Apple Inc. (2015) iOS: understanding iBeacon. https://support.apple.com/en-ap/HT202880. Accessed 3 July 2015
25. Facebook (2015) Engage people who visit your business. https://www.facebook.com/business/a/facebook-bluetooth-beacons. Accessed 18 June 2015
26. Weber RH (2015) Internet of things: privacy issues revisited. Comput Law Secur Rev 31(5):618–627
27. Hodgson K (2015) The internet of [security] things. SDM magazine. Available: http://www.sdmmag.com/articles/91564-the-internet-of-security-things
28. Accenture (2015) Security call to action. Available: https://www.accenture.com/t20160122T014933__w__/usen/_acnmedia/Accenture/Conversion-Assets/Microsites/Documents22/Accenture-Security-Call-to-Action-pdf#zoom=50
29. OWASP (2015) Internet of things top 10 projects'. www.owasp.org/index.php/OWASP_Internet_of_Things_Top_Ten_Project. Accessed Aug 2015
30. IBM (2015) IBM point of view: internet of things security. Available: http://public.dhe.ibm.com/common/ssi/ecm/ra/en/raw14382usen/RAW14382USEN.PDF
31. FTC (2015) Careful connections. Available: https://www.ftc.gov/system/files/documents/plain-language/pdf0199-carefulconnections-buildingsecurityinternetofthings.pdf
32. Ettlinger M, Gordon K (2011) The importance and promise of American manufacturing, center for American process [online]. Available: http://cdn.theatlantic.com/static/mt/assets/businessAmerican_Manufacturing%20.pdf. Accessed 29 Jan 2014
33. Lehtihet A, Wilson D, Susman G (2010) Future of manufacturing in the U.S. [online]. Available: http://www.smeal.psu.edu/cmtoc/research/nist1fut.pdf. Accessed 29 Jan 2014
34. Dumitrache I, Caramihai SI (2010) The intelligent manufacturing paradigm in knowledge society. In: Knowledge management, InTech, pp 36–56, ISBN 978-953-7619-94-7

Chapter 2
Security and Privacy Across Connected Environments

V. Vijayaraghavan and Rishav Agarwal

Abstract The devices in the Internet of Things (IoT) environment find applications in a wide variety of fields, from smart homes and smart cities to smart wearables. Earlier predictions had estimated a huge number of connected devices in use by the year 2015, but it did not happen. A main reason refers to the ubiquity of IoT devices that has its own set of unique challenges and problems which are not easy to surmount. One core issue relates to the security and connectivity vulnerabilities of these devices. With the number of IoT devices steadily on the rise and trends like BYOD (Bring Your Own Device) catching up, the challenges faced by these devices are steadily increasing. To understand the significance of issues relating to the connectivity of IoT devices, we must learn about their unique characteristics and requirements. However, notwithstanding the multiple vulnerabilities, unfortunately, there is no silver bullet to suggest definitive solutions. Apart from securing the devices, there is also an urgent need to update the laws that protect data ownership rights and restrict access to personal data. This chapter is an effort to address privacy and security challenges that IoT devices face. The chapter highlights novel solutions that can be usefully employed to make these devices more secure. It discusses device trust, policies and standards, data anonymization, lightweight authentication, encryption, and Datagram Transport Layer Security (DTLS) techniques.

2.1 Introduction

The Internet of Things (IoT) refers to a network of interconnected "things" that have processing capabilities. These "things" have the ability to transfer data over a network without requiring human-to-human or human-to-computer interaction. A "thing" can be an intelligent object from a smartphone, television, or vehicle to a

V. Vijayaraghavan (✉)
Infosys Limited, Bangalore, India
e-mail: Vijayaraghavan_V01@infosys.com

R. Agarwal
Indian Institute of Technology, Guwahati, Assam, India

© Springer International Publishing AG 2017
Z. Mahmood (ed.), *Connected Environments for the Internet of Things*,
Computer Communications and Networks,
https://doi.org/10.1007/978-3-319-70102-8_2

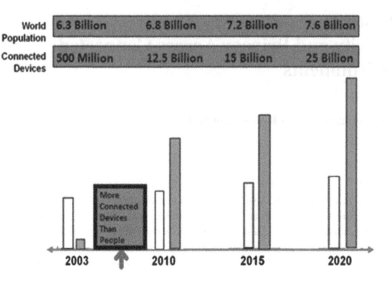

Fig. 2.1 Growth of connected devices

door, window, or even people! In this context, anything that has the ability to process and transfer data over a network can be a "thing."

The use of IoT devices has been on a steep rising curve over the last few years, with the number of IoT devices predicted to reach a figure of 24 million by the year 2020 [1]. Figure 2.1 shows a trend in the number of connected devices over the years inspired by Ericsson Mobility Report 2016 [2]. The IoT sector has been growing at a mind-boggling pace for the past two decades, but it was not always this way. Although, much work had been done to create a network of devices in the 1970s and 1980s, the Internet was still in its infancy. It was only during the 1990s that the idea of ubiquitous computing, wearable devices, and connected environments began taking shape, laying the foundation for IoT. In the year 1994, Xerox EuroPARC's Mik Lamming and Mike Flynn introduced a wearable device called Forget-Me-Not [3]. This device was capable of communicating wirelessly and recording its interactions with the environment around it. In the same year, Steve Mann a Canadian researcher and inventor developed a wearable wireless webcam [4]. Kevin Ashton coined the term "Internet of Things (IoT)" when he gave a presentation to P&G in 1999 [5]. Since then, with advancements in embedded systems and smartphone technology, the idea of IoT started gaining popularity.

Since the start of the new millennia in 2000, more and more people started using personal computers and mobile phones. As the number of people connected to the Internet grew exponentially, so did the number of devices. Today, the devices connected to the Internet comfortably exceed the number of people in the world. IoT devices are ubiquitous, i.e., present everywhere. Most people may not realize, but numerous smart "things" surround them.

Today, IoT devices find application in a wide variety of fields. Building and home automation, smart cities, smart manufacturing, smart automotive, smart wearables, and healthcare are some examples. The rise of the IoT in our daily lives has generated a brand new wave of change for the coming future. Growth in the number of smart objects has not only changed the way we live our lives but is also redefining many sectors like business, manufacturing, etc.

This chapter is organized as follows. Section 2.1 introduces IoT, its evolution, and significant applications. Section 2.2 deals with IoT security risks and its challenges and outlines the data security requirements for the IoT layers. Recommendations for IoT data security, detailed in Section 2.3, discuss devices' trust, policies, and standards. It also discusses lightweight authentication, encryption, and DTLS techniques. Sections 2.4 and 2.5 conclude the chapter and present the future ahead.

2.2   Connected Environments' Security and Privacy

In this section, various risks and challenges that plague the connected environments are highlighted. It also details the data security requirements that need to be satisfied.

2.2.1   Risks and Challenges

IoT devices are set to change the future for better; however, before that happens, there is a need to address some serious issues that plague the rampant applications and usage of these devices. Considering that IoT devices gather a lot of data about its surroundings and the user, any security threat to these devices is a matter of grave concern. What if sensitive data containing information related to user's identity, finance, health, or location is somehow stolen? This data may be invaluable to many organizations, and if the user is lucky enough, it may just be used for advertisements. Realistically though, they may be able to get their hands on enough data to predict the health status of the user, and he/she may have to bear the burden of increased insurance price or even policy cancellation! This is not just applicable to individuals but also corporate organizations. Hackers can target networks with inadequate security within the workplace to steal sensitive information. With trends like BYOD (Bring Your Own Device) catching up, data security risks at workplaces are likely to rise even further. The year 2015 was predicted to be the year of IoT devices, but it failed to have that kind of an impact, with security giants like Kaspersky terming IoT as Internet of Crappy Things [6]. The five major challenges faced by IoT devices are now highlighted below.

2.2.1.1 Device Hardware and Firmware Security

Most IoT devices are resource constrained in nature, i.e., they have limited computational abilities. Most of these devices come with minimalistic architecture, which is just sufficient to fulfill the desired purpose. This approach, although makes devices cheaper to manufacture, leaves out serious loopholes, which can be easily exploited to make undesired use of these devices. Most of the IoT devices do not have a proper authentication mechanism, and it can be easy to gain access to these devices. All these factors make device firmware and hardware susceptible to security threats and other risks. For example, if the device is misplaced, someone with even basic technical knowledge may be able to gain access to data stored in the device by tampering it.

2.2.1.2 Transport Layer Security

Another challenge with IoT devices is to do with the secure transfer of data. Most devices do not have robust encryption techniques to protect sensitive data like location, identity of the user, and other such details, which the device may be recording.

There have been cases where the data is transferred in clear text format. A research paper by Wei Zhou and Selwyn Piramuthu [7] explains vulnerabilities in communication between a fitbit device and its cloud server. It is suggested that the log-in information containing the user password is sent to the website in clear text format and stored in log files. No encryption is applied on the data being synced to the server after log-in. The data is sent as plain HTTP instructions, which could easily be compromised. These limitations in transport layer security are prone to eavesdropping, man in middle, and determined brute-force attacks. Security firm Bitdefender demonstrated deciphering the Bluetooth communication between an android device and a smartwatch [8]. The hackers opted for persistent trial and error. They tried multiple username and password combinations until they were able to gain access to the device contents.

2.2.1.3 Weak Security of Data Stored on Cloud Servers

Most IoT devices store their data on cloud servers with whom they may communicate directly or indirectly with the help of a gateway such as a smartphone. This provides more points of attacks for hackers. Another serious risk that data on cloud servers pose is the amount of personally identifiable information (PII) that they contain. If not properly anonymized and encrypted, data from cloud servers may be analyzed to reveal sensitive personal information. Highly skilled cyber criminals may make use of distributed denial of service (DDoS) attacks, backdoor attacks, SQL injection, etc. to sabotage the information stored on the cloud. All these risks are so real that some organizations are protecting themselves by buying data breach insurance, in case client data falls into the wrong hands.

2.2.1.4 Nonexistent Laws Regarding Data Ownership and Policy Compliance

There is a gray area when it comes to legal policy compliance of IoT devices. This is because there is not much awareness regarding the risks, which these devices pose on the user, and there are not many laws and policies in place to protect the user in cases of security lapse. There is no law to restrict data-hungry enterprises like e-commerce sites, advertising networks, and insurance companies on the amount of data that they can ethically collect. Some acts and policies like Fair Information Practice Principles (FIPPs) and Health Insurance Portability and Accountability Act (HIPAA) do exist which impose certain limit on the use of consumer data for making decisions regarding insurance, credit, or recruitment. However, they have a very limited effect in the IoT sphere. In addition, no clear laws govern the ownership rights on the amount of data collected by these devices. Ownership rights vary from company to company, and in many cases, the owner of a device is not necessarily the owner of the data collected by it. There have been cases where companies have tried to sell consumer data illegally.

2.2.1.5 Lack of Device Interoperability

Another grave challenge faced by IoT devices is the lack of device interoperability. Because of this, devices in the Internet of Things environment cannot always "talk" with each other, i.e., they are incapable of communicating with each other. This is because different manufacturers use different standards, which do not allow such devices to communicate. This causes a huge problem as it hinders the seamless experience and limits the potential of these devices. There is a need for a unified framework that can handle the "heterogeneity" of IoT devices and make connected environments truly smart.

All the above factors have made it imperative to build device trust. To realize the true power of connected environments, the above challenges need to be addressed and resolved.

2.2.2 Data Security Requirements in the IoT

There are many challenges that currently plague IoT devices, as discussed already. Most of these flaws are different in nature, and there is no silver bullet to take care of all of them. Additionally, it is not just the device that must be secured; various nodes through which the data is transmitted or stored also need to be secured. There are many requirements that IoT security must fulfill to overcome these challenges. However, before we get into details of security requirements, it is helpful to categorize various security layers of these devices and study them in detail. IoT security can be classified into four layers [9]:

- Device layer: It is the most basic level of security and deals with the robustness of the device hardware and firmware in protection against attacks to preserve data integrity.
- Transport layer: This layer deals with measures to make device communication secure. Communication could be between different devices, between device and gateway, or between device and cloud server.
- Cloud layer: This layer deals with algorithms and encryption techniques to make data stored on the cloud safe from external attacks.
- Product and data management layer: This layer is very different from the other three layers. It deals with concepts like Product Lifecycle Management (PLM), policy compliance and data ownership, adherence to IoT security standards, etc. This layer helps to ensure that the device is "future ready" and sticks to the contemporary security and legal standards.

A bottom-up approach needs to be followed while securing connected devices beginning with the device layer. Currently, most of embedded devices are poorly built and just focus on getting the job done. Considerable work has to be done to strengthen authentication mechanism of these devices and provide integrity of stored data. Manufacturers must make the device intelligent and robust enough to handle the complexities of connected environments. Devices must be capable of securing the data locally before they can transfer it. IoT devices do not just collect data but also transfer it over networks for multiple applications. Hence, securing the communication channel is very important. However, the requirements of transport layer security for IoT devices are a little different from traditional devices, as they are limited by their resource-constrained nature. It requires the use of algorithms that are lightweight and effective.

As mentioned before, cloud layer security is just one of the concerns. Cloud service providers must uphold certain benchmark for security and make use of good encryption algorithms and strong key management techniques. Data stored on cloud servers must be properly de-identified to make sure that it is not of any use in case of breach.

The topmost security layer is a vital cog in the wheel to obtain secure connected environments. It deals with various device and data management practices, which manufacturers, users, and policy makers might follow to bolster security in the connected space. Manufacturers must have the entire product life cycle in mind and must be willing to provide firmware updates to tackle the risks that outdated firmware poses. There is an urgent need for stricter laws regarding data ownership rights and legal policy compliance by companies. The risk associated with data collected by IoT devices must be identified, and laws must be in place to help the device users in case of crisis. In addition, there is a need for security standards that are universally accepted to alleviate the problem of device heterogeneity. The standards for device communication must be carefully chosen, keeping in mind the security and use of the devices.

2.3 Recommendations for IoT Data Security

It is clear that much work needs to be done to make connected devices platforms secure and trustworthy. In the previous section, we outlined security requirements in IoT ecosystem that must be implemented to alleviate the risks and challenges faced by them. In this section, we provide recommendations to overcome these challenges to secure the respective layers.

For complete security, all four layers need to be strengthened. The device layer can be secured by building trust in the Internet of Things and making device firmware and hardware more secure. We describe various lightweight encryption techniques that can be employed to secure device data and strengthen the transport layer. The cloud layer can be secured with the help of some data de-identification techniques that could be implemented to make sure that sensitive data is protected. We detail policies and guidelines that are recently proposed to protect privacy of consumers from data-hungry organizations. We also suggest guidelines for future policies that can lay down restrictions on data use and put strong legislations on data ownership rights. Lastly, we talk about developing security standards for IoT devices that help to promote device interoperability and unleash the true potential of IoT devices. These measures help to secure the product and data management layer, hence achieving the target of complete security. Figure 2.2 shows different layers of IoT security and highlights their various risks/challenges; it also lists the security recommendations for each layer.

Layer	Risks/Challenges	Solutions
Device Layer	Weak Authentication & Prone to Tampering	Securing boot, securing firmware, remote attestation & TPM
Transport Layer	Weak encryption of data due to resource constrained devices	Lightweight encryption, distributed encryption
Cloud Layer	Weak encryption & improper anonymization	ABE, TPA & Data De-identification
Product & Data Management Layer	Non existent legal policies & data ownership guidelines, lack of device interoperability	Stricter Laws on Data Collection & Data Ownership Rights, Development of IoT Standards like C-RAN & ZigBee

TPM: Trusted Platform Module   ABE: Attribute Based Encryption   TPA: Third Party Auditor
C-RAN: Cloud Radio Access Network

Fig. 2.2 Layers of IoT security

2.3.1   Securing Device Firmware and Hardware

The deficiencies in IoT security have been brought to light on many occasions, and all these have a huge impact on trust between device and user. A pair of cybersecurity engineers demonstrated one such vulnerability by successfully overriding the controls of a Jeep Cherokee that was on a highway, with the driver inside it [10]. The video in the link [10] presents the story. It is almost comical to see the driver lose control over the car fans, music system, and eventually engine on a busy highway. The hackers made use of the cellular connectivity of the car's entertainment system to breach its security.

Traditionally, most of the manufacturers have not put much effort in laying out a systematic plan to provide end-to-end security of devices. They follow more of a patchwork approach in tackling the loopholes, which can be easily exploited. For example, in the above scenario, the car must have surely had various security measures in place to prevent attacks but only to secure individual components rather than it being a planned, integrated security measure at a holistic level.

Events like these have made it essential for manufacturers to reconsider their approach for securing connected systems. They must now think of security as an integral part of the device right from the design stage and put together an end-to-end solution that keeps the entire product life cycle in mind, right from development to decommissioning of the device.

There are various methods to secure the device firmware. Right from securing the boot of the device to software isolation in case of device breach and providing regular updates to tackle new vulnerabilities. These methods, or rather steps, are discussed below:

1. Securing the boot of the device is essentially the root of trust [11] that is necessarily expected from a device. Most of the IoT devices are embedded devices that have a microcontroller. The creators must make sure that the software stored on these microcontrollers is secure and impregnable. This can be done using read-only memory (ROM) or flash memory to store the microcontroller software. Once this software starts running when the device is switched on, it needs to make sure that the device is not loading application software that has been modified or tampered. This can be done by verifying the digital signature of the application. Various self-certification and hierarchical certification techniques are used to verify device signature. A tree with strong roots is difficult uproot. Similarly, a device with trustworthy initial software provides a strong foundation for securing the device.

2. The next step is to code the software as fragments in such a way that all fragments of the code are independently secure. This is called software isolation, and it goes a long way in restricting the severity of breach in case of software compromise. It ensures that a breach in one part of the system is restricted to that part only, hence making it difficult for a hacker to enter the system from one point of attack and then take control of the entire device.

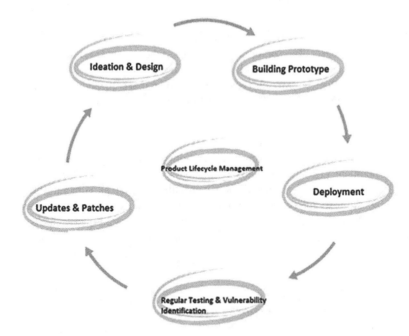

Fig. 2.3 Product lifecycle management

3. Finally, to secure the firmware of the device, manufacturers must have the Product Lifecycle Management in mind. An old firmware is prone to increasingly new attacks, and to tackle this, manufacturers must regularly release patches and updates as soon as new vulnerabilities are identified. They should also employ secure packet management (SPM), which verifies the authenticity of updates being patched with the help of signature keys. Regular security reviews by using mechanisms like side-channel attack, defense verification, trust boundary review, and fault injection could be employed to test the devices. Figure 2.3 shows the various stages of Product Lifecycle Management to consider.

4. After securing the device firmware, it is now essential to secure the device from physical attacks, i.e., securing the device hardware. Devices in connected environments are so widespread and ubiquitous that there can be numerous points of entries for an attacker, and it becomes very difficult to ensure the physical security of the device. However, the security of the device should be so strong that the hackers cannot access sensitive data from the tampered devices. Hackers make use of various reverse engineering techniques like de-packaging of chip, microprobing, layout reconstruction, etc. to tamper the device. Methods like remote attestation and Trusted Platform Modules (TPM) are effective to tackle such problems.

5. Remote attestation is a technique by which a remote server can determine if a connected device can be trusted or not. It checks for the integrity of hardware and

software of the connected client. The manufacturers embed credentials in the device during its development, and this credential essentially is the identity of the device in the server. The server can then request the connected device to confirm its identity from time to time to check and ensure that the device is not tampered.

6. TPM (Trusted Platform Module) is a microcontroller that authenticates the hardware of host. It could be thought of as the hardware counterpart of remote attestation. It checks if the host is authenticated (correct identity) and attested (trustworthy).

The methods and the solutions detailed above can certainly help to secure device and build trust between the device and the user. Some of them are inspired from a report by Wind Company [12], which details many more such strategies for end-to-end security of IoT devices. However, there is no silver bullet to tackle all vulnerabilities. The above suggestions should be kept in mind and implemented as per the requirements of the devices. Manufacturers need to make sure that they not only just create a list of security solutions that they want in their device and implement them individually but also interweave these solutions to create an integrated security solution.

2.3.2   Securing the Transport Layer

Wearable smart devices and other IoT devices collect a lot of sensitive information. If the encryption on the device is not strong enough, there is a risk of personal information getting into the wrong hands. Also, if the transport layer security is weak, then hackers can easily intercept information packets. Securing the transport layer means securing device communication. This is done by encrypting the channels so that interceptors may not able to make sense of the message in transit. Only the end devices must have the capability of decoding messages. As mentioned earlier, most of the IoT devices are made with bare minimum architecture, and this is why most of these devices have low computational power and cannot support complex encryption techniques. Designing lightweight cryptographic techniques entails finding the optimum trade-off between security, cost, and performance.

In this section, we discuss some lightweight encryption techniques that could be implemented to strengthen the transport layer security.

1. Hummingbird technique [13]: It was motivated by the design of enigma machine and was originally created by Engels, Schweitzer, and Smith. It was developed with constrained devices in mind and uses a hybrid structure of block and stream ciphers. Other lightweight algorithms use either one of the above two mentioned cipher structures. The hybrid structure reduces the block size, hence reducing power consumption and improving performance. The encryption/decryption process is inspired from the enigma machine, which used rotors for decoding. Similarly, Hummingbird contains four small block ciphers that are virtual equivalents of the rotor machine, which continuously change their internal states in a random way. The research paper [13] provides an in-depth security analysis of Hummingbird and the protection it offers against attacks like linear and differen-

tial cryptanalysis. A better version of this algorithm, the Hummingbird 2, has also been covered in detail by Engels D. et al. [14]. In this new algorithm, the number of internal states has been increased to 128 bits. Hummingbird algorithm is well suited for devices like RFID tags and wireless sensor nodes.

2. Scalable encryption algorithm (SEA) for small, embedded applications [15]: As the name suggests, this algorithm is scalable with respect to text, key, and processor size as it takes these specifications as a parameter. It is a low-cost solution, targeted at processors with limited instruction sets. The algorithm is denoted as $SEA_{n,b}$ where n is the key size and b is the processor (word) size. This makes the lightweight solution good for any type of processors. Its simplistic implementation and adaptability make it a good choice for a wide array of applications. With concepts like smart homes and buildings gaining popularity, even small devices like switches and bulbs are now connected to a network. The SEA ticks all the right boxes for the requirements of such devices. It makes use of a limited set of elementary operations like bitwise XOR, AND, OR, and Word Rotation, to achieve its purpose. The research paper by Standaert et al. [15] provides an in-depth security and performance analysis and outlines its effectiveness against attacks like linear and differential cryptanalysis, side attacks, square attacks, and interpolation attacks. This algorithm is capable of performing encryption/decryption in a few milliseconds using minimum memory requirements.

3. CryptoCop [16]: It is a lightweight and energy-efficient algorithm for wearable smart devices. From fitness trackers to smart watches, many options are available for the users. Since these devices are worn by the users and most of them have GPS and tracking capabilities, the data stored on these devices can reveal a lot about the user. Hence, it is essential to have good encryption of the device data while keeping in mind the energy and resource consumption. Most algorithms use asymmetric encryption, which is computationally expensive and consumes a lot of energy. In addition, most wearable devices use Bluetooth Low Energy (BLE) for communication, which has typically small packet size. CryptoCop uses symmetric algorithm, which is not just computationally less demanding but also uses smaller block sizes. The algorithm uses Advanced Encryption Standard (AES) in counter mode and uploads the AES keying material to the device only when it is charging. Hence, it is clear that this algorithm is optimized for wearable devices. The research paper [16] demonstrates its feasibility with real hardware on an electrocardiogram sensor. It is also resistant to eavesdropping and surveillance attacks.

The future is built around sensor networks. From the sensors that regulate our room temperature to the sensors that control room lighting and ambience, the functionalities are facilitated by a network of sensors. However, if a third party is able to control or even access the data of these sensors, it could lead to serious privacy violations. SPINS [17] which is security protocols for sensor networks is an interesting solution to the problem. Like other IoT devices, sensor networks do not have hardware capable of performing asymmetric encryption techniques. A sensor network also has an added challenge of broadcasting secure data to each node of the network that is communicated using radio frequency (RF). These problems are addressed by the two blocks of SPINS: SNEP and μTESLA. SNEP takes care of authentication and data freshness, whereas μTESLA provides authenticated broadcasts in resource-constrained devices. The research paper [17] provides an in-depth performance analysis of SPINS and demonstrates it on a prototype sensor network with low-power CPUs.

A very improtant application of IoT is the healthcare sector. Wearable medical devices (WMDs) such as heart rate and blood pressure monitors are becoming increasingly common. Apart from these devices, hospitals and clinics are also getting smarter through the application of connected environments to monitor the patients in real time, store patient information, and respond to emergencies. All these have tremendously improved the quality of healthcare services and helped in providing hassle-free services to the patients. Needless to say, protection of privacy and confidentiality of patients is the topmost priority as medical data is very personal. The elliptic curve cryptography (ECC) in healthcare devices is very effective. We discuss now two separate algorithms for each of the cases of wearable healthcare devices and smart healthcare environments:

- Elliptic curve cryptography (ECC) with symmetric algorithm for wearable healthcare devices [18]: Most of these devices consist of sensors which are attached to the patient's body and communicate using wireless networks like wireless body area networks (WBANs). Figure 2.4 shows an example of WBAN in healthcare. Elliptic curve cryptography is an asymmetric encryption tech-

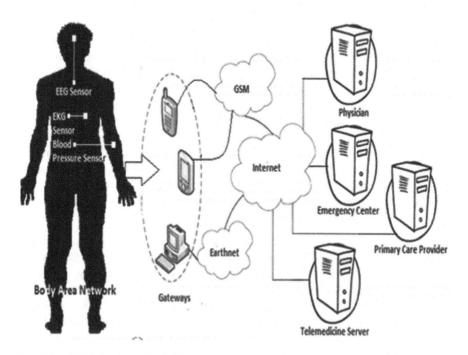

Fig. 2.4 A WBAN example for healthcare

nique, and using 160-bit key, it provides the same security level as that of an RSA system with 1024-bit key offers [18]. Symmetric algorithm is used to encrypt/decrypt medical data and ECC for managing keying information. Hence, the advantages of symmetric and asymmetric encryption techniques are combined to alleviate the security issues of WBANs.

- RFID authentication schemes in healthcare environment using elliptic curve cryptography [19]: Most connected healthcare environments make use of RFID for wireless communication. RFID authentication is one of the critical steps to ensure secure communications in the RFID system. ECC provides good security even though it uses smaller key size than traditional systems making it a natural choice for resource-starved RFID devices. The paper [19] details its working and compares various lightweight and heavyweight implementations of ECC.

Security can be added to different layers of a protocol stack. To achieve end-to-end security, some devices delegate the application layer security to transport layer security. One of such techniques available is lightweight Datagram Transport Layer Security (DTLS) implementation in CoAP-based IoT [20]. Traditionally, DTLS techniques are heavy and not suitable for use in resource-constrained devices. However, this technique provides a lightweight implementation of DTLS, which is bound with Constrained Application Protocol (CoAP). It makes use of pre-shared key (PSK)-based implementation of DTLS technique to make it suitable for IoT application. The research paper [20] also demonstrates the application of this procedure in home automation to control lights, temperature, and humidity sensors.

Apart from algorithms implemented on the device, we can also improve the transport layer by distributing the encryption process between device and gateway. The research paper [21] sheds light on this approach. IoT devices that are resource constrained, i.e., devices with low processing power, memory, and battery life are termed as Class-0 IoT devices. It aims at distributing the security scheme by implementing low processing encryption on the device, whereas resource-hungry processes are delegated to the gateway. The gateway has sufficient resources to perform transport layer security (TLS) techniques to secure the device. This is also demonstrated in the paper [21] by implementing Advanced Encryption Standard (AES) on device to gateway layer.

In this section, we looked at some of the lightweight encryption algorithms available to secure IoT devices. A study reported in [22] provides literature survey on various lightweight encryption algorithms; it also performs in-depth comparisons. Algorithms can thus be chosen based on the device requirements.

2.3.3 Cloud Layer Security and Data De-identification

Many cloud servers have very weak encryption standards. Even if encryption is available, cloud service providers and architects handle the encryption keys. Various steps could be taken to limit the data stored on public cloud servers and also to encrypt it. Developers of device must ensure that all the data being stored is properly de-identified beforehand. Data, if improperly de-identified, has a risk of re-identification.

Attribute-based encryption improves cloud layer security by securing the data stored on cloud servers. A third-party auditor could be used to check cloud servers' reliability. In addition, we discuss a few techniques that can be used to de-anonymize the data stored on cloud servers, as follows:

1. The use of attribute-based encryption (ABE) for fine-grained access control is a popular technique for securing cloud-based servers. The papers [23, 24] detail two different types of approaches of ABE. The first one uses key policy attribute-based encryption (KP-ABE), while the second one uses cipher text policy attribute-based encryption (CP-ABE) along with hierarchical identity-based encryption (HIBE) system. In both the methods, ABE is followed by proxy re-encryption and lazy re-encryption. Here the users are given access control on their own data. High performance, scalability, and fine-grained access control are some of the salient features of these techniques.

2. A novel way to check the cloud service provider's reliably is to introduce a third-party auditor (TPA) that can audit the data stored in cloud server. In most cases, user is not well equipped to understand the difference in security provided by various servers. The concept of public auditability allows the user to outsource this job to a third party to determine the level of security. The report generated by TPA could be used by the user to identify the risks of the cloud server. It also helps the cloud service provider to identify vulnerabilities and fix them. As per the method provided in the paper [25] by Wang et al., the TPA does not even need to request for the local copy of the data. It uses homomorphic authenticator to achieve this. There could be concerns regarding TPA learning about the data stored and misusing it. This can be avoided by using the homomorphic authenticator with random masking. The research paper [25] also lists various requirements that are expected from the TPA and provides a detailed performance review of this technique.

3. As outlined earlier, personal data stored on the cloud layer run into the risk of being identified. Data de-identification techniques are employed before sending data to the cloud. They can be very useful in protecting sensitive user data like medical and location data. The relevant algorithm must be efficient to identify and omit some keywords that are frequently used. For example, in case of medical data, information such as name of the patient, date of birth, etc. must be identified and omitted or hidden. For devices, which store information related to healthcare, a type of k-anonymity algorithm called Optimal Lattice Anonymization (OLA) [26] works efficiently. For location-based services, [27] provides an optimal k-anonymity algorithm that makes use of grid maps and entropy. Figure 2.5 shows an example of k-anonymity technique.

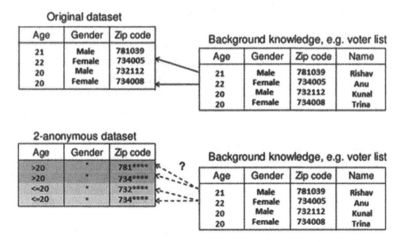

Fig. 2.5 K-anonymity technique example

2.3.4 Policies and Legislation

IoT devices sense, store, and transfer a huge amount of data. Taken together, the range of information collected could easily be in the petabyte range. Analysis performed on such a big data set could reveal many interesting things; and the results could be used by companies to provide better services to consumers, by the governments to get a better understanding of its populace, or by e-commerce sites to understand consumer preferences and display better advertisements. For example, data generated from sensors on a smart highway or smart cars could be analyzed to reveal traffic congestion patterns, peak traffic hours, and other such factors. These data could be used to control the traffic better and help in traffic management. However, the matter of concern is the amount of data collected and accessibility to this data. A lot of data collected by IoT devices are personal and could be analyzed to decode behavioral, mental, and physical aspects of a person. It could also be used to know about people's interest, their location, or their schedule. All this could lead to borderline infringement of user privacy. The worrying part is that there are no rules and legislations that enforce guidelines on how much data can be collected, what legal measures can be taken in case of privacy violation, or even draw clear lines on who owns the data collected by these devices.

Though aforementioned organizations such as the FIPPs and HIPAA do exist, their regulations have not been updated to deal with the issues that wide-scale use of IoT technology has opened up. Most IoT device manufacturers are not covered under these acts and are not liable or answerable in case of data breach that breaks compliance. The importance of formulating strong legislations for these devices has only recently begun that is now catching attention. In January 2015, the Federal Trade Commission (FTC) published a staff report on privacy and security in connected environments [28]. Later, in January 2016, it also issued a report titled, *Big*

Data: A Tool for Inclusion or Exclusion? [29]. It was aimed at big data companies that collect user data in various forms; it attempted to educate them on the potentially applicable laws that must be respected when they make use of user data. Also, in January 2015, the Food and Drug Administration (FDA) released a document called, *General Wellness: Policy for Low Risk Devices* [30]. It outlined the FDA's policy regarding devices that made "general wellness" claims such as fitness trackers, heart rate trackers, etc. It also discussed recommendations for manufacturers to better manage data security and privacy risks of these devices.

All these measures provide a good sign that government organizations finally understand the need to update their laws regarding user data privacy. However, this is just the starting point, and more needs to be done to create clear rules that users can rely upon. There is an urgent need to upgrade policies related to data collection and data ownership:

1. Governments need to come in terms with the new kinds of threats posed to security by the use of wearables. Strong regulations and policies must be put in place to force device manufacturers to uphold certain standards of security to protect user information. Also, these policies must be strong enough to embrace manufacturers and cloud service providers responsible. In cases where insufficient security measures lead to data breach, they must not be able to get away just by shifting blames.
2. Strong data ownership rights must be put in place, and the consumers must be informed about what data is collected from the device and where and how it is stored. The users must have the power to choose what data collected from them are stored on the server, and they must be able to delete them according to their convenience.

All these go a long way toward building trust in the IoT devices and IoT environment. Stricter policies ensure that personal data is not used in an unethical way.

2.3.5 IoT Standards and Device Interoperability

Most IoT devices today are manufactured as stand-alone units that are mostly incapable of communicating with other IoT devices, specifically when the devices are from different manufacturers. All these devices use their own coding schemes for encryption and protocols for transferring data. Many devices relay information to smartphones via gateways, which act as a medium of exchange that translates the sensed data to a format that can be understood by the smartphone. However, these gateways are also device and manufacturer specific and usually support limited devices. This essentially means that the Internet of Things, which aims at connecting various different "things" under a single network is, as of now, divided into small network of objects that cannot talk to each other. This is a huge hindrance to the ultimate objective what IoT tends to achieve.

Let us consider an example of smart homes. Suppose a person has an intelligent smart home assistant installed that allows the use of voice input to control smart lighting system and smart switches and can access the Internet using cellular connection. Also, he has installed a smart television that can be accessed using an application on mobile. In addition, he also owns a futuristic refrigerator with many useful functionalities. Unfortunately, he has to access these devices separately as they do not recognize each other. Now imagine if these devices are built on the same security standards. It would open up an entirely new dimension in which the owner could use these devices. For example, if he asks the smart assistant to locate the nearest grocery store, it could stream the result on the smart TV screen and tell him that he would soon run out of milk and eggs! This is one of the simplest examples and can be enhanced further as more devices are added. The possibilities that open up, as more and more devices become capable of interacting with each other, are endless.

To address the problem of device heterogeneity, there is an urgent need for IoT standards. Though IoT standards are still in the making, we focus our discussion on some of the possible solutions:

- Heterogeneous devices can be connected using a hybrid framework that combines the advantages of Cloud Radio Access Network (Cloud-RAN) and software-defined radio (SDR) [31]. SDR-based radio units (SRUs) are capable of communicating with devices that use different communication technologies. These SRUs can act as gateways that can connect to multiple devices and communicate the information to a centralized server under the Cloud-RAN architecture. Hence, only one SRU can be present locally to connect different devices, and multiple SRUs can be connected using a common centralized server. Figure 2.6 shows an example of Cloud-RAN architecture.

- It is a fact that most users may have no means to judge if a device upholds certain standards. This is not the case for other consumer products. For example, industrial products in India come with an ISI marking, which is a mark that certifies that the product conforms to the standards set by the Bureau of Indian Standards (BIS). Similarly, the International Organization of Standardization (ISO) is a body that aims to promote international industrial and commercial standards. However, there is no such organization for cybersecurity to certify whether products uphold security standards or not. IoT giants have already begun to realize this, and some of them have started working together with the result being popular standards like ZigBee [32]. The research chapter [33] also provides an insightful look at data security and privacy from an IoT perspective.

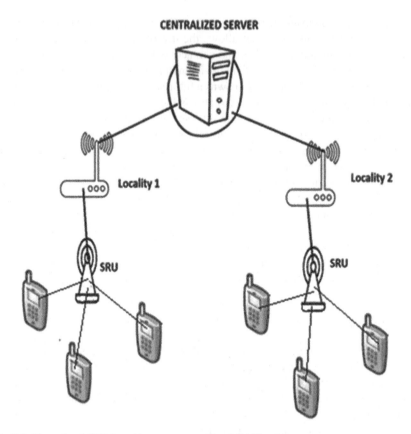

Fig. 2.6 Example of SDR-based heterogeneous Cloud-RAN architecture

2.4   Conclusion

The IoT is thought of as a concept with immense potential and unlimited applications. While this is true for most part, there is still a long way to go before this goal is truly realized. The biggest obstacle on this path is the security challenges surrounding these devices.

Demonstrations about weak security in connected environments have made consumers aware about the security hazards posed by these devices. Growing concerns have made manufacturers take notice, and they have slowly begun to realize the importance of putting privacy and security of their devices on top. This trend has been reciprocated in the mind-set of law and policy makers. They have begun to realize that the need of the hour is to protect the privacy of consumers. Similarly, there is growing awareness regarding the issues of device heterogeneity and boons of interoperability.

All of this provides a good sign that security in connected environments is on a road to recovery. While there is no single framework that can be employed to fix all issues, this chapter highlights different techniques that can be taken inspiration from. The best method to secure devices may depend on the purpose of the device, the environment it is used in, and how much sensitive information it collects. If all these factors are kept in mind, the ultimate goal of connecting all kinds of devices to the Internet can be achieved, which will change our lifestyle for the better.

2.5 Future Direction

At present, we are still finding ways to secure connected platforms and build trust in IoT devices. Manufacturers have to lay a lot more stress on Product Lifecycle Management to constantly update device firmware and keep it protected against vulnerabilities. Also, algorithms that are more lightweight need to be developed specifically for implementation in IoT sphere, keeping in mind its unique requirements and wide range of applications. IoT protocols and standards need to be formulated to bring all IoT devices under one big umbrella. Finally, it is also the responsibility of the user to be aware of the threats that these devices pose to their security and that of people around them. When consumers take their own security seriously, manufacturers and governments will increase their efforts to make these devices secure.

References

1. Meola A (2016) What is the Internet of Things (IoT). http://www.businessinsider.com/what-is-the-internet-of-things-definition-2016-8. Accessed Mar 2017
2. Qureshi R (2016) Ericsson mobility report, June 2016. https://www.ericsson.com/res/docs/2016/ericsson-mobility-report-2016.pdf. Accessed Mar 2017
3. Lamming M, Flynn M (1994) "Forget-me-not" Intimate computing in support of human memory, 94 International Symposium on next generation human interface, Technical Report EPC-1994-103, 2–4 Feb 1994
4. Media (2002) A brief history of wearable computing. www.media.mit.edu/wearables/lizzy/timeline.html#1981b. Accessed Mar 2017
5. Ashton K (2009) That 'internet of things' thing, 22 June 2009. http://www.rfidjournal.com/articles/view?4986. Accessed Mar 2017
6. Drozhzhin A (2015) Internet of crappy things, 19 Feb 2015, https://blog.kaspersky.com/internet-of-crappy-things/7667/. Accessed March 2017
7. Zhou W, Piramuthu S (2014) Security/privacy of wearable fitness tracking IoT devices. In: 9th Iberian Conference on Information Systems and Technologies (CISTI), pp 1–5, 18–21 June 2014
8. Arsene L (2014) Bitdefender research exposes security risks of android wearable devices, 12 Sept 2014. www.darkreading.com/partner-perspectives/bitdefender/bitdefender-research-exposes-security-risks-of-android-wearable-devices-/a/d-id/1318005. Accessed Mar 2017
9. Scully P (2016) Understanding IoT Security – Part 1 of 3: IoT security architecture on the device and communication layers, 29 Nov 2016. https://iot-analytics.com/understanding-iot-security-part-1-iot-security-architecture/. Accessed Mar 2017

10. Greenberg A (2015) Hackers remotely kill a jeep on the highway – with me in it, 21 July 2015. https://www.wired.com/2015/07/hackers-remotely-kill-jeep-highway/. Accessed Mar 2017
11. Loisel Y, di Vito S (2015) Securing the IoT 2 – secure boot as a root of trust. http://www.embedded.com/design/safety-and-security/4438300/Securing-the-IoT--Part-2---Secure-boot-as-rooot-of-trust-. Accessed Mar 2017
12. White Paper (2017) Building trust in the internet of things, (2017), Wind Report
13. Engels D, Fan X, Gong G, Hu H, Smith EM (2010) Hummingbird: ultra-lightweight cryptography for resource-constrained devices. In: Sion R et al (eds) Financial cryptography and data security. FC 2010. Lecture notes in computer science, vol 6054. Springer, Berlin/Heidelberg
14. Engels D, Saarinen MJO, Schweitzer P, Smith EM (2011) The hummingbird-2 lightweight authenticated encryption algorithm. In: Juels A, Paar C (eds) RFID. Security and privacy. RFIDSec 2011. Lecture notes in computer science, vol 7055. Springer, Berlin/Heidelberg
15. Standaert FX, Piret G, Gershenfeld N, Quisquater JJ (2006) SEA: a scalable encryption algorithm for small embedded applications. In: Domingo-Ferrer J, Posegga J, Schreckling D (eds) Smart card research and advanced applications. CARDIS 2006. Lecture notes in computer science, vol 3928. Springer, Berlin/Heidelberg
16. Snader R, Kravets R, Harris AF (2016) CryptoCop: lightweight, energy-efficient encryption and privacy for wearable devices. In WearSys 2016 – Proceedings of the 2016 Workshop on Wearable Systems and Applications, co-locatedsssss with MobiSys 2016, pp 7–12. [2935647] Association for Computing Machinery, Inc. doi:https://doi.org/10.1145/2935643.2935647, 25–30 June 2016
17. Perrig A, Szewczyk R, Tygar J et al (2002) SPINS: security protocols for sensor networks. ACM J Wirel Netw 8(5):521–534
18. Young Sil Lee, Esko Alasaarela, Hoon Jae Lee (2014) An efficient scheme using elliptic curve cryptography (ECC) with symmetric algorithm for healthcare system. Int J Secur Appl 8(3):63–70
19. He D, Zeadally S (2015) An analysis of RFID authentication schemes for internet of things in healthcare environment using elliptic curve cryptography. IEEE Internet Things J 2(1):72–83
20. Lakkundi V, Singh K (2014) Lightweight DTLS implementation in CoAP-based Internet of Things, vol. 00, no, pp 7–11. In: Advanced Computing and Communications (ADCOM), 2014 20th annual international conference, 19–22 Sept 2014
21. King J, Awad AI (2016) A distributed security mechanism for resource-constrained IoT devices. Informatica Int J Comput Inform (Slovenia) 40(1):133–143
22. Eisenbarth T, Kumar S, Paar C, Poschmann A, Uhsadel L (2007) A survey of lightweight-cryptography implementations. IEEE Des Test 24(6):522–533
23. Yu S, Wang C, Ren K, Lou W (2010) Achieving secure, scalable, and fine-grained access control in cloud computing. In: Proceedings of IEEE INFOCOM'10, San Diego, CA, USA, March 2010
24. Wang G, Liu Q, Wu J (2010) Hierarchical attribute-based encryption for fine-grained access control in cloud storage services. In: Proceedings of the ACM conference Computer and Communications Security (ACM CCS), Chicago, IL, 4–8 Oct 2010
25. Wang C, Wang Q, Ren K, Lou W (2010) Privacy-preserving public auditing for storage security in cloud computing. In: INFOCOM'10 proceedings of the 29th conference on information communications, pp 525–533, 14–19 Mar 2010
26. El Emam K, Dankar FK, Issa R, Jonker E, Amyot D et al (2009) A globally optimal k-anonymity method for the de-identification of health data. J Am Med Inform Assoc 16:670–682
27. Felix JGC (2015) Anonymity in preference-aware location-based services without third trusted-party. In: 12th EAI international conference mobile and ubiquitous systems, Coimbra, Portugal
28. FTC (2015) Internet of things, FTC Staff report, January 2015
29. FTC (2016) A tool for inclusion or exclusion, (2016), FTC report *Big Data,* January 2016
30. *General Wellness: Policy for Low Risk Devices* (2016) FDA document, July 2016

31. ERCIM News 101 (2015) Special theme: the internet of things and the web of things, April 2015
32. Zigbee (2017) The ZigBee Alliance. http://www.zigbee.org/zigbeealliance/. Accessed Mar 2017
33. Varadharajan V et al (2016) Data security and privacy in the internet of things (iot) environment. In: Mahmood Z (ed) Connectivity frameworks for smart devices. Springer, Cham, pp 261–281

Chapter 3
Big Data Challenges for the Internet of Things (IoT) Paradigm

Pornpit Wongthongtham, Jaswinder Kaur, Vidyasagar Potdar, and Abhishek Das

Abstract Millions of devices equipped with sensors are connected together to communicate with each other in order to collect and exchange data. The phenomenon of daily life objects that are interconnected through a worldwide network is known as the Internet of Things (IoT) or Internet of Objects. These sensors from a large number of devices or objects simultaneously and continuingly generate a huge amount of data, often referred to as Big Data. Handling this vast volume, and different varieties, of data imposes significant challenges when time, resources, and processing capabilities are constrained. Hence, Big Data analytics become even more challenging for data collected via the IoT. In this chapter, we discuss the challenges pertaining to Big Data in IoT; these challenges are associated with data management, data processing, unstructured data analytics, data visualization, interoperability, data semantics, scalability, data fusion, data integration, data quality, and data discovery. We present these challenges along with relevant solutions.

3.1 Introduction

The Internet of Things (IoT) paradigm asserts that each individual object in everyday life can be equipped with sensors which can acquire useful information about the objects and will be on the network in one form or another [1]. Over the past decade, an increasing number of objects (e.g., smart devices, cars, intelligent roadways, pacemakers and other personal health monitoring units, refrigerator, cattle, smart billboards, etc.) have been connected to the Internet, collecting and exchanging data without requiring human-to-human or human-to-computer interaction. This network infrastructure enables anything and anyone to be connected anytime and anywhere.

P. Wongthongtham (✉) • J. Kaur • V. Potdar
Curtin University, Perth, Australia
e-mail: p.wongthongtham@curtin.edu.au

A. Das
Tripura University (A Central University), Agartala, India

© Springer International Publishing AG 2017

Z. Mahmood (ed.), *Connected Environments for the Internet of Things*,
Computer Communications and Networks,
https://doi.org/10.1007/978-3-319-70102-8_3

At present, there are about 1.5 billion Internet-enabled PCs and over 1 billion Internet-enabled mobile phones [2], and it is expected that 50 to 100 billion smart devices will be connected to the Internet by 2020 [3]. According to IDC, the world-wide IoT market spend will increase from $592 billion in 2014 to $1.3 trillion in 2019 [4]. Sensors from these devices will simultaneously generate a huge amount of data in an automated way. In the future, 40% of all the data in the world will be generated by machine-to-machine communication [4].

We are all constrained by time, limited resources, and capability, making it impossible to manually handle this vast amount of data. This data continues to increase at a rapid pace because embedded sensor devices have steadily been increasing with advances in technology. It is the greatest force driving Big Data analytics. A comprehensive data analytics model or framework is needed to analyze this enormous amount of sophisticated data.

There are three key IoT elements which enable seamless and ubiquitous computing: (a) hardware, comprising sensors, actuators, and embedded hardware; (b) middleware, on-demand storage and computing tools for data analytics; and (c) presentation, perception of visualization and interpretation tools which can be extensively accessed on different platforms and adapted for different applications. IoT middleware solutions are gaining more attention in the marketplace as they simplify the sensor data by performing data binding, filtering, fusing, reasoning, etc. In addition, the variety of IoT applications that are built on top of this middleware poses further challenges. The IoT middleware consists of a mechanism to combine high-tech infrastructure with a service-oriented architecture and sensor networks to provide access to discordant sensor sources in a disposition-independent manner [5]. The IoT middleware needs to assist users to retrieve the data streams required for their application. It is evident that data analytics will be critical for IoT in this Big Data era. In this chapter, we discuss the challenges associated with Big Data in IoT.

The rest of this chapter is organized as follows. Sections 3.2 and 3.3 introduce IoT and Big Data, respectively. Sections 3.4, 3.5 and 3.6 explain the challenges facing IoT Big Data. The challenges include data management issues presented in Sect. 3.4, data analytics challenges presented in Sect. 3.5, and semantics challenges presented in Sect. 3.6. Section 3.7 concludes the chapter.

3.2 Internet of Things

The Internet is the most widely adopted technology, which has radically changed the way people communicate with each other. The Internet as we know it is a large network of interconnected servers that host a huge amount of valuable information. However, the Internet is changing rapidly, and it now connects machines, equipment, sensors, actuators, home appliances, surveillance cameras, and numerous other objects in our environment. This communication network does not require constant human intervention, and this new phenomenon of an interconnected world where everything is connected is referred to as IoT [6]. According to [7], the number of physical things that are now connected to the Internet is greater than the world's population. It is estimated that 25 billion devices were connected to the Internet in 2015, and this number is rising at an alarming rate. It is estimated that by 2020 we will have at least 50 billion devices feeding data to the Internet via IoT [8].

3.2.1 Definitions of the Internet of Things (IoT)

The IoT is syntactically comprised of two terms. The first term, "Internet," focuses on the vision which is network oriented; the second term, "Things," refers to the "objects" which are generic and are integrated to form a common framework. Hence, IoT is defined as "a worldwide network of interconnected objects uniquely addressable, based on standard communication protocols" [9]. Each and every thing connected to the Internet has a unique identifier such as MAC that addresses and communicates using the TCP/IP protocol. Radio-frequency identifiers (RFID) is a good example of the real power of IoT [6].

These "things" or objects interact with each other in order to accomplish a common goal. For example, smart electric cars such as Tesla have 18 sensors that work together automatically. This car can open the doors of a garage before the person arrives home; it can control the temperature, and it provides a framework whereby the user can design his/her own app and use this app to check the battery status and control the speed of the car from anywhere.

IoT is also known as the Internet of Objects; these are daily life objects that are interconnected through a network and possess ubiquitous intelligence [10]. IoT increases the Internet's ubiquity, because it integrates the objects so that they can communicate with other devices/objects and with humans. Yoo, Henfridsson et al. [11] define IoT as the combination of components which are both physical and digital. This combination results in the development of new products and creates innovative business models. Wortmann and Fluchter [12] mentioned that in IoT, physical things are combined with IT in the form of hardware and software, thereby improving the physical function of the associated things by means of additional IT-based services. With the combined IT-based services, the functionality of such things can be accessed locally as well as globally via the Internet. For example, home automation can convert a standard home to a smart home by using IoT devices. In a smart home, the homeowner can switch an air conditioner on or off before arriving home or switch off the lights after leaving home. The owner can also receive notification that an unauthorized person has entered the house and police can be called automatically. Moreover, a light bulb can act as a smart security system. The physical function of a bulb is to illuminate a specific area, but this physical function of a bulb can be enhanced with IoT. With IoT capability, this bulb can be used to detect the presence of a human being and can work as a security system which detects the intruder, turns on the flashing mode, and sends a message to the homeowner's smartphone.

According to Internet Telecommunication, IoT is "a global infrastructure for the information society, enabling advanced services by interconnecting things based on existing and evolving, interoperable information and communication technologies" [12]. Another paradigm of IoT is Cyber-Physical Systems (CPSs) as mentioned by [13].

3.2.2 Cyber-Physical Systems

Cyber-Physical Systems (CPSs) are new generation systems which integrate both physical and computational capabilities and can communicate with human beings by using various modalities [14]. These are engineered systems which are developed from the synergy of both physical and cyber components. CPS can be applied in medical services, robotics, avionics, etc. [15]. Future innovative technical developments are possible with CPS because CPSs have the ability to communicate with the physical world by means of computation [14].

Lee [16] mentioned that in CPS computational processes, network processes and physical processes are integrated. Physical processes are controlled and monitored by the embedded computers and networks by using the feedback loops, whereby computations are affected by the physical processes and vice versa.

CPS needs both the computing and networking technologies to capture the physical dynamics as well as the information. CPS requires the interaction between the computing, physical systems, control systems, and network systems in order to establish the interaction among them. CPS requires new design technologies. In CPS, software is embedded in physical devices whose principal goal is not only computation but also to combine computation with physical processes [17]. Autopilots are a good example of CPS. Autopilots were initially used in missiles but were later adopted in aircrafts. Autopilots include sensors and processors that are used to assist the human operator in controlling the aircraft. The airplane has high nonlinear dynamics, so it requires more complex and advanced technologies such as neural network and fuzzy logic, which ensures smooth trajectory navigation [18].

Nowadays, the terms "IoT" and "CPSs" are used interchangeably, although there are several differences between them. According to [17], CPSs and the IoT are almost similar because both use the same architecture. However, a CPS has several characteristics that distinguish it from IoT:

- In a CPS, every physical device has cyber capability. Every device has embedded software and system resources such as network bandwidth, and each device has limited system resources.
- CPSs require a greater integration of computation and physical processes compared to the IoT.
- CPSs are distributed systems which are networked by means of various network types such as wireless network, wired network, Bluetooth, GSM, and others.
- In a CPS, every component has different spatial and time granularity. Spatiality and time capabilities are the strictest constraints of CPS.

- A CPS requires very high degree of automation. For this purpose, feedback technologies are used in these systems. The advanced feedback technologies establish easy interaction between man and machine.
- Because they are complex, large-scale systems, CPSs are reliable and secure and have adaptive capabilities.

3.2.3 IoT Architecture

Said and Masud [6] suggest two main architectures for IoT: a three-layered architecture and a five-layered architecture. Other than these, several special-purpose architectures tailored for specific contexts are also found in the literature.

3.2.3.1 Three-Layered Architecture

The earliest proposed architecture for IoT was a three-layered architecture comprising a perception layer, network layer, and application layer.

The perception layer is used to identify objects in the IoT system [19]. This layer collects information about every object, and for this purpose, the perception layer uses the data gathered from RFID tags, cameras, sensors, etc. Sensors collect information about temperature, motion, acceleration, humidity in the air, etc., and the perception layer passes this information to the network layer [20].

The network layer is the main component of the three-layered IoT architecture [19]. The function of this layer is to securely transmit to the application layer the information collected by the perception layer, using the software and hardware instruments of the Internet. The medium of transmission could be wired or wireless such as Wi-Fi, Bluetooth, 3G, etc. The network layer also contains the information and management centers [20].

The application layer connects the IoT's social needs with industrial technology. It acts as a middle tier linking the industrial technology with the needs of humans. The applications which can be developed by IoT are smart health, smart home, smart farming, intelligent transportation, etc. [6].

3.2.3.2 Five-Layered Architecture

The three-layered architecture became inadequate with the rapid development of IoT; hence, a five-layered architecture was developed [20]. Currently, a TCP/IP protocol stack is used to facilitate communication between network hosts. Billions of devices are connected within the IoT system, creating a huge amount of traffic and requiring larger storage space. Hence, the next-generation architecture must be able to provide security and privacy for such a huge amount of data and should be scalable and interoperable [19]. So, for this purpose, five-layered architecture was proposed.

The first layer is known as the business layer. The main function of this layer is to define the IoT applications and is also responsible for the management of IoT applications and services. The business layer ensures data privacy and creates business models and graphs according to the information acquired from the application layer. Based on these generated models and graphs, one can predict future actions and goals.

The second layer is the application layer, the purpose of which is to determine the types of applications in IoT. This layer develops intelligent, safe, and authenticated applications of IoT. It works similarly to the application layer of the three-layered architecture. IoT can develop many applications such as smart health, smart home, smart farming, intelligent transportation, etc.

The third layer is the processing layer which handles the information collected by the perception layer. This layer is responsible for storing and analyzing the information. Functions of this layer are very critical and difficult, because the perception layer collects huge amounts of data about system objects. So, to handle such a huge amount of information, this layer uses techniques such as database software, intelligent processing, and cloud computing. This layer is linked to the database, and it stores in the database the information received from the transport layer. This layer performs some computations on the information and makes decisions automatically.

The next layer is the transport layer. It functions like the network layer of the three-layered architecture. This layer is also known as the transmission layer. The transport layer is responsible for receiving the information from the perception layer and transmitting it to the processing layer and vice versa. This layer uses many network technologies such as Wi-Fi, Bluetooth, etc. This layer is responsible for the secure transmission of data between the perception layer and the processing layer.

The last, the fifth, layer is the perception layer. It works similarly to the perception layer of the three-layered architecture. This layer collects information about every object in the IoT system such as the temperature and location of each object. This layer transmits collected data into signals. The layer uses technologies such as RFID, GPRS, etc. for the collection of data.

3.3 Big Data

As mentioned in [21], in the last 20 years or so, there has been a great increase in the volume of data in every field. A report from the International Data Corporation (IDC) in 2011 stated that 1.8ZB data was copied and found in the world, and within 5 years, the amount of data had increased ninefold [22]. For example, if we consider social media as a major source of data, it is anticipated that by mid-2019, there will be nearly 65 million Twitter tweets per day and around 190 million users [23]. So, given the colossal amount of data, "Big Data" is the term used to describe huge datasets. These datasets are very difficult to manage, acquire, perceive, and process by means of traditional tools in real-time environments.

According to [24], Big Data is defined as the data which is so huge that it cannot be captured, processed, and managed using traditional techniques. Big Data includes massive amounts of structured, unstructured, and semi-structured data, which require more real-time analysis than do the traditional datasets. Moreover, Big Data provides the opportunity to explore new values and to acquire an in-depth understanding of data.

Nowadays, because of its high potential, companies and government agencies are becoming more interested in Big Data and have undertaken major research on Big Data and its applications [21]. Big Data is relatively new, although the term has been around for a long time and has appeared in many scientific papers [25]. Big Data is not only about the volume of data; it has many other features apart from size. In the next section, we present various definitions of Big Data.

3.3.1 Definitions and Characteristics of Big Data

According to [26], Big Data consists of three Vs: volume, velocity, and variety. Volume indicates that the data generated by the Internet is very high in volume compared to that of earlier years. Velocity refers to the speed of data generation; i.e., systems generate data at a very high speed compared to the speed of traditional systems. Variety refers to the various forms of data; that is, data is present in many forms on the Internet. These three Vs were originally suggested by Gartner for describing Big Data elements. Gantz and Reinsel [22] added a fourth V to the characteristics of Big Data: value. The fourth characteristic is highly accepted because it defines the actual meaning and requirement of Big Data. Chen, Mao, and Liu [21] added a fifth V: veracity. Hence, Big Data analytics is required to disclose hidden data (or gather actionable insights) from very huge datasets, which are complex, diverse, and very big. The main characteristics of Big Data are described below, in more detail.

3.3.1.1 Volume

Volume indicates the data magnitude and the huge amount of different kinds of data which are generated by various sources, and this data is continuously increasing [27]. The size of Big Data is in terabytes and petabytes. IBM conducted a survey of 1144 respondents in mid-2012 and found that only half of the respondents believed that a Big Data dataset exceeded one terabyte [28]. One terabyte of storage is equivalent to 1500 CDs, which can store around 16 million photographs. According to [29], in one second, Facebook processes one million photographs, and it stores 260 billion photographs in 20 petabytes of storage space. So, one can only imagine the volume of data that is being processed, managed, stored, and analyzed. The volume of data needs to be measured in terabytes or petabytes, because huge amounts of data are generated by different sources such as sensors. Hence, it is difficult, if not impossible, to manage such a huge amount of data using traditional database techniques [30].

As an example, smart traffic management systems are one of the developments of IoT. Nowadays, because of affordable car prices, the number of cars on the road has increased significantly leading to traffic congestion. To manage congestion, traffic management systems are connected to the digital road map of the city, and traffic displays are installed within cities to guide drivers. For traffic management, sensors are connected to the traffic lights, and these sensors send information to a central server about the number of vehicles. The analytical software at central location receives real-time data from sensors, traffic lights, and digital road maps. When the number of vehicles on a road exceeds the total capacity, traffic screens advise drivers to take a detour 1 km before the signal, which reduces both the travel time and the fuel consumption. This is possible because a large amount of sensor data from road sensors is sent to a central management system for real-time analysis. However, such large datasets cannot be managed using traditional database techniques and therefore require Big Data analytics approaches. The analysis of such large datasets can reveal hidden patterns and information which are then used to improve the traffic management systems.

3.3.1.2 Variety

Variety refers to the heterogeneous nature of Big Data such as data that is collected by different types of sources such as sensors, social networks, etc. The collected data could be of any type such as audio, video, text, or data logs, and it could be structured, semi-structured, or unstructured. Structured data is data which is stored in tabular form in spreadsheets or in a relational database. The data which is not organized in a structured way is called unstructured data, such as text in the form of paragraphs on the Internet. Semi-structured data is the data whose formats lie between structured and unstructured data. The format of semi-structured data does not follow strict standards. An extensible markup language, XML, which is used to exchange data on Internet, is an example of semi-structured data. XML documents have data tags, which are readable by machines [27].

The data which are generated by mobile phones, such as game data, text messages, and blogs, are mostly unstructured [31]. For example, in a smart traffic management system, data from different sources such as sensors, traffic lights, and digital road map are analyzed for better traffic management. Every source will produce data in a different form; these different types of data presentations are managed and analyzed in a central location for better decision-making.

3.3.1.3 Velocity

Velocity indicates the speed at which the data are generated and analyzed. With the development of digital devices such as sensors and smartphones, an extraordinary amount of data is created which requires real-time analytics. Data generated through sensors are collected and analyzed in real time [32]. Retailers such as Amazon are also generating data at very high speeds. For example, Wal-mart processes approximately 1 million transactions per hour [33]. Data generated through mobile phones help to produce personalized offers for customers. Another example of the velocity of data is the data generated by traffic sensors. These sensors gather and transfer information in real time, because the data collected by these sensors are useful only if they give information to the driver before she/he reaches the congested area. Hence, data analysis needs to be done at an equally fast speed because data have time value; i.e., after a specific time, the data will no longer be useful.

3.3.1.4 Value

This is the most important characteristic of Big Data. It refers to the exploration of data to discover hidden patterns and values of large datasets of different types by using different techniques [21]. Very valuable data can be acquired by analyzing a huge amount of Big Data. It also has the potential to provide cost-beneficial criteria. For example, sensors in the IoT system of a smart traffic management system send huge amounts of data to a central control system, where the data are processed and analyzed. Data have value only if they can assist in predicting the future and current traffic conditions of traffic lights.

3.3.1.5 Veracity

Veracity refers to the accuracy, reliability, and truthfulness of data, which means that the data are noise-free and nonredundant and can therefore be confidently used for decision-making and for future predictions [34]. Achieving veracity of data is very difficult because data are produced by different sources.

3.3.2 Big Data Analytics

Big Data has demonstrated its great potential to transform decision-making in the business realm. Efficient and effective processes are needed to turn the high volume of rapidly generated and diverse data into significant information that can inform decision-making. Big Data analytics are the techniques used to procure and analyze an intelligence acquired from Big Data. There are four types of analytics which are presented here.

3.3.2.1 Descriptive Analytics

Descriptive analytics are used to diagnose what has happened or is happening [35]. These analytics are applied to categorize, classify, and consolidate massive amounts of historical data in order to understand what the data imply. They include the presentation of raw data in summarized or query form to manage otherwise elusive information. This sort of analysis is mainly concerned with processing the very diverse collected data by monitoring data from device sensors and databases to detect patterns and trends in such data [35]. Descriptive analytics can produce data visualization in the form of tables, drawings, maps, interactive dashboards, charts (fever, pie, bar, etc.), etc. to summarize and report the trends.

3.3.2.2 Diagnostic Analytics

Diagnostic analytics are applied in order to determine why a phenomenon is occurring or has occurred and to analyze the factors leading to this occurrence which may include the inputs and operational policies [27]. Diagnostic analytics can benefit from sensitivity analysis using a simulation model of the system that mimics the current operation.

3.3.2.3 Predictive Analytics

Predictive analytics harnesses sophisticated machine learning and data mining techniques to examine the historical data in an effort to predict the upcoming future. Predictive analytics is capable to detect hidden patterns from data in large scale and cluster these data into segments which share common characteristics. Predictive analytics are used to estimate efficiency based on planned inputs. They can be applied to all domains ranging from weather forecasting and market volatility predictions to predictions of customers' next moves based on their spending and even on what they tweet [27]. It also has applications in other domains such as healthcare, education, marketing, supply chain logistics, etc. In essence, predictive analytics explore and interpret patterns in order to find relationships among the data. Predictive analytics use simulation models to predict a future occurrence using a set of inputs and "what-if" scenarios.

3.3.2.4 Prescriptive Analytics

Prescriptive analytics are concerned with how we can make it happen and what the consequences will be [28]. Prescriptive analytics are used to identify the policies and inputs that will lead to a desired outcome and may include identifying changes in input parameters and policies that will reduce the cycle time and increase through-put in order to reach the desired levels. Prescriptive analytics are intended to provide the optimal solution(s) to an existing problem through the use of optimization and simulation techniques. This significantly helps decision-makers to select the best option.

3.4 Management Challenges of Internet of Things Big Data

In this section, we discuss the challenges of managing IoT data, including data and process challenges.

3.4.1 Data Challenges

Challenges associated with Big Data characteristics are discussed below.

3.4.1.1 Massive Amount of Data Collected

According to [6], the main problem is related to the huge amount of information which is collected through RFID. IoT systems may have millions of devices. Every object in the IoT generates information about itself. This generated information must be gathered and amounts to a massive quantity of data, producing problems of transmission, storage, and processing.

The transmission issue relates to the necessity of transferring all the gathered information in real time, which is very difficult because the bandwidth which is required to transfer that information might not be available at that time. Another problem is related to the storage of information because a large amount of space is required for storage and backup. The last issue is the processing problem. In order to determine the actions that must be taken, the information about things must be handled by web applications, and information must be handled in real time [36].

The volume of data is increasing day by day. As mentioned in [30], 80,000 pet-abytes of data were stored across the world in 2000, and this is predicted to rise to 35 zettabytes by 2020. In today's world, many objects and/or activities are tracked and recorded, such as environmental data, medical data, industrial data, etc. Information is even recorded for every event; for example, speed cameras store information about speed limit breaches, etc. What we observe nowadays is that massive amounts of data are being stored, but the processing of such huge datasets is becoming difficult; hence, the percentage of processed data is decreasing, resulting in blind zones [37].

3.4.1.2 Various Forms of Data Collected

The data which comes from sensors are sometimes combined with other unstructured data, so there is a strong relationship between sensor and other unstructured data. So different forms of data such as structured, semi-structured, and unstructured are collected and stored by Big Data. Of the massive amounts of data that are collected, only 20% is processed; the remaining 80% cannot be processed and analyzed using traditional techniques. Hence, most of the collected data are not useful for decision-making [30]. In addition, there needs to be a technique which can effectively combine structured data with unstructured images, text, or data [38].

3.4.1.3 Data Transmission Speed

The transmission speed of data on the Internet is also known as velocity. In order to explore and acquire some insight about the data, this high-speed data needs to be analyzed in real time. The current software applications can generate data streams at very high speeds which can be very difficult to analyze in real time [39]. This is still a challenge for Big Data. For example, in 1999, the data warehouse of Walmart could store data up to 1000 terabytes, but in 2012 it had increased to 2.5 petabytes of data [40]. This shows a rapid increase in data accessed through the sensors and presents new challenges regarding the storage processing and analysis of such high-speed data in real time.

3.4.1.4 Time Series for Data Analysis

Generally, in the case of sensors, some events are captured at a specific point in time. The data captured by specific events or at specific times are sometimes useless. However, if something serious happens, it must be recorded and addressed. As a starting point, it is good to use a static threshold to analyze the datasets, gathered at particular time intervals. Most technical companies find this difficult to handle [38].

3.4.1.5 Security and Privacy

In the IoT, data are transferred between objects using a wireless medium; therefore, it becomes critical to ensure the privacy and security of information. There could be a number of attacks such as physical attacks or wireless information attacks, which can affect the security and authenticity of the transmitted information. The attacker can attack the IoT devices physically or steal the information during transmission. Most of the IoT devices do not accept security packages, which leads to low self-defense.

Privacy means to ensure three things: firstly who collects the personal information, secondly how this information is collected, and lastly the time when the information is gathered. Moreover, the acquired personal information must be used by an authorized person and should be stored on an authorized server, and only an authorized client should be able to access the information [41].

3.4.2 Process Challenges

Challenges relating to the processing of Big Data are discussed below.

3.4.2.1 Selective Data Acquisition

In today's world, data acquired using sensors and other devices are in petabytes. However, not all collected data are important, so data must be filtered and compressed. These filters decide the data that should be collected and those that should be discarded. For example, if all the sensors except one are giving readings within an acceptable range, then it is possible that that sensor is either faulty or something has gone wrong in that sensing area, which should be investigated. Therefore, the task of designing a smart filter to make such decisions in real time presents a significant challenge [41].

3.4.2.2 Data Extraction

The gathered information is mostly in different formats. For instance, a health record can comprise MRI data, prescriptions, medical reports, x-ray images, etc., all of which information is in different formats. In order for this information to be used effectively, the data must be transformed into a single structured format. Therefore, a new extraction process is needed that can extract the required data from the source and transform it into a structured format suitable for analysis. The correct design and maintenance of this extraction process is a big challenge [41].

3.4.2.3 Data Heterogeneity

Data gathered from diverse sources are heterogeneous in nature; hence, data processing is not a straightforward process because finding, identifying, and understanding information are difficult when the data sources cannot be integrated seamlessly. When data are heterogeneous, analysis becomes difficult because the data have different structures and different semantics. Thus, the integration of heterogeneous data for processing in real time presents a major challenge. New data mapping and data integration systems need to be designed to ensure seamless integration of data from heterogeneous sources.

3.4.2.4 Nature of Big Data

Big Data is unreliable, dynamic, heterogeneous, noisy, and interconnected [42]. Sometimes, noisy data is more useful than small datasets because repeated patterns can be extracted from general statistics. Hidden information can also be revealed through interrelation analysis [30]. Redundant data can sometimes be useful in finding missing data and can also be analyzed to find unreliable relationships and to discover hidden models [43].

3.5 Analytics Challenges of the IoT Big Data

In this section, we discuss several challenges associated with IoT data analytics. These challenges are related to unstructured data analytics (i.e., text analytics, audio analytics, video analytics, and social media analytics) and visualization challenges.

3.5.1 Analytics Challenges over Unstructured Data

The analysis of unstructured data such as text, audio, video, and social media is difficult. Text analytics are those procedures that extract information from textual data. Some examples of textual data are feeds from social networks like Facebook, Twitter, etc. and online forums, blogs, emails, white papers and other documents, etc. It involves statistical analysis, natural language processing, and deep learning. Transforming large volumes of randomly generated text into meaningful abstracts, which support cue-based decision-making, is challenging. Apple's Siri and IBM's Watson are examples of commercial question answering systems which have been implemented in various domains like healthcare, education, finance, marketing, and banking, and these systems rely on complex natural language processing, information retrieval, and knowledge-based approaches [28].

Audio analytics refer to processes that analyze and extract information from raw audio data. It is also known as speech analytics. Business process outsourcing (BPO) uses audio analytics for the effective analysis of recorded calls, which in turn helps to improve customer experience, appraise agent performance, elevate sales turnover rates, cue into customer behavior, identify service problems, and monitor compliance with security and privacy policies, among other tasks [27]. Audio analytics systems are designed to scrutinize a live call, forecast recommendations based on customers' past interactions, and provide feedback to BPO agents in real time.

Video analytics are those procedures that monitor, analyze, and extract meaningful information from raw video streams. The increased ubiquity of CCTV cameras and video sharing websites is leading to the proliferation of computerized video analysis. However, a key challenge is the enormity of the video data. Big Data analytics overcomes the need for manual processing to automatically scrutinize and derive intelligence from millions of hours of streaming video. In modern times, video analytics have been applied in automated surveillance systems, in order to detect trespassing in restricted zones, identify unknown objects, and recognize spying or suspicious activities. On detection of a threat, an automated alarm goes off to notify the security personnel in real time. In retail outlets, data generated by CCTV cameras may provide business intelligence to discover the demographics, choices, behaviors, buying patterns, etc. of consumers [27].

Social media analytics are the processes that analyze and extract meaningful information from social media channels such as Facebook, Twitter, LinkedIn, Instagram, Wikipedia, wikiHow, YouTube, ResearchGate, Ask.com, etc. Social media analytics is a relatively new area. The challenges of the modern social analytics are its data-centric nature and its research which is interdisciplinary and may include the domains of psychology, sociology, computer science, mathematics, economics, and statistics. The primary application of social media analytics has been in marketing and business management. Content generated by users (e.g., photos, videos, emotions, thoughts, etc.) and the relationships and synergy between the network entities (e.g., people, businesses, and merchandise) are the different sources of information in social media.

3.5.2 Visualization Challenges

Visualization helps to improve the human cognitive process by quickly identifying interesting and significant events and patterns in collected data [44–47]. Some other benefits of visualization include better understanding of large datasets, quick recognition of errors and outliers in datasets, facilitation of hypothesis formation from data, etc. [48]. A wide range of studies on visualization have been carried out, proposing techniques and methods to facilitate the process in order to obtain insights from data; some of these techniques include visualization of unstructured temporal data with a parallel rendering algorithm [49], taxonomies of interaction techniques [50], the focus-on-context technique [51], tree maps for visualizing hierarchical data structure while making use of all of the available space [52], and artificial reality in visualization [53].

The total amount of data generated is expected to experience a significant growth. However, approximately 3% of the collected data was tagged, and approximately 0.5% of the world's digital data was analyzed [54]. Approaches are needed to represent data in a more intuitive way to improve the understanding of data and provide adequate support for decision-making. Visualization is expected to assist in tackling some of these challenges. Visualization challenges include its applicability for a large volume of data, the possibility of visualization of data being presented in different data formats, speed, and effectiveness of data presentation.

3.6   Semantics Challenges of the IoT Big Data

In this section, we present challenges related to IoT data semantics. These challenges are associated with data interoperability, data semantics, data scalability, data fusion, data integration, data quality and trustworthiness, and data discovery.

3.6.1   Data Interoperability Challenges

To make the data interoperable, semantic description of and an ontology for the data are required. Ontologies describe formally shared conceptualizations of a domain of interest [55]. Solodovnik [56] described the concept of ontology from its philosophical origins to its adoption within the IT field as follows: *Philosophically, ontology is a systematic explanation of being that describes the features of Reality. Nowadays Ontology is proliferating in organizing Knowledge of different domains managed by advanced computer tools. Ontology qualifies and relates semantic categories, dragging, however, the idea of what, since the seventeenth century, was a way to organize and classify objects in the world. Ontology maximizes the reusability and interoperability of concepts, capturing new Knowledge within the most granular levels of information representation. Ontology is subjected to a continuous process of exploration, formation of hypothesis, testing and review.*

Data will be interoperable for users, who use the same ontology. In most cases, ontology and semantic description are defined only for a specific project, but for achieving global semantic interoperability, a common definition of ontology and semantic description framework must be adopted. For this reason, the ontologies must be reusable by a large number of applications. The sharing of the ontologies of current and previous applications is an effective means of achieving semantic interoperability on a global level.

There are millions of heterogeneous devices in our environment. These heterogeneous devices must be connected in such a way that they can communicate easily. We need semantic interoperability which enables all the stakeholders to interpret and access the data from these heterogeneous devices without any issue. Within the IoT, objects/things are required to exchange data with other things and users on the Internet. This data must be processed and interpreted by machines in such a way that information communication can be automated in the IoT. Data semantic annotation provides information that is machine interoperable, and this information can reveal the source of data, relationship of data with surroundings, provider of data, quality of data, and description of technical and nontechnical terms [57]. Therefore, the accessing and processing of data from a number of heterogeneous devices are going to become increasingly challenging in the years to come.

3.6.2   Data Semantics Challenges

Millions of heterogeneous devices are connected to different types of sensors in order to collect real-world data and to communicate with other devices. Interoperable service-oriented technologies are intended to share the real-world data among these heterogeneous devices to integrate and fuse these semantic data [58]. Data semantics is one of the major elements of data analysis. It is a challenging task to deal with different data structures and information types and to analyze the data as the structure of information is very complex. Also, the system does not have adequate knowledge enabling it to describe fully the semantic meaning of the analyzed information. Computer cognitive resonance techniques have been proposed by [59], which can solve the problem by using a cognitive information system that uses features extracted from records and knowledge in the database. It is quite conducive to the analysis of the semantic data of different information records. The integration of various heterogeneous collections of data has become a colossal issue as the existing data sources are very sparse and incomplete which makes it an onerous task to find a logical connection between the data.

3.6.3   Data Scalability Challenges

It is challenging for data engineers to create domain knowledge models and semantic annotation frameworks which can describe a huge number of devices in the IoT. Domain knowledge must be associated with semantic descriptions of data because IoT data can refer to separate phenomena. In many applications, to define IoT data's spatial aspects, linked open data (an approach that interconnects different resources of IoT) are used as domain knowledge. However, linked sensor data is mostly inconsistent and contains numerous errors. As a solution for this problem, most of the applications design and maintain their own domain knowledge. However, this limits their interoperability. Another big challenge concerns granularity description; if the terms and concepts are very specific, then the domain knowledge is very extensive. The semantic web community has done a great deal of work in developing an efficient technique for storing and querying large semantic data in a distributed environment. However, the challenges in handling semantic data are the scale of data developed by IoT resources, the changing status of resources and data, and the volatility of the IoT environment. Research should address these issues and develop solutions to define linked IoT data which can analyze the links between the resources, and semantic repositories must be developed which can access and query the sensory data [57].

3.6.4   Data Fusion Challenges

Data fusion is used as a means of improving the quality of the data. Data fusion focuses on the computation of structured and comparable semantic data in order to obtain appropriate decisions. Semantic data fusion is challenging as data are acquired from multiple sensors, and different types of algorithms are used to improve the quality and accuracy of the data. Data fusion in the IoT, based on such multi-sensor data, produces new information. Information fusion is the major part of the information and comprises of several theories, techniques, and algorithms. It can improve the accuracy and produce more accurate results as the data is produced from multiple sensors and cognate information which is obtained from the affiliated databases. The major function of information fusion is to integrate diverse types of semantic data, without which the related data and information cannot be integrated, because it is impossible to process information fusion computation using a variety of algorithms as heterogeneous data cannot be correlated.

3.6.5   Data Integration Challenges

Mostly, IoT data are generated from sensor devices, humans, or a physical entity. To create multiple environment abstraction, this data can be merged with other data. This data can be combined with the processing chain in an application which already exists, and this data can support situation awareness. It is necessary that different types of data be combined seamlessly [60]. Semantic description assists this combination process by facilitating interoperability among different sources of data. However, to enable IoT data integration, the mapping and analysis of different semantic description models are required.

The combination of appropriate data that reside in a huge number of data sources which are heterogeneous in nature may conflict in terms of value and structure. This type of data integration allows the user to have a unique view of the data. Semantic technology is the fundamental technology of data integration. Data integration systems are commonly defined as a triple GSM, where G is the global schema, S is the discordant set of source schemas, and M is a mapping that maps queries between the source and the global schemas. For each of G and S, their respective relations are defined in languages which consist of symbols. In this way, huge amounts of linked data are transformed from the raw IoT data. Using the basic idea of data integration, different models at schema level are merged together when users need an integration of the relevant heterogeneous data. As a result, the data at the instance level are presented in a unified view to achieve data integration. By means of mapping, different models at schema level can be merged. These mappings are obtained in several ways. Predefined mapping is the first method of mapping which may produce highly accurate data, but is not efficient. The second method is based on mapping which is determined with the help of computation by following several principles such as the linked open data cloud. Schema level mapping is one of the main functions of integrating data.

3.6.6   Data Quality and Trustworthiness Challenges

Sensor devices generate IoT data which have errors and quality issues. Quality means that data must be complete and accurate and must be available when required. The quality of data collected through sensors can change over time. For example, this occurs if there is any environmental change, due to any faulty device or due to any error in the settings of device. It is not possible to avoid inaccuracy in IoT data. To retrieve and process quality data, readings from IoT devices need to be detected and filtered, in addition to having semantic descriptions of the attributes of quality. This could also assist with error detection. Another main issue is trust, especially when data are generated by many different sources. Trustworthiness of data and sources can be achieved by identifying the data provider and verifying data accuracy and reliability, along with the semantics which describe the quality and trust attributes of sources and providers. Although semantics can be used to define trust and reliability attributes, several major issues still need to be addressed such as the development of a trust model, feedback, and the development of a verification mechanism [57].

3.6.7   Data Discovery Challenges

The efficient handling of data and storage is becoming more difficult with time as the volume of data and semantic description is increasing day by day. Sensor data must be stored with semantic descriptions, and this data can be stored temporarily or for a lengthy period. The main challenges include designing and developing repositories, publishing the semantic data, accessing the semantic data in distributed environments, and developing effective indexing and discovery mechanisms. To address these issues, an effective mechanism for information indexing, search, access, and query is required. Such mechanism could be used for the discovery of relevant data from many sources, real-time query and aggregation of multiple data streams, description of various events and data which are generated by many sources, and data discovery when semantic data is distributed among multiple repositories. Cloud computing is a good technical approach which can overcome some of these issues, but in order to handle, process, and maintain data, the solution must be scalable and efficient; it is not sufficient to simply develop a centralized and non-scalable solution and put it in the cloud [57].

3.7 Conclusion

New properties are emerging in IoT with every passing day. Inter-conceivable service-oriented technologies are imperative for sharing real-world data among discordant devices to integrate and fuse multisource IoT data. The IoT can offer only trivial and insignificant benefits if it cannot integrate and incorporate useful information from the data generated by multiple interconnected devices. This is where Big Data analytics plays a critical role and bring out the value from the information and data gathered by IoT devices. Hence, research in the field of Big Data analytics and IoT is becoming important as it has diverse application areas, especially in the context of smart cities. This chapter introduced and described number of challenges at the intersection of IoT and Big Data to provide a holistic view on how to manage these challenges effectively. Managing such large datasets poses substantial difficulties under computing and time constraints. We elaborated the challenges associated with data management (such as size and forms of data, time series analysis, security, and privacy), data processing (such as data acquisition, extraction, and heterogeneity), unstructured data analytics, data visualization, and data semantics (such as interoperability, data fusion, data integration, data quality, and data discovery). We then described the latest solutions to address these upcoming challenges to provide guidance for future research in this field. Overall, this chapter will guide researchers by providing the most up-to-date information on challenges and solutions at the intersection of IoT and Big Data.

References

1. Aggarwal CC, Ashish N, Sheth A (2013) The internet of things: a survey from the data-centric perspective. In: Managing and mining sensor data. Springer, Boston, pp 383–428
2. Perera C, Vasilakos AV (2016) A knowledge-based resource discovery for internet of things. Knowl-Based Syst 109:122–136
3. Sundmaeker H, Guillemin P, Friess P, Woelfflé S (2010) Vision and challenges for realising the internet of things. The Cluster of European Research projects on the Internet of Things, European Commission
4. Verizon (2016) State of the market: internet of things 2016
5. Gubbi J, Buyya R, Marusic S, Palaniswami M (2013) Internet of things (IoT): a vision, architectural elements, and future directions. Future Gener Comput Syst 29:1645–1660
6. Said O, Masud M (2013) Towards internet of things: survey and future vision. Int J Comput Netw IJCN 5:1–17
7. Said O, Tolba A (2012) SEAIoT: scalable e-health architecture based on internet of things. Int J Comput Appl 59
8. Evans D (2012) The internet of things how the next evolution of the internet is changing everything (April 2011). White Paper. Cisco Internet Business Solutions Group (IBSG)
9. Atzori L, Iera A, Morabito G (2010) The internet of things: a survey. Comput Netw 54:2787–2805
10. Xia F, Yang LT, Wang L, Vinel A (2012) Internet of things. Int J Commun Syst 25:1101
11. Yoo Y, Henfridsson O, Lyytinen K (2010) Research commentary—the new organizing logic of digital innovation: an agenda for information systems research. Inf Syst Res 21:724–735

12. Wortmann F, Flüchter K (2015) Internet of things. Bus Inf Syst Eng 57:221–224
13. Salim F, Haque U (2015) Urban computing in the wild: a survey on large scale participation and citizen engagement with ubiquitous computing, cyber physical systems, and internet of things. Int J Hum-Comput Stud 81:31–48. https://doi.org/10.1016/j.ijhcs.2015.03.003
14. Baheti R, Gill H (2011) Cyber-physical systems. Impact Control Technol 12:161–166
15. ZHANG Y, XIE F, DONG Y et al (2013) High fidelity virtualization of cyber-physical systems. Int J Model Simul Sci Comput 4:1340005
16. Lee EA (2006) Cyber-physical systems-are computing foundations adequate. 2
17. Wan J, Yan H, Suo H, Li F (2011) Advances in cyber-physical systems research. TIIS 5:1891–1908
18. Chao H, Cao Y, Chen Y (2010) Autopilots for small unmanned aerial vehicles: a survey. Int J Control Autom Syst 8:36–44
19. Khan R, Khan SU, Zaheer R, Khan S (2012) Future internet: the internet of things architecture, possible applications and key challenges. IEEE:257–260
20. Wu M, Lu T-J, Ling F-Y et al (2010) Research on the architecture of internet of things. IEEE:V5-484–V5-487
21. Chen M, Mao S, Liu Y (2014) Big data: a survey. Mob Netw Appl 19:171–209
22. Gantz J, Reinsel D (2011) Extracting value from chaos. IDC Iview 1142:1–12
23. Schonfeld E (2010) Costolo: twitter now has 190 million users tweeting 65 million times a day. Techcrunch June 8
24. Manyika J, Chui M, Brown B et al (2011) Big data: the next frontier for innovation, competition, and productivity
25. Hashem IAT, Yaqoob I, Anuar NB et al (2015) The rise of "big data" on cloud computing: review and open research issues. Inf Syst 47:98–115
26. Zikopoulos P, Eaton C (2011) Understanding big data: analytics for enterprise class hadoop and streaming data. McGraw-Hill Osborne Media, New York
27. Gandomi A, Haider M (2015) Beyond the hype: big data concepts, methods, and analytics. Int J Inf Manag 35:137–144
28. Schroeck M, Shockley R, Smart J et al (2012) Analytics: the real-world use of big data: how innovative enterprises extract value from uncertain data, executive report. IBM Institute for Business Value Saïd Business School, University of Oxford
29. Beaver D, Kumar S, Li HC et al (2010) Finding a needle in haystack: facebook's photo storage, pp 1–8
30. Nasser T, Tariq RS (2015) Big data challenges. J Comput Eng Inf Technol 4:3
31. Russom P (2011) Big data analytics. TDWI Best Pract Rep Fourth Quart:1–35
32. Cukier K (2010) Data, data everywhere: a special report on managing information. Economist Newspaper, London
33. Ragothaman B, Prabha MS, Jose E, Sarojini B (2016) A survey on big data and internet of things. World Sci News 41:174
34. Shao G, Shin S-J, Jain S (2014) Data analytics using simulation for smart manufacturing. In: Proceedings 2014 winter simulation conference. IEEE Press, pp 2192–2203
35. Lakshman TV, Madhow U (1997) The performance of TCP/IP for networks with high bandwidth-delay products and random loss. IEEEACM Trans Netw ToN 5:336–350
36. Vilamovska A-M, Hatziandreu E, Schindler HR et al (2009) Study on the requirements and options for RFID application in healthcare
37. Deshpande B (2016) 3 challenges unique to IoT analytics. https://www.owler.com/reports/simafore/3-challenges-unique-to-iot-analytics/1476315363392
38. Yassin AT (2014) Analyzing 6Vs of big data using system dynamics. In: 2nd scientific conference of the College of Science 2014
39. McNulty E (2014) Understanding Big Data: The Seven Vs. http://dataconomy.com/2014/05/seven-vs-big-data/
40. Chan H, Perrig A (2003) Security and privacy in sensor networks. Computer 36:103–105

41. Labrinidis A, Jagadish HV (2012) Challenges and opportunities with big data. Proc VLDB Endow 5:2032–2033
42. Katal A, Wazid M, Goudar RH (2013) Big data: issues, challenges, tools and good practices. IEEE:404–409
43. Pradeepa A, Thanamani A (2013) Significant trends of big data analytics in social network. NGM Coll, India
44. Bauer MI, Johnson-Laird PN (1993) How diagrams can improve reasoning. Psychol Sci 4:372–378
45. Larkin JH, Simon HA (1987) Why a diagram is (sometimes) worth ten thousand words. Cogn Sci 11:65–100
46. Mayer RE, Gallini JK (1990) When is an illustration worth ten thousand words? J Educ Psychol 82:715
47. Card SK, Mackinlay JD, Shneiderman B (1999) Readings in information visualization: using vision to think. Morgan Kaufmann, San Francisco
48. Ware C (2012) Information visualization: perception for design. Elsevier, Amsterdam
49. Ma K-L, Stompel A, Bielak J et al (2003) Visualizing very large-scale earthquake simulations. In: Supercomput. 2003 ACMIEEE conference IEEE, pp 48–48
50. Yi JS, ah Kang Y, Stasko J (2007) Toward a deeper understanding of the role of interaction in information visualization. IEEE Trans Vis Comput Graph 13:1224–1231
51. Lamping J, Rao R, Pirolli P (1995) A focus+ context technique based on hyperbolic geometry for visualizing large hierarchies. In: Proceedings of the SIGCHI conference on human factors in computing systems. ACM Press/Addison-Wesley Publishing Co, pp 401–408
52. Johnson B, Shneiderman B (1991) Tree-maps: a space-filling approach to the visualization of hierarchical information structures. In: Proceedings of 2nd conference on visualization. IEEE Computer Society Press, pp 284–291
53. Erickson T (1986) Artificial realities as data visualization environments: problems and prospects. Virtual Real-Appl Explor:3–22
54. Tam NT, Song I (2016) Big data visualization. In: Information science and applications ICISA 2016. Springer, pp 399–408
55. Gruber TR (1993) Toward principles for the design of ontologies used for knowledge sharing
56. Solodovnik I (2010) ONTOLOGY: from philosophy to ICT and related areas
57. Payam B, Wei W, Cory H, Kerry T (2012) Semantics for the internet of things: early progress and back to the future. Int J Semantic Web Inf Syst IJSWIS 1:1–21. https://doi.org/10.4018/jswis.2012010101
58. Nugraheni E, Akbar S, Saptawati GAP (2016) Framework of semantic data warehouse for heterogeneous and incomplete data. In: Region 10 symposium. TENSYMP 2016 IEEE. IEEE, pp 161–166
59. Ogiela L, Ogiela MR (2015) Semantic data analysis algorithms supporting decision-making processes. In: Broadband Wireless Computing and Communication Applications. BWCCA 2015 10th international conference on IEEE, pp 494–496
60. Sheth AP (2011) Computing for human experience: semantics empowered cyber-physical, social and ubiquitous computing beyond the Web

Chapter 4
Using Cloud Computing to Address Challenges Raised by the Internet of Things

Marinela Mircea, Marian Stoica, and Bogdan Ghilic-Micu

Abstract The growing number of connected smart devices and the expansion of data storage capacities and data analytics make the fabric of the global interconnection of the manifold universe of human existence. On top of that, the premise of this type of global network of technology infrastructure enables the development of efficient and dynamic enterprise services. The Internet of Things (IoT) interconnects real-world objects through a large variety of technologies, devices, and protocols. Besides its benefits, the IoT is faced with problems and challenges related to scalability, interoperability, reliability, efficiency, availability, storage, and security (known as the Big 7 of IoT), which experts try to overcome with various solutions. This chapter addresses one of the solutions, namely, Cloud Computing. It dwells on the seven challenges in IoT and the extent to which Cloud Computing can address them (the Big 7 of IoT). It is an analytic approach that focuses on the new paradigms emerging from coupling Cloud and IoT together, which has resulted in the Cloud of Things or CloudIoT.

4.1 Introduction

History credits Johannes Gutenberg with the invention of the printing press 562 years ago, though the movable type first originated in China in the twelfth century. We cannot say the same about the Internet, which has no single recognized parent, but we can say for sure that the development of the Internet has influenced mankind as least as much as the printing press, if only for the field of information and the art of solving codes. It only took a small technology-enabled step to take us in the realm of the Internet of Things or IoT for short. From an economic angle, the IoT is by far the biggest business ever in electronic communication devices. Moreover, it is the founding stone of a digital industrial world, the successor of the

M. Mircea (✉) • M. Stoica • B. Ghilic-Micu
Department of Economic Informatics and Cybernetics, The Bucharest University
of Economic Studies, Bucharest, Romania
e-mail: mmircea@ase.ro

© Springer International Publishing AG 2017   63
Z. Mahmood (ed.), *Connected Environments for the Internet of Things*,
Computer Communications and Networks,
https://doi.org/10.1007/978-3-319-70102-8_4

information and knowledge society. Just like any other element of novelty, the IoT comes with a host of advantages but also challenges that experts are trying to overcome through various solutions.

Cloud Computing comes with large storage capacities and data processing applications and provides on-demand tailored services. In the last 10 years, however, Cloud technology has been "troubling the waters" of enterprise architecture (at least in the sense of its technology component), human resources, and investment policies. In their fast-paced development, modern technology paradigms do not only shake the technical side of an enterprise, but they also enable a change in the way individuals live and work. The current economic, social, and political context can furnish the IoT with the features of a "selective black hole." From the jungle of technology and methodological instruments, it would only absorb those elements which, if implemented, would answer the problems and challenges facing us today as well as in the future (provided we can speak of some predictability of the IoT).

The IoT involves a big volume of data and a wide range of sources of information. Among the problems the IoT is faced with are the collection, acquisition, processing, archiving, and sharing of this volume of data. Cloud Computing is part of the solution and offers unlimited on-demand storage capacity, reduced costs, fast access, and ease of use. Additionally, many of the IoT applications can be developed, run, and managed online by using Cloud-based Big Data Analytics and Cloud Storage facilities. The IoT can also benefit from the agility, scalability, storing capacity, and performance of Cloud Computing. Cloud Computing-based IoT architecture answers more than one challenge/problem and leads to better agility of the connected environment. Furthermore, interdependencies created in the operation of the two paradigms may result in symbiotic products designated in terms such as Cloud of Things (CoT) or CloudIoT.

IoT and Cloud Computing are emerging technologies with features of their own, which may create added value when used together. The IoT enables objects to be virtually represented and connected over the Internet, while Cloud Computing allows for the effective use of the services attached to these things, as a means of payment for the service provided [1]. Cloud Computing is an important element in the IoT architecture. Cloud services are globally accessible, irrespective of place and time, allowing for the data to be transferred and the objects making the network to interact. It also offers fast scalability, by adjusting the storage and computing capacities to the needs of the network.

Researchers and practitioners alike consider Cloud Computing and the IoT to be two complementary technologies [1, 2]. This consideration is the main reason why we are faced with so many proposals to integrate the two paradigms, which would bring benefits to specific areas, such as smart cities, smart energy, smart grids, smart healthcare, and smart metering [3–5]. Moreover, the features of the CloudIoT paradigm can help reduce the difficulties and the challenges stemming from the connected media [6]. Many times integration is no longer an option but a must. Because of the large volume of data generated by the IoT and the need for large storage and use capacities of virtual resources, integration with Cloud Computing becomes both important and necessary [7]. The need to integrate IoT and Cloud Computing is also analyzed in [8], where the authors are highlighting the features of integration and complementarity.

The main focus of this chapter lays both on the problems and challenges of the IoT and the ways Cloud Computing can meet them via the three traditional services it supplies: Software as a Service (SaaS), Platform as a Service (PaaS), and Infrastructure as a Service (IaaS). This chapter is split into four parts that form a linear approach to the topic, viz., Introduction; Problems and Challenges of the Internet of Things: The Big 7 of IoT; Combining Cloud Computing and the IoT to Address the Inherent Challenges of IoT; and Conclusions.

This chapter opens with a short introduction of the topic, focusing on the need and the benefits of integrating Cloud Computing and the IoT. It continues with the analysis of scalability, interoperability, reliability, efficiency, availability, storage, and security in the IoT and the identification of major problems and challenges these features are faced with in the connected environment. The third part dwells on the benefits of Cloud Computing and IoT integration and the solutions to the problems and challenges identified in the previous section. This chapter ends with conclusions, limitations, and future research directions.

4.2   Problems and Challenges of the Internet of Things: The Big 7 of IoT

The IoT makes it possible for objects to interact by sharing information and providing services through Internet protocols. The magnitude of the connected environment together with the multitude of heterogeneous objects requires solutions to at least the following seven major challenges: scalability, interoperability, reliability, efficiency, availability, storage, and security. According to Gartner, by 2020, the IoT will include 26 billion units, which creates new challenges in all data center-related aspects [9]. The IoT developments also require real-time processing of Big Data volumes, which causes an increase in the load in data centers and generates new challenges with respect to security, capacity, and data analytics [10]. The challenges are discussed below.

4.2.1   Scalability in IoT

A scalable IoT system must allow for the connection of new devices, new users, and new analytical capabilities as well as for the technology able to ensure long-term support. Scalability in IoT must also consider the possibility to provide good-quality service (response time, analytics) under the circumstances of a growing number of new users and/or devices. Given the rapid growth of the connected devices, the frequent changes in technology, the large number of interactions within the IoT, as well as the growing demand for services, scalability in the IoT is still a major challenge of our society today.

It is not by chance that developments in technology in the past years have focused on higher storage and better data processing capabilities. One of the modern technologies prone to ensuring the needed scalability features in IoT is found in non-relational databases and the systems processing GIS data.

4.2.2 Interoperability in IoT

Considering the heterogeneity of the different systems integrated in the IoT, interoperability is another major challenge that the IoT must face for the successful delivery of services and data sharing. In spite of the fast development of the IoT systems, interoperability between the IoT systems comes at a high cost, even as high as \$4 trillion or 40% of the overall IoT worth by 2015, according to McKinsey report [11].

Good IoT interoperability requires platform-related standards enabling communication, operability, and integration of different kinds of devices. Despite the efforts of the past few years, interoperability still stays a major challenge in IoT. Network data acquisition, data sharing, processing, and use have so far been very challenging. Interoperability can be analyzed in the light of factors such as the level of data perception (technical, syntactical, semantic, organizational) or the moment when interoperability is achieved (static, dynamic) [12].

There are four directions in the analysis of information: technical (the way data are represented on the physical media), syntactical (syntactical constructions used to represent the information in the collection, transmission, recording, and processing of data), semantic (the meaning of the data), and organizational (the overall amount of information an organization holds). With information at its core, interoperability can be analyzed along the four lines of information perceived: technical, syntactic, semantic, and organizational [13].

At the technical level, interoperability is analyzed at the level of hardware/software components, systems, and platforms that enable machine-to-machine communication (M2M). This type of analysis focuses on protocols and communication infrastructure. Syntactic interoperability focuses on the data formats transferred though the communication protocols. Many communication protocols convey data or contents by using high-level syntax such as HTML or XML. Semantic interoperability is related to the human interpretation of the content (information) being shared. Semantically, information can be defined in terms of data significance and can be discussed in terms of information flows. Organizational interoperability pertains to the capability of organizations to effectively communicate and transfer data (information) among different types of systems, infrastructures, across various geographic regions and cultures. Successful organizational interoperability relies on the success of technical, syntactic, and semantic interoperability. Organizational interoperability also relies on the success of the information process. The process of

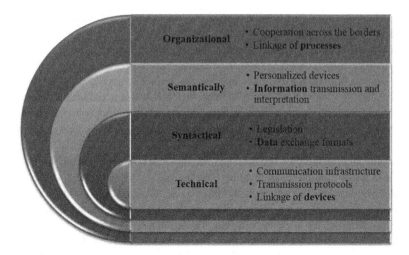

Fig. 4.1 Challenges by levels of interoperability in IoT

information communication should ensure the lowest possible redundancy between the sender and receiver entities, thus enabling the reception and comprehension of the message.

Starting from the four levels of interoperability, Fig. 4.1 identifies the challenges in interoperability peculiar to each level (devices, data, information, and processes).

The IoT consists in a large variety of applications, which gives rise to challenges in point of *static interoperability* (fulfillment of all conformity requests). Some level of non-interoperability is often accepted (for some of the protocols, for instance), provided it is addressed on the way (*dynamic interoperability*). Features of dynamic interoperability are found in intelligent gateways and middleware from heterogeneous and complex IoT environments [12].

4.2.3   Reliability in IoT

In a system, reliability is defined as the ability of the system to consistently implement a request/mission without fail/fault, a definition that also suits the IoT environment. Since the IoT consists in a vast volume of information where data needs to be accessed, processed, and manipulated correctly, new architectures are required to disseminate and process information in a reliable and effective manner.

Most of the IoT applications are required to operate for a specific time horizon, which asks for a longer-term investment. Under the circumstances, the network should be adaptable enough to adjust to the conditions of the environment or the required changes in the network components. Standardization efforts are critical in securing good reliability. Kempf et al. (2011) outline four major research areas in standardization: reliability in the design of system architecture, reliability in the development of the system, support for mobile network sensor gateway communication, and reliability at transfer level [14].

Reliability in IoT can be analyzed starting from the levels of IoT architecture. According to the literature, IoT architecture evinces more than one type (for instance, IoT-A, Internet-of-Things Architecture; IIRA, Industrial Internet Reference Architecture) and the same stands for reference models. In this context, it is important to look at reliability in IoT at the level of the devices, network, and the provided services.

Considering the number and diversity of connected devices, *reliability of devices* turns into a true challenge. Depending on the type and role of a device, the system should provide correct, continued, and intensive data access and good data processing, even when there is no power, no or weak Wi-Fi signal, when a server or an access point fails.

The high number of users that are connected to the Internet for various online services in combination with the multitude of devices connected to the IoT network is challenging to network operators, as they should secure uninterrupted broad network access. *Network reliability* is vital for the success of IoT and should be analyzed both at the level of each network provider and the IoT as a whole. At IoT level, there can be several types of networks or network operators in place, which may result in additional challenges in securing uninterrupted broad access.

Reliability in the provided services deals with ensuring a good availability, collection, storage, and processing of large volumes of data taken from the IoT devices, with no error of failure. In the light of these considerations, reliability in IoT is closely connected with interoperability.

4.2.4 Efficiency in IoT

Ensuring efficiency in IoT is yet another challenge of a connected environment. The network should be capable to support different real-time analyses of a big volume of data available in the network, to satisfy the diversity of data processing requests, and to process data as fast as it arrives, irrespective of their storage place (data decentralization). Another challenge is linked to ensuring advanced data processing and analysis with a view to support the machine learning processes embedded in smart devices.

That is why the IoT structure should be supplemented with specific elements of artificial intelligence, such as neural networks or intelligent agents. From the same perspective of efficiency, we may look at the economic angle of the IoT network and measure the effect of its operation in a well-defined context against the effort fed into its operation. Moreover, by assigning the IoT a cybernetic paradigm, it turns into an element of the higher-order feedback loop showing a systemic behavior in relation to its environment. A systemic approach to the IoT automatically endows it with a different perspective of efficiency.

4.2.5 Availability in IoT

So far as the availability/access is concerned, several factors come into play [15]: time, place, service provision, network, object, and user. Figure 4.2 presents the availability requirements in IoT as well as the challenges facing such requirements.

In addition to the six availability factors in IoT that we mentioned before, we should also consider the aspects pertaining to the environment, which emerge more and more in the current trends in technology developments, such as green computing, green cloud, and even green IoT, why not? This green feature is rooted first of all in the topic of exhaustible resources and renewable energy sources at the same time.

Fig. 4.2 Availability challenges in IoT

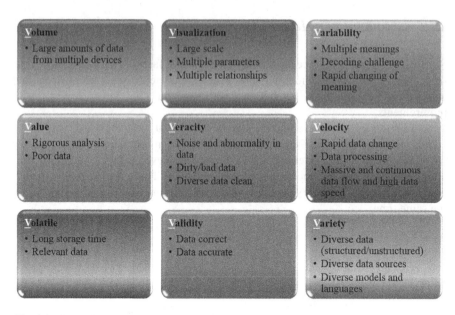

Fig. 4.3 The addiction for nine Vs of data storage challenges in IoT

4.2.6 Storage in IoT

The IoT generates large volumes of data that should be processed and analyzed in real time. This leads to a high volume of operations to be executed in data centers, which comes with new challenges in point of security, network capacity, and analytical capabilities. On top of that, the multitude of heterogeneous devices combined with a large volume of data creates challenges in data storage management. Storage management should consider at least the following IoT data-related challenges (the nine Vs of Big Data): volume, variety, velocity, variability, visualization, veracity, validity, volatile, and value (Fig. 4.3).

We can see that in terms of data storage capacity, next to the fundamental features defining the concept of Big Data (volume, velocity, variety), the IoT evinces six other different aspects. Each of them comes with two or three sensitive challenges that require a collective interpretation in the general context of the IoT.

4.2.7 Security in IoT

The IoT supposes the existence of numerous connected devices, which gives rise to multiple entry points and necessarily higher security risks. Moreover, more than one level of software, integration middleware, APIs, machine-to-machine communication, etc. necessarily result in a complex environment and high security risks [16].

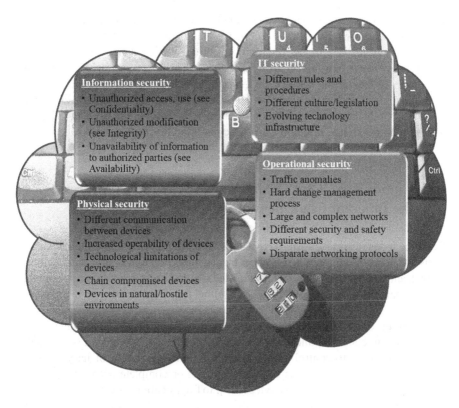

Fig. 4.4 Security challenges in IoT

Security in IoT is both a challenge and a top priority. Since technology is a scale phenomenon in our daily lives, we must ensure the security of the devices and the services provided to consumers. There are several dimensions to the analysis of security in IoT [17] including information security, information technology (IT) security, physical security, and operational security. Starting from the four dimensions, Fig. 4.4 illustrates some of the security challenges in IoT.

Information security is first aimed at ensuring the confidentiality, integrity, and availability of data. In the context of the IoT, another major security element is for the data to preserve their non-repudiation features. Beyond the four dimensions in the analysis of data security in IoT, the topic remains critical. Security is the main reason why we see so much concern for quality assurance and the development of standardization in IoT frameworks and architectures. Security also makes the main barrier in the way of what is now the effort to expand the IoT in the area of government.

IoT security challenges also stem from the strongly heterogeneous nature of the IoT components as such. In other words, the IoT may shift all the vulnerabilities of the digital world to the real world. Any IoT component, either an individual or an object, is subject to some level of exposure.

Given the major challenges and problems the connected environment is confronted with, experts have never stopped looking for solutions to address them. Cloud Computing is a modern solution bringing important benefits through the three types of services it offers (IaaS, PaaS, SaaS). The next paragraphs dwell on the advantages of integrating Cloud Computing and the IoT in countering the problems and challenges described before. Focus is laid on the analysis of Cloud Computing in the light of the benefits and solutions it offers at the level of the Big 7 of IoT (scalability, interoperability, reliability, efficiency, availability, storage, and security).

4.3   Combining Cloud Computing and the IoT to Address the Inherent Challenges of IoT

The three types of services offered by Cloud Computing bring important benefits in terms of storage, computing, resource management, analytics, the management, control, and coordination of network-adjusted systems and services. Service providers offer benefits to IoT at the level of each cloud type: IaaS allows for the management of the network and hardware equipment; PaaS facilitates the management of the operating systems and the application environment; SaaS can manage everything related to clients, applications included [18]. Cloud Computing also offers the IoT the possibility to control access to the resources, by means of IaaS services; provide data access, by means of PaaS services; or complete access to software applications, by means of SaaS services [19]. IoT applications offered through SaaS are built on PaaS infrastructure, and they make it possible to conduct enterprise processes by means of IoT services and software.

The IoT can make the most of the three models of Cloud Computing: public cloud (where the service provider makes resources available to the general public over the Internet), private cloud (the services and infrastructure are part of a private network), and hybrid cloud (both public and private options). The selection of the cloud models to be used in the IoT depends on specific requirements and security.

The combined use of Cloud Computing and IoT can embrace two convergent approaches [20]: bring IoT functionalities into cloud (cloud-centric IoT) or bring cloud functionalities into IoT (IoT-centric cloud). Figures 4.5 and 4.6 present the two approaches to the combination between Cloud Computing and IoT along the three types of cloud services and models. The combination between Cloud Computing and the Internet of Things translates in paradigmatic research in the literature, such as Cloud of Things, CloudIoT, or Cloud-based IoT.

The next sections dwell on the analysis of Cloud Computing from the point of view of its benefits in coping with the seven challenges in IoT (scalability, interoperability, reliability, efficiency, availability, storage, and security) previously described.

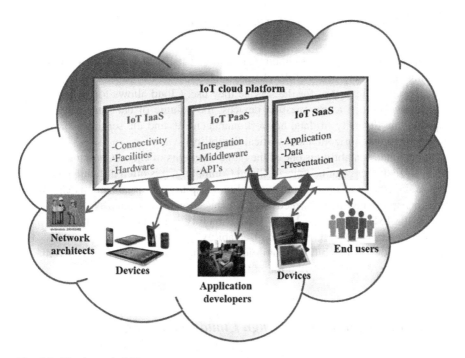

Fig. 4.5 Cloud-centric IoT

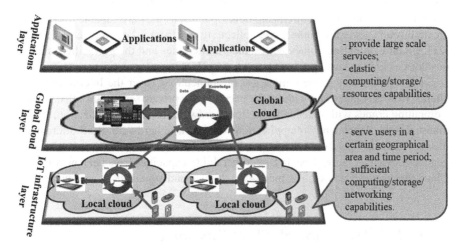

Fig. 4.6 IoT-centric Cloud Computing

4.3.1   Scalability Through Cloud Computing

One of the main features of Cloud Computing is its flexibility in adapting to the growing or declining needs of the clients. Such a feature can cause cost to go down in IoT, where clients pay for the service they use. Cloud allows for scalability on several levels, such as the existing devices, the volume of data and data storage capacity, the diversity of data, network management, and the services attached to the applications (horizontal and vertical flexibility).

On-demand scalability is one of the biggest benefits of Cloud Computing. When we analyze the range of benefits of Cloud Computing, it is often difficult to conceptualize the power of on-demand scalability. Despite that, organizations can enjoy huge benefits when they correctly implement automated scalability. It is obvious that in the IoT context, the benefits of scalability come hand in hand with their inherent complexities. On-demand scalability of only some applications, for instance, asks for scalability capabilities throughout the entire cloud environment (e.g., multiple-instance distribution of traffic).

4.3.2   Interoperability Through Cloud Computing

The IoT comprises a variety of objects that are connected to the Internet in different ways, such as 2G/3G/4G, NFC, Wi-Fi, ZigBee, Bluetooth, WSAN, and Z-Wave. Moreover, many devices operate via a single channel, which generates difficulties in their interaction. One solution is to develop hubs, as they are capable to communicate through several channels and collect signals from a large range of devices [21]. Cloud Computing comes with standard interfaces and the portability of various devices among various Cloud providers [22].

SaaS services enable the remote use of applications (over the Internet) by IoT clients, from any place and without the need to have private servers installed. Cloud Computing comes with independence from hardware through virtualization, which minimizes the dependency of applications on the basic hardware. PaaS offers middleware and interoperable architectures for data sharing and services among heterogeneous devices. Lately, these IoT interoperability capacities have been provided in Cloud through services such as metal-as-a-service and container-as-a-service.

4.3.3   Reliability Through Cloud Computing

One way in which Cloud is part of the solution to better device reliability is the increase in the battery life of devices (for instance, by eliminating the heavy tasks allocated to the devices) or the possibility to put in place a modular architecture [23, 24]. Reliability of services is improved, too, as Cloud Computing provides a disruption-tolerant infrastructure by better availability of the site-redundant Cloud services [22]. Cloud Computing also uses various mechanisms to ensure data synchronization (ACID, atomicity, consistency, isolation, durability; BASE, basically available, soft state, eventual consistency), which improves transactional reliability and consistency. Network reliability can be improved by good traffic management. Cloud Computing offers control mechanisms that can manage excessive data traffic and check the activities to initiate new instances to be shared in traffic [25].

4.3.4 Efficiency Through Cloud Computing

Cloud Computing comes with different advantages resulting in increased efficiency in IoT, such as multi-zone management, allowing for high-level availability, performance, scalability, savings, or better use of energy [22]; on-demand unlimited processing capabilities, addressing the needs of IoT processing and allowing for highly complex analyses [26, 27]; real-time data processing [26, 28]; the management of complex events; real-time data access for objects [28]; and remote monitoring, control, coordination, and communication of objects [29].

4.3.5 Availability Through Cloud Computing

Cloud data are homogeneously treated through standard API interfaces [29], and they can be accessed and visualized from anywhere [28]. The Cloud environment offers effective solutions allowing to connect, follow, and manage any object (thing), irrespective of place and time, by using customized gateways and embedded applications [28]. Starting from the seven components of the availability of Cloud Computing services [30], Table 4.1 presents the benefits they bring to IoT.

4.3.6 Storage Through Cloud Computing

The IoT challenge related to the growing need for storage space can find a solution in Cloud storage, since it comes with reliability and security and it can scale-up to the needs of the IoT network. Through its storage methods, Cloud Computing offers unlimited, low-cost means to manage and analyze both structured and unstructured data.

Cloud infrastructure offers storage and processing capabilities able to address the need for IoT applications to work with Big Data. Yang et al. (2017), analyze the ways in which Cloud Computing can meet the challenges of Big Data (5 V) [32]:

Table 4.1 Benefits of Cloud Computing availability to the IoT environment

Availability component	Benefits of Cloud Computing to IoT environment
Continuity and functionality	Disaster recovery plan, at a low cost (data recovery off-site)
	Operational recovery, focused on the recovery of the technology or the applications (on-site)
	Redundant infrastructure (components, routes, power supply)
	Continuous data availability (disaster recovery copies; replacement of onsite copies in case of incident; archiving data according to organizational policies and the legislation into force; data replication)
	Service continuity, which makes it possible to provide the service in another component of the application (in case the initial component fails)
	Loose dependencies among services, which avoid a cascading disaster
	Restarting the service in case of an incident and enabling service and data access
Quality	Flexible, anywhere and anytime real-time access to shared computing resources (networks, servers, applications, storage, services)
	Multi-tenant virtual Cloud Computing platform
	Efficient processing of the users' requests in the context of big spatial data and of numerous competing requests [31]
	Platform for large-scale data analysis
	Complex data processing algorithms
	On-demand and unlimited virtual processing power [32]
Monitoring and incident management	Environment for Cloud-based implementation, machine health prognostics for Big Data, and complex processing (e.g., [33])
	Metrics and incident response plans, incident monitoring, notification, and sensing tools provided by the Cloud operator
Security and data access	Cloud Computing intensifies data sharing, by applying modern analytic tools and managing controlled access and security [34]
	Third-party provision facilitates good security, incident management, compliance, access, and identity control [35]; security layers, responsibilities, and exceptions are enclosed in SLAs (service-level agreement)
	Secured access depends on the Cloud model (public, supplied by the Cloud provider; private, supplied by the organization; hybrid,supplied by both the organization and the third-party provider)
	Ensuring several layers of control, depending on requirements (physical security, network security, system security, application security) as well as security measures implemented at individual and process levels (such as separation of duties and change management) [35]

- Volume – a large volume of data processed by powerful computing resources;
- Variety – the variety of multiple-entry sources is addressed through flexible (computing and analytical) resources and self-service advantages;
- Velocity of observation and forecasting is handled by the flexibility and on-demand features of Cloud Computing;

- Veracity of the Big Data is relieved by self-service to select the best-matched services and pay-as-you-go cost model;
- Value represented as accurate forecasting with high resolution, justifiable cost, and customer satisfaction with on-demand, flexibility, and pay-as-you-go features of Cloud Computing.

Cloud Computing also meets the other challenges in Big Data (see Fig. 4.3), namely:

- Variability – scenario-building techniques related to the multiple significance of data, with fast adjustment possibilities based on the current tasks called for through the data involved;
- Visualization – approaches, methods, and techniques for the smart visualization of multidimensional data [36];
- Validity – mechanisms to ensure the accuracy and correctness of the data in the models; possibilities to block potential error propagation, including errors generated by the multiple significance of data;
- Volatile – flexible approaches to archiving to facilitate the secure classification, indexation, search, and recovery of data during the operation of automatic monitoring and reporting [37], for extended (not long term) periods of time and digital long-term preservation, which includes the preservation of information and data, as well as the complete management of the support infrastructure, data, information, and storage services (long term) [38].

4.3.7 Security Through Cloud Computing

Cloud Computing offers advanced secure multi-tenant environment with multi-role support and complete isolation of applications. It also ensures data integrity and security mechanisms for the stored resources [22]. Cloud data can be protected through the implementation of high-level security [26]. Nevertheless, Cloud Computing security is still an important challenge that, unfortunately, can propagate even toward the IoT. As highlighted before, for both Cloud Computing and the IoT, security impediments amount to barriers in the development and large-scale adoption of the two paradigms in more sensitive fields such as the government.

Starting from the major challenges and problems of the IoT as well as the benefits of Cloud Computing described before, Table 4.2 presents a summary of how Cloud Computing can offer a solution to the Big 7 of IoT.

4.4 Conclusions

The approach to the Big 7 in IoT suggested in this chapter is not necessarily exhaustive. It is obvious that beyond the Big 7 of IoT, there are aspects that need further analysis in line with developments in technology, methodology, concepts, and legal requirements. Moreover, one should not lose sight of the political dimension of the

Table 4.2 Problems and challenges of IoT and Cloud Computing solutions

The Big 7 of IoT	IoT problems and challenges	Cloud Computing benefits and solutions
Scalability	The connection of new devices and new users	Flexibility in adapting to the growing or declining needs of the clients
	New analytical capabilities	Allows for scalability on several levels, such as the existing devices, the volume of data and data storage capacity, the diversity of data, network management, and the services attached to the applications (horizontal and vertical flexibility)
	The frequent changes in technology, the large number of interactions within the IoT, as well as the growing demand for services	
Interoperability	The level of data perception (see Fig. 4.1): technical (communication infrastructure, linkage of devices), syntactical (legislation, data exchange formats), semantic (customized devices, information transmission and interpretation), organizational (cooperation across borders, linkage of processes);	Enable the remote use of applications (over the Internet) by IoT clients
		Standard interfaces and the portability of various devices among various Cloud providers
		Independence from hardware through virtualization
	The moment when interoperability is achieved (static, dynamic)	Middleware and interoperable architectures for data sharing and services among heterogeneous devices
Reliability	Devices (number and diversity of connected devices)	Device reliability (increase in the battery life of devices, the possibility to put in place a modular architecture)
	Network (high number of users, the multitude of devices, several types of networks)	
		Network reliability (good traffic management)
	The provided services (availability, collection, storage, and processing of large volumes of data)	Reliability of services (a disruption-tolerant infrastructure, various mechanisms to ensure data synchronization, which improves transactional reliability and consistency)
Efficiency	Supports different real-time analyses of a big volume of data	Multi-zone management
		On-demand unlimited processing capabilities
	Satisfies the diversity of data processing requests and process data as fast as it arrives	Real-time data processing
	Ensuring advanced data processing and analysis with a view to supporting the machine learning processes embedded in smart devices	The management of complex events
		Real-time data access for objects
		Remote monitoring, control, coordination, communication of objects

(continued)

Table 4.2 (continued)

The Big 7 of IoT	IoT problems and challenges	Cloud Computing benefits and solutions
Availability	Anything (many things)	Effective solutions allowing to connect, follow, and manage any object (thing), irrespective of place and time, by using customized gateways and embedded applications
	Any time (all day and night)	
	Anywhere (many and diverse locations)	
	Any service (many services)	The benefits that cloud services bring to IoT (details in Table 4.1)
	Any network (multi-protocol, technology, operating systems)	
	(details in Fig. 4.2)	
Storage	IoT data-related challenges (the nine V's of Big Data): volume, variety, velocity, variability, visualization, veracity, validity, volatile, value (details in Fig. 4.3)	Cloud Computing can meet the challenges of Big Data
		Cloud Computing benefits for the nine V's of Big Data: volume, variety, velocity, variability, visualization, veracity, validity, volatile, value
Security	Information security	Advanced secure multi-tenant environment with multi-role support and complete isolation of applications
	Information technology security	
	Physical security	Ensures data integrity and security mechanisms for the stored resources
	Operational security	
	(details in Fig. 4.4)	Implementation of high-level security

IoT paradigm that comes to strengthen once again the complexity of the approaches, at least from the perspective of globalization, the free movement of workers, or the phenomenon of migration. In this context, it is worth mentioning that national policies regarding information security, information protocols, and, last but not least, legal initiatives of the Big Brother family aimed at monitoring communications over the Web. On the other hand, the evolutionary perspective of the IoT placed it in the early 1990s in terms of *domotic* or *imotic* perspectives. One way or another, aspects still regard the same and only issue: the automation of daily human activities or the so-called digital human universe.

An important conclusion of our scientific study is that we must reiterate the vital role of individuals in the IoT context. An individual is not a mere or common component of the IoT environment but the very entity that controls the environment by means of technology. The challenges in IoT regard numerous and sometimes complex aspects. Despite that, the critical dimension lies with the security aspects, and it is security that makes the main barrier in the development of the IoT. We have seen that communications, computing power, and sensing capacity are key elements in the IoT environment. These three elements form what the literature calls the primitives of IoT trustworthiness. Recent NIST research from 2017 suggests five such primitives: sensor, aggregator, communication channel, eutility (related to installed computing power), and decision trigger [39]. Moreover, with respect to the issue of security, NIST identifies six elements that play a major role in stimulating trustworthiness in an IoT network: the environment, cost (in time and money), geographical location, the owner of the primitive, the unique identification number of the communication device, and the snapshot used to synchronize events.

Integration between Cloud Computing and IoT helps in solving some of the challenges the IoT is faced with, but it is not a panacea. Like any other technology solution, Cloud Computing not only comes with benefits but also with challenges and problems, which is something to consider in the creation of CloudIoT. One of the important problems facing both the IoT and Cloud is standardization. Speaking of security, for instance [40], we cannot fail to see that the standard package ISO 27000-27019 on information security management systems (updated in February 2016) is already obsolete in some respects. This happens first of all due to the fast-paced development of modern communication technologies and solutions. Second, hybrid solutions, such as Cloud sourcing or Cloud of Things, are, in their turn, sources of mistrust and are not covered by standards.

In spite of that, considerable effort is consistently being made to bring the IoT in all spheres of human existence. Therefore, we must highlight some of the manifest trends in politically and economically stable countries to promote the IoT government paradigm. Accordingly, the 2020 horizon will mark the beginning of a new era – the digital industrial society – thus escalating the stage of knowledge-based information society. Beyond the aspects linked to technology or legislation, the question whether to develop the IoT in symbiosis with Cloud Computing must also consider the environment, and that is unknown, if we think of the 2020 horizon. Green computing philosophy thus expands its scope toward what we call green Cloud Computing today and what we may call the green Internet of Things in the near future.

References

1. Zhou J, Leppänen T, Harjula E, Ylianttila M, Ojala T, Yu C, Jin H, Yang LT (2013) CloudThings: a common architecture for integrating the internet of things with Cloud Computing. In: Proceedings of the 2013 IEEE 17th international conference on computer supported cooperative work in design, pp 651–657, Canada, 27–29 June 2013
2. Chao HC (2011) Internet of things and Cloud Computing for future internet. In: Chang RS, Kim T, Peng SL (eds) Security-enriched urban computing and smart grid. Springer, Berlin/Heidelberg
3. Alhakbani N, Hassan MM, Hossain MA, Alnuem M (2014) A framework of adaptive interaction support in Cloud-based Internet of Things (IoT) environment. In: Fortino G, Di Fatta G, Li W, Ochoa S, Cuzzocrea A, Pathan M (eds) Internet and distributed computing systems. Springer, Cham, pp 136–146
4. Aitken R, Chandra V, Myers J, Sandhu B, Shifren L, Yeric G (2014) Device and technology implications of the Internet of Things. In: VLSI technology: digest of technical papers, pp 1–4, 2014 Symposium on VLSI technology digest of technical papers, 11 Sept 2014

5. Gomes MM, Righi RR, da Costa CA (2014) Future directions for providing better IoT infrastructure. In: Proceedings of the 2014 ACM international joint conference on pervasive and ubiquitous computing, pp 51–54, UbiComp'14 Adjunct, Seattle, 13–17 Sept 2014

6. Botta A, de Donato W, Persico V, Pescapé A (2016) Integration of Cloud Computing and internet of things: a survey, Futur Gener Comput Syst 56:684–700

7. Aazam M, Khan I, Alsaffar AA, Huh E-N (2014) Cloud of Things: Integrating Internet of Things and Cloud Computing and the issues involved. In: Applied sciences and technology, pp 414–419, 11th International Bhurban conference on Applied Sciences & Technology (IBCAST) Islamabad, 14th–18th January 2014

8. Liu Y, Dong B, Guo B, Yang J, Peng W (2015) Combination of Cloud Computing and Internet of Things (IOT) in medical monitoring systems. International Journal of Hybrid Information Technology 8(12):367–376

9. Gartner (2014) The impact of the internet of things on data centers. Gartner report, 18 March, 2014. http://www.gartner.com/newsroom/id/2684915. Accessed 3 Feb 2017

10. Davis R (2014) 7 big problems with the internet of things. 19 March 2014, http://www.cmswire.com/cms/internet-of-things/7-big-problems-with-the-internet-of-things-024571.php. Accessed 3 Feb 2017

11. Iconectiv (2016) Overcoming interoperability challenges in the internet of things. Telcordia Technologies, September 2016. http://www.iconectiv.com/sites/default/files/2016-09/appid_wp_overcoming-interoperability-challenges-iot.pdf. Accessed 3 Feb 2017

12. IERC (2015) Internet of things IoT semantic interoperability: research challenges, best practices, recommendations and next steps. European Research Cluster on the Internet of Things, March 2015. http://www.internet-of-things-research.eu/pdf/IERC_Position_Paper_IoT_Semantic_Interoperability_Final.pdf. Accessed 3 Feb 2017

13. Van der Veer H, Wiles A (2008) Achieving technical interoperability – the ETSI approach, ETSI 3rd edition, April 2008. http://www.etsi.org/images/files/ETSIWhitePapers/IOP%20whitepaper%20Edition%203%20final.pdf. Accessed 3 Feb 2017

14. Kempf J, Arkko J, Beheshti N, Yedavalli K (2011) Thoughts on reliability in the internet of things, March 2011. https://www.iab.org/wp-content/IAB-uploads/2011/03/Kempf.pdf. Accessed 3 Feb 2017

15. Bagula BA (2016) Internet-of-things and big data: promises and challenges for the developing world, 11 May 2016. http://unctad.org/meetings/en/Presentation/ecn162016p16_Bagula-UWC_en.pdf. Accessed 3 Feb 2017

16. Kocher C (2014) The internet of things: challenges and opportunities, 17 Nov 2014. http://sandhill.com/article/the-internet-of-things-challenges-and-opportunities/. Accessed 3 Feb 2017

17. Liwei R (2015) IoT security: problems, challenges and solution. http://www.snia.org/sites/default/files/DSS-Summit-2015/presentations/Liwei-Ren_Iot_Security_Problems_Challenges_revision.pdf. Accessed 20 Jan 2017

18. Singh J, Pasquier T, Bacon J, Ko H, Eyers D (2016) Twenty security considerations for cloud-supported internet of things. Internet Things J 3(3):269–284

19. Soldatos J (2016) IoT tutorial: chapter 4 – internet of things in the Clouds, 30 May 2016. https://www.linkedin.com/pulse/iot-tutorial-chapter-4-internet-things-clouds-john-soldatos. Accessed 3 Feb 2017

20. Abraham S (2016) IoT – Internet of Things, 26 Sept 2016. http://www.slideshare.net/SherinCAbraham/internet-of-things-with-cloud-computing-and-m2m-communication. Accessed 3 Feb 2017

21. Workflow Studios (2016) Taming the internet of things with the Cloud, 22 March 2016. http://workflowstudios.com/taming-the-internet-of-things-with-the-cloud/. Accessed 3 Feb 2017

22. Llorente I (2012) Key challenges in Cloud Computing to enable future internet of things, 18 Jan 2012. http://www.slideshare.net/llorente/challenges-in-cloud-computing-to-enable-future-internet-of-things-v03. Accessed 3 Feb 2017

23. Yun M, Yuxin B (2010) Research on the architecture and key technology of Internet of Things (IoT) applied on smart grid. In: Advances in energy engineering (ICAEE), pp 69–72. International Conference on Advances in Energy Engineering, Beijing, 19–20 June 2010

24. Wang C, Bi Z, Xu LD (2014) Iot and Cloud Computing in automation of assembly modeling systems. IEEE Trans Ind Inf 10(2):1426–1434
25. Bauer E, Adams R (2012) Reliable cloud computing – key considerations, 16 July 2012. https://insight.nokia.com/reliable-cloud-computing-key-considerations. Accessed 3 Feb 2017
26. Dash SK, Mohapatra S, Pattnaik PK (2010) A survey on application of wireless sensor network using Cloud Computing. Int J Comput Sci Eng Technol 1(4):50–55
27. Parwekar P (2011) From internet of things towards cloud of things. In: Computer and Communication Technology (ICCCT), 2011 2nd international conference on computer and communication technology, pp 329–333, Allahabad, 15–17 Sept 2011
28. Rao BP, Saluia P, Sharma N, Mittal A, Sharma SV (2012) Cloud computing for internet of things & sensing based applications. In: Sensing Technology (ICST), 2012 sixth international conference on sensing technology, pp 374–380, West Bengal, 18–21 Dec 2012
29. Fox GC, Kamburugamuve S, Hartman RD (2012) Architecture and measured characteristics of a cloud based internet of things. In: Collaboration Technologies and Systems (CTS), 2012 International Conference on Collaboration Technologies and Systems, pp 6–12, Colorado, 21–25 May 2012
30. Czarnowski A (2014) Service availability (in the clouds), 24 Mar 2014. http://ec.europa.eu/justice/contract/files/expert_groups/discussion_paper_service_availability_en.pdf. Accessed 3 Feb 2017
31. Zhong Y, Han J, Zhang T, Li Z, Fang J, Chen G (2012) Towards parallel spatial query processing for big spatial data. In: 2012 IEEE 26th International Parallel and Distributed Processing Symposium Workshops & PhD Forum (IPDPSW), pp 2085–2094, Shanghai, 21–25, May 2012
32. Yang C, Huang Q, Li Z, Liu K, Hu F (2017) Big data and cloud computing: innovation opportunities and challenges. International Journal of Digital Earth 10(1):13–53, 03 Nov 2016
33. Yang C, Liu C, Zhang X, Nepal S, Chen J (2015a) A time efficient approach for detecting errors in big sensor data on Cloud. IEEE Transactions on Parallel and Distributed Systems 26(2):329–339
34. Radke AM, Tseng MM (2015) Design considerations for building distributed supply chain management systems based on Cloud Computing. Journal of Manufacturing Science and Engineering 137(4):1–7
35. Cloud Security Alliance (2011) Security guidance for critical areas of focus in cloud computing V3.0. https://downloads.cloudsecurityalliance.org/assets/research/security-guidance/csaguide.v3.0.pdf. Accessed 3 Feb 2017
36. Bernatavičienė J, Dzemyda G, Kurasova O, Marcinkevičius I, Medvedev V, Treigys P (2016) Cloud Computing approach for intelligent visualization of multidimensional data. In: Advances in stochastic and deterministic global optimization, pp 73–85, 5 Nov 2016
37. IBM (2011) Cloud-based data archiving service, July 2011. http://www-935.ibm.com/services/be/en/it-services/cloud-based_data_archiving.pdf. Accessed 3 Feb 2017
38. Chad T, Yangaro S (2013) Digital data archive and preservation in the cloud – what to do and what not to do. http://www.snia.org/sites/default/education/tutorials/2013/spring/cloud/ChadThibodeau-SebastianZangaro_Digital_Data_Archive_and_Preservation.pdf. Accessed 3 Feb 2017
39. NIST (2017) National Institute of Standards and Technology, Draft NIST-IR-8063, 30 Jan 2017. http://csrc.nist.gov/publications/PubsDrafts.html#NIST-IR-8063. Accessed 3 Feb 2017
40. ISO (2016) ISO/IEC 27000:2016(en). International Organization for Standardization, Standard for Information Technology – Security techniques – Information security management systems. https://www.iso.org/obp/ui/#iso:std:iso-iec:27000:ed-4:v1:en. Accessed 3 Feb 2017

Chapter 5
Overcoming Service-Level Interoperability Challenges of the IoT

Darko Andročec

Abstract The Internet of Things (IoT) is a complex ecosystem of devices, solutions, services and applications. IoT is highly heterogeneous because devices focus on proprietary technology and interfaces. To realize its full value, interoperability of 'things' becomes an important component of the ecosystem, which must be satisfactorily achieved. At present, however, it is impossible to manage individually a vast amount of different IoT devices and their application programming interfaces (APIs). Interoperability is therefore one of the main problems of the IoT paradigm. Much of the existing IoT interoperability research elaborates on techniques and methods to achieve interoperability. Multiple IoT standards exist today and new ones are being created. Different IoT standards compete; and a generally globally accepted standard does not currently exist. There are, in fact, many unsolved interoperability issues occurring at different levels, including data, service, network and application. This chapter focuses on service-level IoT interoperability problems and solutions. It reviews the use case of possible interoperability resolutions. The chapter also identifies future research problems related to IoT service-level interoperability.

5.1 Introduction

One of the most important properties of the Internet of Things (IoT) environment is the seamless interoperability between devices, also called 'things', and the services that these devices provide. Unfortunately, there are numerous challenges in this regard. However, with the development of standards and IoT protocols, innovation is at its peak. Yet, a satisfactory solution has not prevailed as many IoT providers and device manufacturers use their own protocols and APIs. In such ecosystems, it is difficult to achieve technical and semantic interoperability of devices and IoT

D. Andročec (✉)
Department of Information Systems Development, Faculty of Organization and Informatics, University of Zagreb, Varaždin, Croatia
e-mail: dandrocec@foi.hr

© Springer International Publishing AG 2017   83
Z. Mahmood (ed.), *Connected Environments for the Internet of Things*,
Computer Communications and Networks,
https://doi.org/10.1007/978-3-319-70102-8_5

services to effectively communicate. IoT interoperability has become a complex practical and research problem.

This chapter provides a discussion of the main challenges of IoT interoperability, with a focus on service-level IoT interoperability. Service-level interoperability aims to semantically annotate services to enable their automatic or semi-automatic composition and orchestration based on their functional and nonfunctional properties. Semantic Web services aim at an automated solution to the following problems: description, publishing, discovery, mediation, monitoring and composition of services.

Known solutions to the problems will also be presented. Most researchers use Semantic Web technologies to tackle IoT interoperability problems. An IoT interoperability use case will also be presented to illustrate the implementation of IoT interoperability solutions at the service level. It will discuss the development of underlying IoT ontology, annotation of things and automatic or semi-automatic composition of IoT services.

The remainder of the chapter will outline interoperability: specifics of IoT interoperability and both recent and ongoing IoT interoperability research projects. Next, common interoperability issues and challenges will be presented and systematized. Known interoperability solutions will be discussed. The chapter will conclude with an IoT service-level interoperability use case and conclusions.

5.2 Interoperability

Interoperability can be defined in several ways. IEEE [1] is credited with one of the simplest definitions: *the ability of two or more systems or components to exchange information and to use the information that has been exchanged.* Brownsword et al. [2] provide the following working definition of interoperability: *the ability of a collection of communicating entities to (a) share specified information and (b) operate on that information according to an agreed operational semantics.* Pokraev et al. [3] claim that *interoperability implies that systems are able to interact (i.e., exchange messages), read and understand each other's messages and share the same expectations about the effect of the message exchange.*

From these definitions, three main aspects of interoperability can be identified: syntactic interoperability (compatible formats), semantic interoperability (meaning of the information) and pragmatic interoperability (effect of the exchanged information) [3].

Vernadat [4] similarly defines interoperability as *the ability for a system to communicate with another system and to use the functionality of the other system.* Park and Ram [5] note that interoperability is the most critical issue facing businesses that use data from different information systems. According to Park and Ram [5], two types of interoperability are found: semantic and syntactic interoperability. Semantic interoperability, which exists at the knowledge level, bridges semantic conflicts due to differences in meanings, perspectives and assumptions. Syntactic interoperability, which is interoperability at the application level, aims at software component cooperation with different implementation languages and development platforms [5].

Interoperability is a multidimensional concept that can be looked at from multiple perspectives. Therefore, interoperability frameworks were developed using the following elements: vocabulary, concepts, principles, guidelines and recommendations. Some of the most important frameworks are ATHENA interoperability framework (AIF), IDEAS interoperability framework, LISI reference model, enterprise interoperability framework and GridWise interoperability context-setting framework [6].

Apart from interoperability frameworks, some comprehensive interoperability models are presented in current literature. For example, Naudet et al. [7] developed a general ontology of interoperability. This ontology described the ontological metamodeling system, as well as its problems and solutions. It can be used to diagnose and resolve interoperability problems. The aforementioned authors concluded that there were two alternative technical solutions to interoperability problems: bridging and homogenization [7]. Bridging uses an intermediate system (often called an adapter) between systems having interoperability problems. The intermediate system relies on the translation protocol (e.g. using mappings) to achieve interoperability between interacting systems [7]. Homogenization, which implies the unified model, acts directly on models or their representations [7]. It requires syntactic or semantic transformations using the defined unified model. In the following subsections, IoT interoperability will be described in more detail. Main IoT interoperability research projects will be listed.

5.2.1 IoT Interoperability

The IoT promises a world of networked intelligent devices (things). These things communicate mutually and constantly, as well as generate data as a basis for smart applications and services. Achieving point-to-point communication relies on interoperability [8]. Technical IoT interoperability requires that things can speak and be heard. Semantic IoT interoperability requires that things speak the same language [8]. One of the most critical semantic interoperability elements is a means for device identification. Currently, companies develop their own things to rely on proprietary standards or closed systems. Therefore, it is difficult to enable interoperability. A similar situation is emerging in other fields (e.g. cloud computing) as company products and services compete for the market share. Interoperable IoT systems can increase the ability to build innovative IoT services.

5.2.2   Research Projects on IoT Interoperability

IoT interoperability is a popular research theme. It is well founded because of promises of IoT possible future capabilities of citizens' life improvements, (e.g. by European past FP7 and current Horizon 2020 initiatives). This chapter will list important research projects, as well as their achievements or future goals. The OpenIoT [9] FP7 project provided an open IoT platform to enable semantic IoT service interoperability in the cloud. Based on W3C Semantic Sensor Networks (SSN) ontology, it enabled semantic annotations of sensors. OpenIoT used Linked Data technologies to link related sensor data. The project's focus was to achieve interoperability among sensors' data. Another FP7 project, IoT.est. [10], developed a framework for IoT service creation and testing to enable test-driven and semantic control of IoT service lifecycle. The EU FP7 project IoT@Work [11] aimed at self-anagement features in factory automation systems. The main concept of the project is Plug&Work, which represented the ability of devices to autoconfigure themselves for different automation applications. The GAMBAS consortium [12] developed the middleware and Java-based SDK for smart city applications to address context data acquisition and interoperable data integration. IoT6 [13] designed IPv6-based SOA to achieve interoperability among smart thing components, applications and services. The SmartAgriFood FP7 project [14] addressed the food and agribusiness as a use case for the future Internet. Interoperability was identified as one of the most important requirements for agri-food logistics.

IoT interoperability is a popular research theme as confirmed by recent Horizon 2020 European research projects. The first BIG IoT (Bridging the Interoperability Gap of the Internet of Things) plans to implement BIG IoT APIs for use by various IoT platforms [15]. It seeks to create marketplaces for IoT services and applications [15]. Through the common API, it is easier to develop software for different IoT platforms. Three key IoT interoperability pillars have been identified, viz. (1) common API, (2) well-defined information models and (3) an IoT marketplace [15]. BigIoT is a part of IoT-EPI (European Initiative for IoT Platform Development).

The next ongoing project is INTER-IoT [16]. This aims to design, implement and test an open cross-layer framework for interoperability across the software stack among different IoT platforms [15]. The project's main use cases are (e/m) Health and transportation and logistics.

VICINITY (open virtual neighbourhood network to connect IoT infrastructures and smart objects) [17] plans to build a device and standard agnostic platform for interoperability. This project focuses on a virtual neighbourhood where users control and share smart objects.

Using semantic-based technologies, FIESTA-IoT [18] seeks to create an interconnection and interoperability of diverse IoT platforms and test-beds. It focuses on the federation of different IoT test-beds and enables experimentation as service for IoT experiments. The annotation process enables data in standards semantics by using FIESTA-IoT ontology.

symbIoTe [19] provides an interoperability framework for cooperation of vertical IoT platforms, IoT platform federations and cross-domain IoT application development. The framework is built using an IoT stack connecting the cloud to smart objects and IoT gateways. It aims to design an architecture for the interconnection of existing IoT platforms at different levels (e.g. application, cloud, smart space and device domain) [19].

5.3   Interoperability Issues and Challenges

Interoperability is a multidimensional concept with multiple levels of problems, issues and conflicts. The European interoperability framework identified four levels of interoperability, viz. legal, organizational, semantic and technical. This chapter focuses on the technical and semantic interoperability issues, especially at the service level. Table 5.1 lists some related works for classifying interoperability issues. The main categories of interoperability issues defined by Sheth and Kashyap [20] are domain definition incompatibility (attributes have different domain definitions), entity definition incompatibility (descriptors used for the same entity are partially compatible), data value incompatibility (inconsistency between related data), abstraction level incompatibility (the same entity is represented at different levels of abstraction) and schematic discrepancy (data in one database corresponds to schema

Table 5.1 Database and service interoperability issues

Author/s	Domain	Identified interoperability issues
Sheth and Kashyap [20]	Issues among multiple databases	Domain definition incompatibility, entity definition incompatibility, data value incompatibility, abstraction level incompatibility, schematic discrepancy
Parent and Spaccapietra [21]	Data interoperability problems during database integration	Heterogeneity conflicts, generalization/specialization conflicts, description conflicts, structural conflicts, fragmentation conflicts, metadata conflicts, data conflicts
Park and Ram [5]	Semantic conflicts among databases	Data-level conflicts (data-value conflicts, data representation conflicts, data-unit conflicts, data precision conflict), schema-level conflicts (naming conflicts, entity-identifier problems, aggregation conflicts, schematic discrepancies)
Haslhofer and Klas [22]	Metadata interoperability at model level	Naming conflicts, identification conflicts, constraints conflicts, abstraction level incompatibilities, multilateral correspondences, meta-level discrepancy, domain coverage
Ponnekanti and Fox [24]	Web service interoperability	Missing methods, extra fields, different types for service inputs/outputs, cardinality mismatches
Nagarajan et al. [23]	Web services heterogeneities	Attribute level incompatibilities, entity definition incompatibilities and abstraction level incompatibilities

elements in another). Parent and Spaccapietra [21] distinguished seven categories of database interoperability problems:

- Heterogeneity conflicts (different data models)
- Generalization/specialization conflicts (different generalization/specialization hierarchies and different classification abstractions)
- Description conflicts (types have different properties and/or their properties are described differently)
- Structural conflicts (different structures of related types)
- Fragmentation conflicts (the same object is depicted by decomposition into different elements)
- Metadata conflicts
- Data conflicts (data instances have different values for the same properties)

Data-level conflicts [5] include data-value conflicts (the data value has different meaning in different databases), data representation conflicts (such as different representations of date and time), data-unit conflicts (different units used in different databases) and data precision conflicts. Data-level conflicts can occur at the attribute level or at the entity level. Structural heterogeneities [22] occur at the model level in the form of naming conflicts (different names of model elements representing the same real object), identification conflicts (model elements identifiable by their name or identifier), constraints conflicts (different definition of constraints in different models), abstraction level incompatibilities (different generalization of aggregation of the same real-world object), multilateral correspondences (an element from one model corresponds to multiple models in another model), meta-level discrepancy (the same elements in one model could be modelled differently in another model) and domain coverage (real-world concepts described in one model are missing from the other model).

The main classes of heterogeneities in Web services are [23] attribute level incompatibilities (different descriptions used to model similar attributes), entity definition incompatibilities (different descriptions are used to model similar entities) and abstraction level incompatibilities (different levels of abstraction).

The general database and service interoperability issues as shown in Table 5.1 are relevant for the IoT domain. Much of the things are sensors generating a large amount of data. For this reason, data interoperability is very important for the IoT context. Things as a service have the basic properties of services. Therefore, IoT service interoperability issues are similar to other service-oriented architectures' issues.

There are also IoT-specific interoperability issues. European Research Cluster on the Internet of Things (IERC) listed the following IoT technical interoperability challenges [25]: (1) efforts to address interoperability protocols, (2) reduction of ambiguities in specifications and (3) tests to ensure minimum levels of interoperability. There is also a list of the most important IoT semantic interoperability challenges [25]: integration of things and IoT data, linking and annotation of IoT data sources, management of virtual sensors, efficient discovery of things and IoT data sources and development of tools for analysis and visualization of semantic

IoT. These challenges can be mapped into requirements for IoT services and applications using semantic technologies. In the next section, prominent solutions for the interoperability issues will be listed.

5.4   Interoperability Solutions

Linked Data can be used to link heterogeneous data formats since there is not a general agreement on annotating IoT data [25]. Proposing abstract models for semantic descriptions in IoT is useful in solving some interoperability problems. The following subsections will list Semantic Web initiatives and languages, as well as existing work on IoT interoperability at the service level. Semantic Web (ontology-driven approach) is the most promising technology in solving IoT service-level interoperability issues. Semantic annotations can be solved by naming conflicts on an attribute and entity level, as well as attribute entity conflicts [23]. Mapping of schema isomorphism conflicts in both directions requires additional context information [23]. Mappings of data representation conflicts, data scaling conflicts, generalization conflicts and aggregation conflicts are possible in only one direction (from a more detailed version to the more general) [23].

5.4.1   IoT Standards Initiatives

Several standardization organizations and groups are working to create open standards for IoT. Although there are many standards, a single standard has not prevailed. The active IoT standard initiative is discussed in Table 5.2. The list is based on the Postscapes website [26]. Additional information was included after studying the standards and initiatives.

5.4.2   Semantic Web Services

Many service-level interoperability problems can be solved by using Semantic Web services. Current Web services provide only syntactical descriptions. Thus, Web service integration must be done manually. Semantic Web services are the integration of Semantic Web and service-oriented architecture implemented in the form of Web services. Semantic Web services aim at an automated solution to the following problems: description, publishing, discovery, mediation, monitoring and composition of services.

New languages should be used to implement Semantic Web service. OWL-S (Semantic Markup for Web Services) [27] is the ontology of services that enables

Table 5.2 IoT standard initiatives

Organization	Initiative	Brief description
IEEE	IEEE P2413	This draft standard defines an architectural framework for the IoT
	802.15.4	IEEE Standard for Low-Rate Wireless Networks
IETF	CoRE (Constrained RESTful Environments)	CoRE provides a framework for resource-oriented applications intended to run on constrained IP networks with limited packet sizes and a high degree of packet loss
ITU	JCA-IoT	The ITU's joint coordination activity on IoT
More than 200 participating partners and members	OneM2M	The global standards initiative for machine-to-machine communications and the IoT. Formed in 2012 by eight of the world's ICT standards development organizations, oneM2 M provides a necessary framework for interoperability between the many M2 M and IoT technologies being introduced
IMC	IMC IoT M2 M Council	It offers detailed case studies of IoT and M2 M technologies usage
OCF (Open Connectivity Foundation)	OIC specification	OIC is based on the resource-oriented architecture and defines a resource model for IoT resources definition, endpoint and resource discovery, advertisement, monitoring and maintenance
W3C	Semantic Sensor Network Ontology	This ontology is developed by the W3C Semantic Sensor Networks Incubator Group (SSN-XG). The ontology describes sensors and observations, and related concepts, and it does not describe domain concepts, time and locations
	Web of Things Community Group	The aim of the group is to accelerate the adoption of Web technologies as a basis for enabling services for the combination of the Internet of Things with rich descriptions of things and the context in which they are used
XSF (XMMP Standards Foundation)	XMPP	The open standard for instant messaging, presence and real-time communication and collaboration
OMG (Object Management Group)	DDS	DDS is a middleware protocol and API for IoT data-centric connectivity
OMA (Open Mobile Alliance)	LWM2M	A common set of standards for managing light weight and low capability IoT devices on a variety of networks
OASIS	MQTT	A lightweight publish/subscribe reliable messaging transport protocol for M2 M/IoT. It is approved by ISO/IEC JTC1
	AMQP	Advanced Messaging Queuing Protocol
ISO/IEC	IoT Special Working Group	ISO work group on IoT
AIM	IoT Committee	The committee's mission is to educate and support AIM members about IoT

users and/or software agents to discover, invoke and compose Web services. This ontology, defined by using a Web Ontology Language (OWL), has three main parts:

- The service profile for specifying the service's purpose and functionality
- The process model for describing the operation of the service
- The grounding containing details on how to use a service

The next initiative, the Web Service Modelling Ontology (WSMO) [28], describes aspects related to Semantic Web services. As extension of the Web Service Modelling Framework (WSMF), it consists of four elements: ontologies, goals, Web service descriptions and mediators. WSMO refines and extends this framework by developing the ontology for the core elements of Semantic Web services. It also develops the description language consisting of nonfunctional, functional and behavioural aspects of Web services.

WSMO and OWL-S are heavyweight solutions for Semantic Web services. They introduce new languages founded on expressive formalisms, as well as promote the semantics-first modelling approach [29]. Heavyweight solutions are complex in terms of modelling and computation [30]. Lightweight approaches reduce the complexity and enhance existing SOA capabilities by adding intelligent and automated integration to existing service descriptions [31]. Lightweight service ontologies use bottom-up modelling. The most known lightweight approaches include WSMO-Lite, SAWSDL, MicroWSMO, hRESTS and SA-REST. Lightweight service annotation models are cost-effective because it is faster to work on semantic annotation.

5.4.3   Existing Works on Service-Level IoT Interoperability

Many works exist on service-level IoT interoperability and its solutions. A federated discovery service proposed by Gomes et al. [32] encompassed an ontology-based information model to semantically describe resources and IoT services. The service used SSN and SAN ontology, Basic Geo Vocabulary and OWL-S for modelling services. Nambi et al. [33] created a unified knowledge base for IoT to use and extend existing resources, locations, context, domains, policies and service ontologies. Nambi et al. [33] considered these as a main tool for service composition and discovery. Spallazi et al. [34] extended the semantic sensor network ontology with concepts and roles describing actuators. Androcec and Vrcek [35] proposed a framework for things as a service interoperability including composition of sensors and actuators at service level, as well as their integration with existing cloud services. Qu et al. [36] proposed the specification of dynamic services for things by extending OWL-S with service status ontology to describe information like the waiting queue and current status of the entities involved in the services. Hur et al. [37] presented a semantic approach to automatically generate a service description and deployment of different things to various IoT platforms. They also proposed the semantic service description ontology to support the translation of a platform-specific configuration into semantic metadata using a common knowledge scheme.

Fattah et al. [38] introduced a concept of composite virtual objects to compose services and create collaboration among physical objects. Soldatos et al. [39] presented design principles for IoT in cloud environments in which their framework used linked sensor data and W3C semantic sensor networks ontology. Akasiadis et al. [40] presented an approach for developing applications on an IoT platform to build a complex service to determine the number of people inside a smart room. Sezer et al. [41] developed a smart home sensor ontology based on SSN ontology and their simulation environment. Li et al. [42] proposed an architecture for integrating semantics into M2 M/IoT service delivery platforms in which semantics integrate with various APIs. oneM2 M is developing a service layer for resource-oriented architecture and service-oriented architecture.

Thoma et al. [43] described an approach to integrate smart objects and enterprise IT systems using Linked USDL for semantic endpoint descriptions. Their solution was evaluated with CoAP, UDP and 6LoWPAN. Jia et al. [44] presented the architecture of cross-layer IoT services platform based on semantics. They defined an IoT service ontology model and semantic-based IoT service description language OWL-Siot. The ebbits platform [45] provided a middleware for the integration of heterogeneous industrial devices and sensors, as well as a model-driven development toolkit. Ryu et al. [46] proposed an integrated semantic service platform to support ontological models in different IoT services of a smart city. The main problems addressed were semantic discovery, dynamic semantic representation and semantic IoT data repositories. Qu et al. [47], showing the framework with entities represented as Semantic Web services, automatically created a sequence of IoT services. They used the following set of ontologies: goal, role, constraint, message, status, space-time and activity ontology. Kim et al. [48] presented a semantic ontology model for IoT devices, resources and services. Virtual objects included things with their profiles.

Kovatsch et al. [49] used RESTdesc description format and semantic reasoning to create IoT mashups of resource-constrained IoT devices. Additionally, they developed a semantic IDE tool for the experimentation and design of RESTdesc descriptions for IoT devices. Hasemann et al. [50] used RDF documents to describe IoT devices, including services, sensors and capabilities. A sensor can autoconfigure itself, connect to the internet and provide Linked Data without manual intervention. Vecchio et al. [51] semantically described physical devices as virtual objects and exposed their functionalities as IoT services. Furthermore, they used a cognitive management framework to tune key application parameters and provide self-configuration functionality of virtual objects. Chun et al. [52] proposed the IoT directory supporting semantic description, discovery and integration of an IoT object. It took into consideration complex relationships among things that change with time. Desai et al. [53] proposed a gateway and Semantic Web-enabled IoT architecture to provide interoperability between systems. This utilized established communication and data standards, including XMPP, CoAP and MQTT. The mentioned gateway performs translation between different messaging protocols.

Kiljander et al. [54] presented a semantic-level interoperability architecture for pervasive computing and IoT. They divided IoT into numerous local smart spaces managed by a semantic information broker. Wang et al. [55] proposed a sensing network ontology description model for IoT. Their work provided another way to semantically annotate sensing devices and their generated data. Den Hartog et al. [56] identified 48 semantic assets describing properties of smart appliances in smart homes. Based on these concepts, they designed reference ontology for smart things. Ara et al. [57] proposed a web of objects-based user-centric semantic service composition methodology for IoT. They designed an ontology model for a virtual object and composite virtual object. They used a service composition algorithm to create composite services and semantic descriptions. The next section will present a use case showing how to solve IoT service-level interoperability issues.

5.5 Use Case

In this section, a service-level IoT interoperability use case is presented. First, the section will develop the ontology used to semantically annotate things, their services and existing cloud APIs. Next, the section will present a procedure to annotate and compose things as a service. Semantic Web technologies are utilized in the use case. It will show that most of the service-level interoperability problems can be completely or partially solved using an ontology-driven approach, as well as Semantic Web languages, technologies and tools. The aim of service interoperability is to enable automatic or semi-automatic composition of services. The use case will show how this can be achieved with IoT services. To compose IoT services, the service-level incompatibilities presented in Table 5.1 must be taken into consideration.

5.5.1 Development of the Thing-as-a-Service Ontology

For the purpose of this research, the Ontology Development 101 [58] methodology was selected. The open-source tool, Protégé, and OWL were also selected. The representation of IoT devices and things as services is determined as the domain of the ontology. This ontology is used to semantically annotate things as a service. The information in the ontology should provide answers to the following questions: What concepts describe IoT devices and things as services? How are mappings of data types supported among heterogeneous things and existing cloud services?

As a basis for the ontology, this chapter used concepts defined in the W3C defined SSN ontology [59]. The paper [59] is often cited in relevant research papers; existing IoT interoperability projects use or extend this ontology to semantically describe sensors. Next, the chapter used the actuator concepts from semantic actuator network ontology developed by Spalazzi et al. [34]. This ontology described

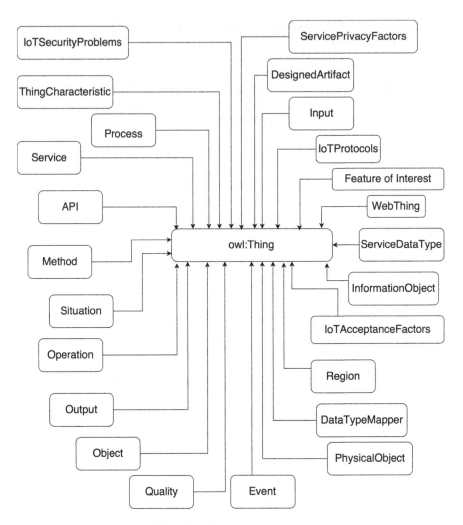

Fig. 5.1 The main hierarchy of the IoT ontology

actuators, operations and related concepts. It extends the aforementioned SSN ontology. A total of 173 defined classes were organized in 24 top-level classes (see Fig. 5.1). Some top-level classes are directly inherited from SSN and SAN ontology, including *DesignedArtifact*, *Feature of Interest*, *InformationObject*, *Input*, *Method*, *Object*, *Output*, *PhysicalObject*, *Process*, *Region*, *Event*, *Quality* and *Situation*. Class *API* represents vendor application programming interfaces. *DataTypeMapper* are instances used for data type mappings. Subclasses of *IoTAcceptanceFactors* represent IoT acceptance factors. *IoTProtocols* contains subclasses describing main IoT protocols. *IoTSecurityProblems* list the most important IoT security problems. The OWL class *Service* describes REST services, SOAP services, cloud services and things as a service. *ServiceDataType* describes data types used and inputs or outputs of services. *ServicePrivacyFactors* list main privacy factors for using IoT services. *ThingCharacteristic* describes the characteristics of physical objects (things); *WebThing* is a digital representation of a physical object accessible via REST API. Table 5.3 lists sample classes from the ontology. The properties of classes that describe the internal structure of concepts along with their corresponding domains and ranges were also defined.

Due to a lack of gold standards and corpus of data, the human evaluation and application-based evaluation were chosen. Some tools eliminated OWL syntax errors and known ontology anomalies. First, the logical consistency of the developed ontologies was checked by means of the Pellet reasoner (incorporated in the used Protégé 5 tool). Furthermore, the Web-based tool, Ontology Pitfall Scanner! (OOPS!) [60], detected possible ontology anomalies. The tool identifies 41 ontology pitfalls. The ontology was evaluated using the public OOPS! tool. Seven cases of one minor problem were found (see Fig. 5.2). Evaluation results by tool show that minor problems were not actual problems. Correcting them improved the ontology. Next, ontology was evaluated by human experts. They were sent a brief ontology description with figures of class hierarchy and a link of the complete ontology stored on GitHub. They were then asked to answer questions on completeness, conciseness, consistency and flexibility of the ontology. After their initial feedback, the ontology was revised and improved. Experts e-mailed additional comments as newer versions of the ontology were created.

The ontology can be used to semantically annotate various smart things. The ontology can be viewed at https://github.com/dandrocec/IoTOntology.

The ontology is richer than any existing IoT ontology. It contains concepts that can be used to annotate services and existing cloud services (via cloud provider APIs). It can annotate privacy, security and supported protocols as nonfunctional properties of things and services. Main IoT security problems are listed as subclasses of *IoTSecurityProblems* OWL class and are derived from OWAPS IoT security guidelines [61]. IoT acceptance factors and service privacy factors are listed in the ontology as subclasses of *IoTAcceptanceFactors* and *ServicePrivacyFactors*. IoT protocols are defined as subclasses of the following OWL classes: *IoTDataProtocols*, *IoTDiscoveryProtocols*, *IoTInfrastructureProtocols* and *IoTTransportProtocols*.

5.5.2 Achieving Service-Level IoT Interoperability

Concepts from the ontology are used to semantically annotate things and services, as well as their functional and nonfunctional properties. To test semantic annotations, two simple things were used: (1) Arduino Yun with temperature sensor and (2) littleBits with cloudBits to connect to their cloud platform and two LED actuators. The basis of the solution was the usage of thing-as-a-service framework as presented in [35]. Additionally, the JSON-LD [62] file was stored on things to describe the sensors/actuators, supporting IoT protocols, and known interoperability/privacy

Table 5.3 Sample classes from the ontology

Class	Super class	Description
API	Thing	It represents vendors' application programming interfaces (APIs)
DataTypeMapper	Thing	Its instances are used for data type mappings
Operation	Thing, Situation	Operation
ActuatorOperation	Operation	Operation that results in a change of the world's state, i.e. hasEffect object property has a value
SensoryOperation	Operation	Operation that returns a parameter
Output	Thing	Any information that is reported from a process
PhysicalObject	Thing	Physical object
Actuator	PhysicalObject	An actuator can do (implements) acting: an actuator is any entity that can follow an acting method and thus control some *Property* of a *FeatureOfInterest*. Actuator may be physical device or any other thing that can follow an acting method to control a *Property*
Acting Device	Actuator, Device	An acting device is a device that implements acting
Service	Thing	Service
CloudService	Service	Cloud service
IaaSService	CloudService	Infrastructure as a service
PaaSService	CloudService	Platform as a service
SaaSService	CloudService	Software as a service
RESTService	Service	REST service
SOAPService	Service	SOAP service
ThingAsAService	Service	Thing as a service
ServiceDataType	Thing	Data types for input and outputs of the services
ComplexServiceDataType	ServiceDataType	Complex service data type
SimpleServiceDataType	ServiceDataType	Simple service data type
WebThing	Thing	A Web Thing (or simply Thing) is a digital representation of a physical object accessible via a RESTful Web API
SemanticWebThing	WebThing	It additionally supports semantic annotations using this (open IoT) ontology

Evaluation results

It is obvious that not all the pitfalls are equally important; their impact in the ontology will depend on multiple factors. For this reason, each pitfall has an importance level attached indicating how important it is. We have identified three levels:

- **Critical** ◉ : It is crucial to correct the pitfall. Otherwise, it could affect the ontology consistency, reasoning, applicability, etc.
- **Important** ◉ : Though not critical for ontology function, it is important to correct this type of pitfall.
- **Minor** ○ : It is not really a problem, but by correcting it we will make the ontology nicer.

[Expand All] | [Collapse All]

Results for P04: Creating unconnected ontology elements.	7 cases	Minor ○
Ontology elements (classes, object properties and datatype properties) are created isolated, with no relation to the rest of the ontology.	
• This pitfall appears in the following elements: › http://www.foi.unizg.hr/ontologies/ThingAsAServiceOntology.owl#ServicePrivacyFactors › http://www.foi.unizg.hr/ontologies/ThingAsAServiceOntology.owl#ThingCharacteristic › http://www.foi.unizg.hr/ontologies/ThingAsAServiceOntology.owl#IotSecurityProblems › http://www.foi.unizg.hr/ontologies/ThingAsAServiceOntology.owl#IoTAcceptanceFactors › http://www.foi.unizg.hr/ontologies/ThingAsAServiceOntology.owl#IoTProtocols › http://www.loa-cnr.it/ontologies/DUL.owl#Event › http://www.loa-cnr.it/ontologies/DUL.owl#Quality	

Fig. 5.2 OOPS! evaluation results

problems. JSON-LD is an attempt to create a simple method to add semantics to existing JSON documents. In that way, a particular thing can connect to concepts from the described ontology. Next, sensors were connected using a customized open-source project, Global Sensor Networks (GSN) [63]. GSN provided virtual sensors to abstract implementation details on accessing sensor data and user needs to specify XML-based deployment descriptors. This task could be done semi-automatically when the server received a JSON-LD identification file from the thing that contains whether the thing contains sensors and of what types. It is possible to uniquely access data when different types of sensors are registered in GSN.

On the next level, Web services can represent different things, sensors and actuators. GSN contains REST API. Therefore, these services can access sensors. For actuators, services can be built semi-automatically by using JSON-LD descriptions of things and services. When services are semantically annotated, things can be composed as services. This considers security and privacy features, as well as supported protocols. Simple scenario tested the aforementioned approach. Web services read data from temperature sensors connected to Arduino Yun, motion trigger sensors connected to littleBits cloudBit and push data to LED actuators connected to littleBits cloudBit [35]. For example, a Java Web service client application was created to check if motion was detected. If so, the Web service for LED actuators was called to activate LEDs connected to littleBits [35].

5.6   Conclusion

Various capabilities of things, a variety of possible IoT services and nonaccepted standards exist. Therefore, IoT interoperability will remain for a certain amount of time, as well as complex research and practical problems. This chapter listed IoT service-level interoperability issues and challenges. Existing work on data (database) and service interoperability was listed and systematized using tables. IoT services have similar issues to other types of services. In addition, they have a variety of IoT capabilities, sensor data formats and protocols supported by things. IoT standards initiatives were also listed. There are several promising IoT standard initiatives. Yet, one standard has not prevailed. IoT remains a dynamic field. Many companies and start-ups develop individual innovative things and IoT services, including proprietary protocols, services and APIs.

Solutions to known interoperability problems are listed. Semantic Web and Semantic Web services are the most used solutions to IoT interoperability problems at the service level. The chapter listed the most recent works on the resolution of IoT interoperability problems by means of Semantic Web. The use case presented how to practically achieve IoT interoperability on a small practical example.

Most of the solutions use ontology. While there are many IoT ontologies, there is no consensus on which to use. Mapping of existing IoT ontologies is a promising future work. Many solutions are based on W3C SSN ontology [59]. However, it only describes basic concepts on sensors. Therefore, it should be upgraded to include actuators, complex things and services. This was achieved in this chapter's use case. The next problem was choosing an IoT service based on functional and nonfunctional properties. Other promising future research topics include the availability of search and register IoT services. Self-identification and auto-configuration of things remain unsolved. End users see basically IoT as a set of services, so achieving the interoperability of IoT services is very important

Acknowledgement This chapter has been fully supported by the Croatian Science Foundation under the project IP-2014-09-3877.

References

1. IEEE (1991) IEEE Standard computer dictionary: a compilation of IEEE standard computer glossaries. New York
2. Brownsword LL, Carney DJ, Fisher D, et al (2004) Current perspectives on interoperability, pp 1–51
3. Pokraev S, Quartel D, Steen MWA, Reichert M (2007) Semantic service modeling: enabling system interoperability. In: Doumeingts G, Müller J, Morel G, Vallespir B (eds) Enterprise Interoperability. Springer, London, pp 221–230
4. Vernadat F (1996) Enterprise modeling and integration: principles and applications. Chapman & Hall, London/New York

5. Park J, Ram S (2004) Information systems interoperability. ACM Trans Inf Syst 22:595–632. https://doi.org/10.1145/1028099.1028103
6. Loutas N, Kamateri E, Tarabanis K, D'Andria F (2011) D 1.2 Cloud4SOA cloud semantic interoperability framework
7. Naudet Y, Latour T, Guedria W, Chen D (2010) Towards a systemic formalisation of interoperability. Comput Ind 61:176–185. https://doi.org/10.1016/j.compind.2009.10.014
8. Kominers P (2012) Interoperability case study: internet of things (IoT), p 19
9. Soldatos J, Kefalakis N, Hauswirth M et al (2015) OpenIoT: open source internet-of-things in the cloud. In: Podnar Žarko I, Pripužić K, Serrano M (eds) Interoperability open-source solution internet things. Springer International Publishing, Cham, pp 13–25
10. De S, Carrez F, Reetz E et al (2013) Test-enabled architecture for IoT service creation and provisioning. In: Galis A, Gavras A (eds) Future internet. Springer, Berlin/Heidelberg, pp 233–245
11. Gusmeroli S, Piccione S, Rotondi D (2012) IoT@Work automation middleware system design and architecture. In: 2012 IEEE 17th conference emerging technology and factory automation ETFA. IEEE, Krakow, pp 1–8
12. Apolinarski W, Iqbal U, Parreira JX (2014) The GAMBAS middleware and SDK for smart city applications. In: 2014 IEEE international conference pervasive computing and communcations workshop PERCOM Workshop. IEEE, Budapest, Hungary, pp 117–122
13. Ziegler S, Crettaz C, Ladid L et al (2013) IoT6 – moving to an IPv6-based future IoT. In: Galis A, Gavras A (eds) Future internet. Springer, Berlin/Heidelberg, pp 161–172
14. Verdouw CN, Sundmaeker H, Meyer F et al (2013) Smart agri-food logistics: requirements for the future internet. In: Kreowski H-J, Scholz-Reiter B, Thoben K-D (eds) Dynamics in logistics. Springer, Berlin/Heidelberg, pp 247–257
15. Bröring A, Schmid S, Schindhelm C-K, et al Enabling IoT ecosystems through platform interoperability. http://www.arne-broering.de/BIG%20IoT%20-%20Vision.pdf. Accessed 19 Jan 2017
16. Ganzha M, Paprzycki M, Pawlowski W, et al (2016) Semantic technologies for the IoT – an inter-IoT perspective. In: 2016 IEEE first international conference internet--things design. implement IoTDI. IEEE, Berlin, Germany, pp 271–276
17. Hovstø A, Oravec V, Samovich N, et al (2016) Deliverable D1.1 requirements capture framework, pp 1–61
18. Lanza J, Sanchez L, Gomez D et al (2016) A proof-of-concept for semantically interoperable federation of IoT experimentation facilities. Sensors 16:1006. https://doi.org/10.3390/s16071006
19. Soursos S, Zarko IP, Zwickl P, et al (2016) Towards the cross-domain interoperability of IoT platforms. In: 2016 European conference networks and communcations EuCNC. IEEE, Athens, Greece, pp 398–402
20. Sheth AP, Kashyap V (1993) So far (Schematically) yet so near (Semantically). In: Proceedings IFIP WG 26 database semantics conference on interoper database system North-Holland Publishing Co., pp 283–312
21. Parent C, Spaccapietra S (2000) Database integration: the key to data interoperability. In: Advances object-oriented data model. Springer, Heidelberg, pp 221–253
22. Haslhofer B, Klas W (2010) A survey of techniques for achieving metadata interoperability. ACM Comput Surv 42:1–37. https://doi.org/10.1145/1667062.1667064
23. Nagarajan M, Verma K, Sheth AP, Miller JA (2007) Ontology driven data mediation in web services. Int J Web Serv Res 4:104–126. https://doi.org/10.4018/jwsr.2007100105
24. Ponnekanti SR, Fox A (2004) Interoperability among independently evolving web services. In: Middle-ware 04 proceedings 5th ACMIFIPUSENIX international conference on middleware, Springer, Toronto, Canada, pp 331–351
25. Serrano M, Barnaghi P, Carrez F, et al (2015) IoT semantic interoperability: research challenges, best practices, recommendations and next steps. IERC
26. Postscapes (2017) Internet of things toolkit. In: Internet things toolkit – stand. initiat. http://postscapes2.webhook.org/internet-of-things-resources/#technical. Accessed 23 Jan 2017

27. Martin D, Burstein M, Hobbs J, et al (2004) OWL-S: semantic markup for web services
28. Roman D, Lausen H, Keller U, et al (2007) D2v1.4. Web service modeling ontology (WSMO). 29 June 2013
29. Fensel D, Kopecky J, Komazec S (2010) Light-weight annotations
30. Pedrinaci C (2009) Lightweight semantic annotations for services on the web
31. Vitvar T, Kopecky J, Viskova J, et al (2009) Chapter 5 semantic web services architecture with lightweight descriptions of services. In: Advanced computing. Elsevier, Amsterdam, pp 177–224
32. Gomes P, Cavalcante E, Rodrigues T et al (2015) A federated discovery service for the internet of things. In: Proceedings 2Nd workshop middleware context-aware application IoT. ACM, New York, pp 25–30
33. Nambi SNAU, Sarkar C, Prasad RV, Rahim A (2014) A unified semantic knowledge base for IoT. In: 2014 IEEE world forum internet things WF-IoT. IEEE. Seoul, pp 575–580
34. Spalazzi L, Taccari G, Bernardini A (2014) An internet of things ontology for earthquake emergency evaluation and response. IEEE, pp 528–534
35. Androcec D, Vrcek N (2016) Thing as a service interoperability: review and framework proposal. IEEE, pp 309–316
36. Qu C, Liu F, Tao M, Deng D (2016) An OWL-S based specification model of dynamic entity services for Internet of Things. J AMBIENT Intelligence Humaniz Comput 7:73–82. https://doi.org/10.1007/s12652-015-0302-y
37. Hur K, Jin X, Lee KH (2015) Automated deployment of IoT services based on semantic description. In: Internet things WF-IoT 2015 IEEE 2nd world forum on, pp 40–45
38. Fattah SMM, Kim HS, Chong I (2016) Design of composite virtual objects for service entity creation in WoO based IoT environment. In: 2016 International conference on information networking. ICOIN, pp 372–374
39. Soldatos J, Kefalakis N (2014) Design principles for utility-driven services and cloud-based computing modelling for the internet of things. Int J WEB GRID Serv 10:139–167. https://doi.org/10.1504/IJWGS.2014.060254
40. Akasiadis C, Tzortzis G, Spyrou E, Spyropoulos C (2015) Developing complex services in an IoT ecosystem. In: Internet things WF-IoT 2015 IEEE 2nd world forum on, pp 52–56
41. Sezer OB, Can SZ, Dogdu E (2015) Development of a smart home ontology and the implementation of a semantic sensor network simulator: an internet of things approach. In: International conference on collaboration technologies and systems. CTS 2015, pp 12–18
42. Li H, Seed D, Flynn B, et al (2016) Enabling semantics in an M2M/IoT service delivery platform. In: 2016 IEEE Tenth International conference semantic computing ICSC, pp 206–213
43. Thoma M, Braun T, Magerkurth C (2014) Enterprise integration of smart objects using semantic service descriptions. In: 2014 IEEE wireless communcation and network conference WCNC, pp 3426–3431
44. Jia B, Liu S, Yang Y (2014) Fractal cross-layer service with integration and interaction in internet of things. Int J Distrib Sens Netw 10(3):760248. https://doi.org/10.1155/2014/760248
45. Conzon D, Brizzi P, Kasinathan P, et al (2015) Industrial application development exploiting IoT vision and model driven programming. In: 2015 18th International conference on Intelligence in next generation networks. ICIN, pp 168–175
46. Ryu M, Kim J, Yun J (2015) Integrated semantics service platform for the internet of things: a case study of a smart office. Sensors 15:2137–2160. https://doi.org/10.3390/s150102137
47. Qu C, Liu F, Tao M (2015) Ontologies for the transactions on IoT. Int J Distrib Sens Netw. https://doi.org/10.1155/2015/934541
48. Kim Y, Lee S, Chong I (2014) Orchestration in distributed web-of-objects for creation of user-centered IoT service capability. Wirel Pers Commun 78:1965–1980. https://doi.org/10.1007/s11277-014-2056-9
49. Kovatsch M, Hassan YN, Mayer S (2015) Practical semantics for the Internet of Things: Physical states, device mashups, and open questions. In: 2015 5th International conference on the internet of things (IOT), pp 54–61

50. Hasemann H, Kroller A, Pagel M (2012) RDF provisioning for the Internet of Things. In: 3rd IEEE International conference on the internet of things (IOT), pp 143–150
51. Vecchio M, Sasidharan S, Marcelloni F, Giaffreda R (2013) Reconfiguration of environmental data compression parameters through cognitive IoT technologies. In: 2013 IEEE 9th International conference wireless mobile computing networking and communication WiMob, pp 141–146
52. Chun S, Seo S, Oh B, Lee KH (2015) Semantic description, discovery and integration for the internet of things. In: IEEE International conference on semantic computing (ICSC), pp 272–275
53. Desai P, Sheth A, Anantharam P (2015) Semantic gateway as a service architecture for IoT interoperability. In: 2015 IEEE International conference mobile services. IEEE, New York, pp 313–319
54. Kiljander J, D'elia A, Morandi F et al (2014) Semantic interoperability architecture for pervasive computing and internet of things. IEEE Access 2:856–873. https://doi.org/10.1109/ACCESS.2014.2347992
55. Wang X, An H, Xu Y, Wang S (2015) Sensing network element ontology description model for internet of things. In: 2015 2nd International conference on information science control engineering. ICISCE. IEEE, Shanghai, pp 471–475
56. den Hartog F, Daniele L, Roes J (2015) Toward semantic interoperability of energy using and producing appliances in residential environments. In: 2015 12th Annu. IEEE consumer communcatons network conference CCNC, pp 170–175
57. Ara SS, Shamszaman ZU, Chong I (2014) Web-of-objects based user-centric semantic service composition methodology in the internet of things. Int J Distrib Sens Netw. https://doi.org/10.1155/2014/482873
58. Noy NF, McGuinness DL (2001) Ontology development 101: a guide to creating your first ontology
59. Compton M, Barnaghi P, Bermudez L et al (2012) The SSN ontology of the W3C semantic sensor network incubator group. Web Semant Sci Serv Agents World Wide Web 17:25–32. https://doi.org/10.1016/j.websem.2012.05.003
60. Poveda-Villalón M, Suárez-Figueroa MC, Gomez-Perez, Asuncion A (2012) Validating ontologies with OOPS! In: EKAW12 Proceedings 18th international conference on knowledge engineering. knowledge managagement. Springer, Galway, pp 267–281
61. OWAPS (2016) IoT security guidance. In: IoT security guidelines. https://www.owasp.org/index.php/IoT_Security_Guidance. Accessed 30 Jan 2017
62. Lanthaler M, Gütl C (2012) On using JSON-LD to create evolvable RESTful services. ACM, New York, p 25
63. Aberer K, Hauswirth M, Salehi A (2006) The global sensor networks middleware for efficient and flexible deployment and interconnection of sensor networks. Ecole Polytechnique Federale de Lausanne, Lausanne

Part II
Methods and Frameworks

Chapter 6
Simulating Sensor Devices for Experimenting with IoT Cloud Systems

Tamas Pflanzner, Marta Fidrich, and Attila Kertesz

Abstract As a growing number of powerful devices join the Internet, a new world of smart devices is being formed. This new trend is due to the emergence of the Internet of Things (IoT) paradigm, which also has a significant impact on the global Internet traffic. There are also more and more cloud providers offering IoT-specific services, since cloud computing has the potential to satisfy IoT needs such as hiding data generation and processing and visualization of tasks. While each cloud provider offers its own set of features, two critical features they all have in common are the ability to connect devices and to store the data generated by those devices. Using the capabilities of smartphones, many things can be simulated simultaneously supporting most types of IoT devices. In this chapter, we introduce and categorize IoT cloud providers and classify common IoT applications. Based on these findings, we propose a mobile IoT simulator called MobIoTSim that helps researchers to learn IoT device handling without buying real sensors and to test and demonstrate IoT applications utilizing multiple devices. We also show how to develop gateway services in cloud environments that can be connected to MobIoTSim to manage the simulated devices and evaluate device handling scalability. By using this tool, developers can examine the behavior of IoT systems and develop and evaluate IoT cloud applications in a more convenient and efficient way.

6.1 Introduction

The Cluster of European Research Projects on the Internet of Things considers the Internet of Things (IoT) as a vital part of future Internet [1]. They define IoT as a dynamic global network infrastructure with self-configuring capabilities using interoperable communication protocols. *Things* in this network interact and communicate among themselves and the environment, exchange sensor data, and react

T. Pflanzner (✉) • M. Fidrich • A. Kertesz
Software Engineering Department, University of Szeged, Szeged, Hungary
e-mail: tamas.pflanzner@inf.u-szeged.hu

© Springer International Publishing AG 2017
Z. Mahmood (ed.), *Connected Environments for the Internet of Things*,
Computer Communications and Networks,
https://doi.org/10.1007/978-3-319-70102-8_6

autonomously to events by triggering actions mostly without direct human intervention.

According to a Gartner report [2], there will be 30 billion devices always online and more than 200 billion devices discontinuously online by 2020, which calls for an ecosystem that provides means to interconnect and control these devices. With the help of cloud solutions, user data can be stored in a remote location and can be accessed from anywhere. The concept of cloud computing has been pioneered by commercial companies with the promise to allow elastic construction of virtual infrastructures, which attracted users early on. Its technical motivation has been introduced in [3]. Gubbi et al. [4] have suggested that to support the IoT vision, the current computing paradigm needs to go beyond traditional mobile computing scenarios, and cloud computing has the potential to address these needs as it is able to hide data generation, processing, and visualization tasks. For this reason, there are more and more cloud providers offering IoT-specific services (e.g., Google Cloud Platform and IBM Bluemix platform). Some of these IoT features are unique, but every IoT cloud provider has the basic capabilities to connect and store data from devices. Many things have to be managed at the same time, and a wide range of devices and data formats are available; therefore, creating and examining such applications are not trivial. The aim of our research is to support the proliferation of IoT with the help of mobile and cloud technologies, thus to enable experimenting with complex systems consisting of interdependent components that work together to enable the creation and management of user applications. To manage the heterogeneity of protocols and data structures used in the IoT cloud systems, smartphones and tablets can provide useful assistance [5].

The main contributions of this chapter are (i) to introduce and categorize IoT cloud providers, (ii) to present a classification of common IoT applications, (iii) to propose a mobile IoT simulator called MobIoTSim that helps researchers to learn IoT device handling without buying real sensors and to test and demonstrate IoT applications utilizing multiple devices, (iv) to introduce how to develop cloud gateway services to manage the simulated devices, and (v) to evaluate the scalability of MobIoTSim device management feature.

The remainder of this chapter is structured as follows: Section 6.2 introduces related works. Section 6.3 gathers cloud providers offering IoT features, and Section 6.4 presents a classification of various IoT applications. Section 6.5 introduces our proposed IoT device simulator called MobIoTSim and demonstrates its utilization with cloud gateways, evaluates its performance, and highlights future development plans. Finally, the contributions are summarized in Section 6.6.

6.2   Related Works

Recently, there has been an increasing competition between the leading vendors in the cloud market, such as Amazon, Microsoft, Google, and Salesforce. Each of them promotes its own, mostly incompatible cloud standards and formats [6], preventing them from agreeing on a widely accepted, standardized way to utilize clouds in the IoT field. However, an interoperable cloud environment would benefit customers, as they could migrate their virtual machines, data, and applications between cloud providers without setting data at risk. The integration of IoT and clouds has been envisioned by Botta et al. [7] by summarizing their main properties, features, underlying technologies, and open issues. A solution for merging IoT and clouds is proposed by Nastic et al. [8]. They argue that system designers and operations managers face numerous challenges to realize IoT cloud systems in practice, due to the complexity and diversity of their requirements in terms of IoT resources consumption, customization, and runtime governance. These related works also serve as a motivation to our research by raising the need for managing a large number of protocols and data formats by means of simulation.

The existing simulators used to examine IoT systems are general network simulators, e.g., NetSim [9], Qualnet [10], and OMNeT++ [11]. With these tools IoT-related processes can be examined such as device placement planning and network interference. The OMNeT++ discrete event simulation environment [11] is a generic tool for simulating communication networks, multiprocessors, and other distributed systems. It can be used in numerous domains from queuing network simulations to wireless and ad hoc network simulations, from business process simulation to peer-to-peer networks.

There are some more specific IoT simulators closer to our approach. Han et al. have designed DPWSim [12], which is a simulation tool kit to support the development of service-oriented and event-driven IoT applications with the aim to support the OASIS standard Devices Profile for Web Services (DPWS). Though this enables the use of web services on smart and resource-constrained devices, it also limits its application scope. The SimpleIoTSimulator [13] is an IoT Sensor/device simulator that is able to create test environments made up of thousands of sensors and gateways on a computer. It supports many of the common IoT protocols (e.g., CoAP, MQTT, HTTP). Its drawback is that it needs a 64-bit Red Hat Enterprise Linux environment to be installed. Our approach is more focused on IoT device simulation with smartphones, which is easier to be combined with real-world applications. The Automaton Simulator [14] seems to be the closest to our concept. It simulates virtual sensors, actuators, and devices with unique behaviors. With this tool complex, dynamic systems can be created for specific applications. Unlike our open mobile solution, it is a commercial, web-based environment with very limited documentation.

The motivation behind our research is that more and more cloud platform providers have started to offer IoT-specific services to ease the development of IoT cloud applications, but cases where many heterogeneous things need to be managed are hard to realize and examine. For example, smart city application scenarios using LoRa [15] or SIGFOX [16] technologies are very expensive and time-consuming to set up with real devices; hence, a base station costs more than a thousand Euros with a lot of configuration work. Therefore, we propose to use simulated devices with a cloud gateway in order to ease the development and testing of such systems.

6.3 Providers Enabling IoT Clouds

The IBM Bluemix platform [17] is an IoT-enabled cloud solution offered by IBM. It can be used for quick development of cloud-based applications that take advantage of the data generated by the sensors and devices. Products of several major device manufacturers are supported, such as ARM, the Electronics B&B, Intel, Multi-Tech Systems, and Texas Instruments, but other individual cases can also be solved on the platform. Data generated by the equipment is sent by the popular and lightweight MQTT protocol to the cloud. The service allows the users to configure, manage the devices, and to store the history of generated data or stream real-time data to the application. The data transfer can be done through secure APIs.

To illustrate the inner workings of the platform, a real-time data visualization demo is also provided. To use it, first a data provider should be configured, which is in the simplest case a smartphone, but it is possible to use a TI SensorTag, ARM Mbed, Raspberry Pi, Intel, and other devices. The opened browser page on the smartphone can send real-time data of the phone's movement to the cloud application. The framework also provides a predefined web-based sensor simulator [18] that is able to act as three simulated sensors, sending temperature and humidity values through websockets.

The Bluemix platform offers several specialized services to support the development of cloud applications. Some examples of these services are Push for messaging, Cloudant NoSQL DB to manage NoSQL databases, Geospatial Analytics for location tracking, and IBM Analytics for Hadoop computations. The supported languages for application development are Java, JavaScript, GO, PHP, Python, and Ruby. In terms of costs, a price calculator helps to determine a monthly fee for a 30-day trial period. Twenty devices can be connected and 100 MB of data can be sent to the devices for free, which is enough for about 50,000 messages. 1GB storage space can also be used in this period.

The Google IoT solution [19] is part of the Google Cloud Platform, which includes various Google services. The scalability is an excellent feature in this platform. It allows devices to be connected, and it collects data and visualizes them. The data sent from the devices are received by the Google Load Balancer and forwards to instances of the AppEngine applications. In general, the main part of the application is the AppEngine, which may use other services. Compute intensive tasks are supported by the Compute Engine. The Cloud Storage and the Cloud SQL manages data. It is possible to send data with streams to the BigQuery service, which is ideal if we want to work with real-time data. In IoT systems, the visualization is an important feature; it is supported in real time using the Google Charts. Google is also strong in managing a large amount of data processing, which is important, since there are many devices generating huge amount of data in IoT systems. Google Firebase plays an important role in the management of the devices. It was originally designed to assist mobile devices (like MBaaS). It provides synchronized real-time database and authentication and is capable of offline operations.

Amazon Web Services is a collection of services that make up a cloud computing platform, which are based on 11 geographical regions across the world. The most central and well-known services are Amazon EC2 (Elastic Compute Cloud) and Amazon S3 (Simple Storage Service). The products are offered to large and small companies as a service to provide large computing capacity faster and cheaper than the client company building and maintaining an actual physical server farm. AWS automatically handles the details such as resource provisioning, load balancing, scaling, and monitoring. One can create applications in PHP, Java, Python, Ruby, node.js,. NET, Go, or in a Docker container that runs on an application server with a database. An environment using the default settings will run a single Amazon EC2 micro instance and an Elastic Load Balancer. Additional instances will be added if needed, to handle any peaks in workload or traffic. Each Amazon EC2 instance is built from an Amazon Machine Image which can be an Amazon Linux AMI or an Amazon Windows Server 2008 R2 AMI by default.

Amazon is also a cloud platform provider, since it has many components to build applications with. This allows for more general usage, but not so many details, which could make the developer's job easier. With the three main components (Cognito for user management, Mobile Analytics, and Simple Notification Service), the mobile solution is a valuable part for the whole Amazon cloud offering. This is still not mature enough for enterprise usage, because the lack of integration and security.

Amazon IoT connects devices to services and other devices with a secure way. The device state is synchronized, so messages can be sent even if the device is offline. The Rule Engine helps to convert the data for services.

Azure [20] is a cloud computing platform, which allows developers to publish web applications running on different frameworks, written in different programming languages such as any. NET language, node.js, php, Python, and Java. Azure Web Sites support a website creation wizard that can be used to create a blank site or use one of the several pre-configured sites. Developers can add or modify content of the website via multiple deployment methods: TFS, FTP, CodePlex, GitHub, Dropbox, Bitbucket, Mercurial, or git. Developers can select the place where their website will be hosted from several Microsoft data centers around the globe. Azure Traffic Manager routes traffic manually or automatically between websites in different regions. Web sites are hosted on IIS 8.0, running on a custom version of Windows Server 2012. The component relating to IoT called IoT Hub can communicate with devices with protocols like MQTT, AMQP, and HTTP, but it is possible to implement other protocols too.

The main IoT-related properties of these cloud providers are shown in Table 6.1. Summarizing the comparison tables, Google, Amazon, Azure, and Bluemix have the highest variety of IoT-related services. The MQTT (or other IoT protocol) should be a basic functionality to an IoT cloud platform, but many providers have just a REST interface. IoT applications in Google can be composed of many connected services, which make it complex providing more freedom for the developers. They are also very good at scaling and performance, and this complexity is compensated by the simplicity of Firebase.

Table 6.1 Cloud IoT features

Provider	Bluemix	Google	Amazon	Azure
Open source	no	no	no	no
Hosting	closed	closed	closed	closed
Server languages	many	many	many	many
Client languages	Java, JS	Java, Python	C, JS	C, Java, JS
Mobile SDK	Android, iOS	Android, iOS	Android, iOS	Android, iOS, WP
Protocols	MQTT	REST	MQTT, REST	MQTT, AMQP, REST
Data store	yes	yes	yes	yes
BLOB	no	yes	yes	yes
GEO	yes	yes	yes	yes
Push. not	yes	yes	yes	yes
Trigger	yes	yes	yes	yes
Visualization	yes	yes	yes	N/A
Protocols	MQTT	REST	MQTT, REST	MQTT, AMQP, REST

From this survey, we can see that the most popular cloud providers have already realized the need for IoT support, and most of them provide reasonably good solutions for IoT application development. Nevertheless, interoperability issues still exist, and applications managing a large number of different IoT devices are hard to develop and evaluate. Bluemix has also identified the need for a sensor or device simulator, but its tool is meant to serve simple demonstration purposes. Our aim is to design a generic solution to this problem.

6.4 A Survey of Common IoT Cloud Applications

In order to reveal current IoT application properties, we studied and investigat-ed 16 IoT cloud uses from various application areas, including smart home, smart city, and smart region. Telemedicine [21] is also an important area; it was originally created to treat patients far away from local health facilities or in areas with shortages of medical professionals. Nowadays, it is becoming a tool for convenient medical care: waste less time in waiting rooms or get quick care for minor but urgent cases. More precisely, telemedicine is a type of medical service where the service provider and the recipient do not meet directly; contact is established through some sort of data transfer system. Technically, telemedicine is a screening, diagnostic, therapeutic, or rehabilitation aiding system supported by info-communication tools, where the necessary presence of the medical staff is provided from a distance through online connection.

Functionality of telemedicine services can fall into the following categories:

- Decision support: digital encyclopedias, medical leaflets, and guidelines.
- Teleconsultation systems are primarily made to assist the communication of physicians with all the parties involved.
- Monitoring applications provide information on bioparameters with the help of sensors.
- Register/diary applications require patients to give data regularly in order to provide useful information for the physician for an upcoming visit.
- Educational applications teach patients or professionals.

Telemedicine has several advantages, like more convenient, accessible care for patients, saves on healthcare costs, extends access to consults from specialists, increasing patient engagement, and better quality patient care. On the other hand, it also has some shortcomings, such as it requires technical training and equipment; some telemedicine models may reduce care continuity and may reduce in-person interactions with doctors, and navigating the changing policy and reimbursement landscape can be tricky.

With the recent growth of wearables, mobile medical devices, and consumer-friendly health apps, patients are starting to use technology to monitor and track their health. As people are becoming more proactive, they will be more open to various alternatives to manage their health. The key to success of telemedicine is having the right health tracking tools and the smart modules that able to analyze bioparameters and medical data, such as blood pressure or glucose level. With recent advances in Artificial Intelligence, smart modules are becoming smarter and smarter. Telemedicine is going to be part of the everyday life.

Next, we introduce and describe the applications we found in this area, and in the following sections, we present a number of use case scenarios to gather the IoT properties of these products and offerings and compile them into a taxonomy.

Use Case 1

The Mimo [22] project develops smart products that are created for babies for better sleep and for parents for more sleepless nights. It measures the baby's breathing, temperature, body position, and activity level. It can send alerts and nightly reports to a smartphone. It uses ultralow-power Bluetooth connection. The caretakers can see the sensor information in real time. There are some extra products, for example, if the baby temperature is not optimal, a smart thermostat can change the room temperature, or if the baby is moving, a webcam can be used to check on the baby.

Use Case 2

The Vitality GlowPack [23] solutions can be used instead of the standard pill bottle top, to upgrade it to a smart pill bottle. It connects via Bluetooth to the user's smartphone, and an application reminds the patient to take the pills at the right time. There is a lamp unit with the product; if the bottle is not opened when the patient needs to take the medicine, the lamp and the bottle top start to flash and then flash with playing music, or if these are not effective, the user can get an SMS or phone call. Usually there are two or three times a patient needs to take the medicine, so there is no much need for a high-speed network. There are some other applications to extend the use of the bottle cap, for example, the patient can alert a user if a drug interaction is needed or can notify the user that two pills cannot be taken at the same time. If there is a connection between the smart top and the local pharmacy, it can ask for a refill if the application is low on medicine.

Use Case 3
AmSmart [24] is a smart home and home security solution. It includes high-quality home alarm system, IP cameras with HD quality, automated door opening, smart-plugs, and heat and light control. The system can be controlled with a smartphone. If the alarm goes off, it is automatically sent to predefined receivers like guards, neighbors, or family members.

Use Case 4
Smart outlets [25] are designed to implement the smart electrical outlet concept. A user can remotely control the appliances or set timers from a smartphone. The number of IoT devices can be different, but on average we can say it is a medium-sized environment. It can communicate with different networks, but the Wi-Fi is the main profile. The monitoring and energy saving opportunities are big with this product.

Use Case 5
Key Finder Tags [26] are location sensors that attach to one's utilities as key fobs or stick-on tags. Some have its own cellular data connection and GPS so they can report the position from everywhere. The simple versions only have Bluetooth connection and can make a beeping sound or light signals. The smartphone can request the device to show its position. Some advanced tags are with a really useful reverse function, so if the user has the smart key fob, but can't find the phone, after pushing the fob, the phone will signal its position.

Use Case 6
Wireless plant sensors [27] help to take care of our plants. These indoor or outdoor sensor systems use Wi-Fi connection to send status info about the plants and have different algorithms for different plant types to water them. To set a timer is a simple solution to not forget to water the plants. The size of the system may vary from few home plants to an industry size system.

Use Case 7
The Bigbelly [28] smart waste and recycling system helps to figure out if a particular trash needs to be emptied. It is a solar-powered system, so no electricity is necessary for fullness level sensing or communication with the Bigbelly cloud. The system is designed to provide smart trash cans for a whole city.

Use Case 8
Outdoor lighting is an important part of the strategic asset base for cities, municipalities, and large enterprises. Echelon [29] offers a sophisticated, comprehensive, open standards-based approach to outdoor lighting control that makes it easy and affordable for lighting owners to increase the efficiency, safety, and versatility of their municipal and commercial lighting systems.

Use Case 9

Open Source Lion Tracking Collars [30] is an open-source wildlife tracking collar system to help conservationists protect the last 2000 lions living in the wild in Southern Kenya and safeguard the Maasai herder cattle, restoring Maasai land to a working ecosystem.

Use Case 10

The smart parking [31] system can detect if the parking spot is reserved with a magnetic sensor. The cellular network is an option to send the data to the Save9 cloud and use it to provide smart parking solutions.

Use Case 11

The optic chemical sensors [32] are silicon devices mainly based on microelectrodes and specific sensing layers, such as silicon nitride for pH measurement. These devices for water monitoring can be integrated into a multi-parametric microsystem together with conductivity, redox potential, temperature, and other sensors for water monitoring applications.

Use Case 12

With the Phenonet Project [33], plant breeders can evaluate the performance of different wheat varieties using measurements taken from remote sensors. These sensors monitor things like soil temperature, humidity, and air temperature and are often used for crop variety trials. This allows farmers to forecast harvest time, improve plant health, plant irrigation time, and determine frost and heat events.

Use Case 13

AquamatiX [34] help cities to better control the flow of water by embedding sensors in water pipes throughout the distribution network and connecting them to pump control systems. These sensors monitor water flow, feeding the data back to facilitate optimized water pumping throughout the system. By minimizing the amount of water in the pipes, cities can reduce the amount lost to leakage and prevent the formation of new leaks. In the process, the system also saves energy by reducing the need for pumping. Moreover, by distributing water monitoring throughout the network, these technologies can detect abrupt events, like bursts, facilitating faster response and minimizing water loss.

Use Case 14

The newest Samsung smart refrigerators [35] have a big touchscreen, where the family calendar can be seen, notes, or photos. Three cameras are built in, and every time the door closes, fresh photos are sent to the user's smartphones. This can be very helpful in the middle of a shopping.

Use Case 15

The latest GE Evolution Series Tier 4 Locomotive [36] is loaded with 250 sensors to measure staggering 150,000 data points in a minute. This data combined with other incoming streams of data from informational and operating systems help in anticipating events and help take driving decisions in real time.

Use Case 16

Based in Ireland, the CleanGrow's [37] project helps with monitoring the crop nutrients making use of a carbon nanotube-based sensor system. This information helps farmers to alter maturity rate or color of the crop production. As opposed to analog devices used conventionally, the CleanGrow device uses a nanotube sensor that detects quantity and presence of specific ion in the production.

Summary

Finally, we categorized the previously seen IoT applications according to four categories: context, number of devices, sensors, and connection type. In Table 6.2, we map the IoT use cases introduced in the survey to the categories of the taxonomy.

It can be seen from the table that the number of users is usually small scale and the number of devices is usually medium scale. This can be explained with the complexity of deploying large-scale systems. The sensor types and the context of the use cases are really diverse, this comes from the nature of these systems (available everywhere), and they are generally used to help us in our everyday lives. Usually, we expect from devices to have low energy consumption, because usually they work with a battery. Regarding networking capabilities, we can examine the data generation frequency and data sizes of the transferred messages; they are generally low and small per device. Concerning the type of the networks, it can be seen that the wireless networks are dominating, and the bandwidth and error rate of these network are not as good as in wired networks.

Table 6.2 Comparison table of IoT use cases

Use case	Context	No. of devices	Sensors	Connection type
1	Body/health	Small scale	Motion	Short range/Bluetooth
2	Body/health	Small scale	Open/close	Short range/Bluetooth
3	Building/home	Medium scale	Photo	Long range/Wi-Fi
4	Building/office	Medium scale	Electric	Long range/TCP/IP
5	Building/home	Small scale	GPS	Short range/Bluetooth
6	Industry	Medium scale	Photo	Long range/Wi-Fi
7	City	Medium scale	Load	Long range/cellular
8	City	Large scale	Light	Long range/Wi-Fi
9	Environment	Medium scale	GPS	Long range/cellular
10	City	Large scale	Magnetic	Long range/cellular
11	City	Small scale	Chemical	Long range/cellular
12	Environment	Medium scale	Humidity	Long range/cellular
13	City	Medium scale	Flow	Long range/cellular
14	Building/home	Small scale	Photo	Long range/Wi-Fi
15	Industry	Large scale	GPS	Long range/cellular
16	Environment	Large scale	Chemical	Long range/cellular

6.5   The Mobile IoT Device Simulator

The main purpose of our mobile IoT device simulator, called MobIoTSim, is to help cloud application developers to learn IoT device handling without buying real sensors and to test and demonstrate IoT applications utilizing multiple devices. The structure of the application lets users create IoT environment simulations in a fast and efficient way with the options for custom settings.

6.5.1   Requirements for an IoT Cloud Simulator

We identified the following incremental challenges relating to IoT networks:

- IoT devices are battery powered.
- They communicate using low-power wireless technologies (e.g., IEEE 802.11, IEEE 802.15.4, Bluetooth).
- There are different resource constraints of devices (e.g., on CPU, memory, connectivity).
- IoT networks are very dynamic as network conditions can change rapidly.
- They are heterogeneous: there is a large spread on device capabilities (e.g., powerful cameras, low-cost temperature sensors); additionally there are sources (sensors) and sinks of information (actuators).
- They are very dynamic: the networking environment in an IoT environment is largely unstructured and can vary rapidly.

There are different kinds of IoT environments; hence, their static or dynamic properties and the number of utilized devices can affect the design of such a simulator. For example, a connected house can be regarded as a static environment, because its devices are usually in one place, possibly with wired connection, providing reliable network stability. The dynamic environment is more complex to simulate, in such cases we would like to simulate a broader part of the environment considering Wi-Fi interference, battery lifetime, and locations of the devices.

We are not aiming at simulating whole IoT systems and networks, but we still want to aid the design, development, and testing processes of these systems. Our goal is to develop a mobile IoT device simulator that can emulate real devices and sensors, thus it can be used in the previously mentioned processes instead of real resources.

The requirements for basic functionalities of such a simulator are to send and receive messages, generate sensor data (for one or more devices), and react to received messages. These capabilities are sufficient to use the simulator in IoT system analysis. Requirements for advanced functionalities such as simulating network errors, recording and replaying concrete simulation cases, and connecting real IoT devices to the simulator can contribute to the analysis of more realistic system.

In our work, we planned to support the basic functionalities with the following settings:

- A simulated device should have an ID or tokens for authentication.
- The generated sensor data should be made available in binary, plain text, or JSON format with metadata like date, time, and device state.
- Finally MQTT or REST communication protocols should be supported.

6.5.2 Architecture and Usage

Our mobile IoT device simulator can simulate one or more IoT devices, and it is implemented as a mobile application for the Android platform. Sensor data generation of the simulated devices are random-generated values in the range given by the user. The data sending frequency can also be specified for every device. The application uses MQTT protocol to send the data with the use of the Eclipse Paho open-source library. The data is represented in a structured JSON object compatible with the IBM IoT Foundation message format [38].

Screenshots of the simulator can be seen in Fig. 6.1. After starting the MobIoTSim Android application, the user can navigate to the cloud settings or the device's screens. The first one can be used to define the connection parameters of a gateway residing in a cloud. These parameters are organization ID, URL, port and connection type for communicating with its MQTT server and optional parameters: application ID, auth key, and auth token, e.g., for accessing visualized data. Users can also select predefined settings from templates, an example parameter setting for the Bluemix Quickstart demo gateway can be seen in Fig. 6.1a.

The devices screen shows the list of currently simulated devices. Each device can be started/stopped or edited (see Fig. 6.1b). A new device can be added by clicking on a button below the list. The creation of a new device and editing the details of an existing device are managed by the same screen, the device settings screen (see Fig. 6.1c). Here, the user can specify a device type, an ID of the device, a token (to authenticate with the MQTT server of the gateway), the data generation frequency, and the parameters with the range for random numeric value generation. For cloud application testing, a great feature is to record sensor data and networking events, and later it can be replayed again many times, with exactly the same scenario.

In order to exemplify the usability of MobIoTSim, we connected it to the Quickstart application (i.e., demo gateway) of the IBM IoT Foundation with an MQTT server [39] (with the settings shown in Fig. 6.1a). Once we registered a simulated device to the MQTT server of the IBM IoT Foundation system and started it in MobIoTSim (like MobIoT_test01 as shown in Fig. 6.1b), the data generated by the device is continuously sent to the demo gateway. A screenshot of the received and visualized data in the IBM IoT Foundation demo gateway can be seen in Fig. 6.2.

We also developed an own gateway service in the IBM Bluemix platform that is able to manage more devices simultaneously and to send a notification to the

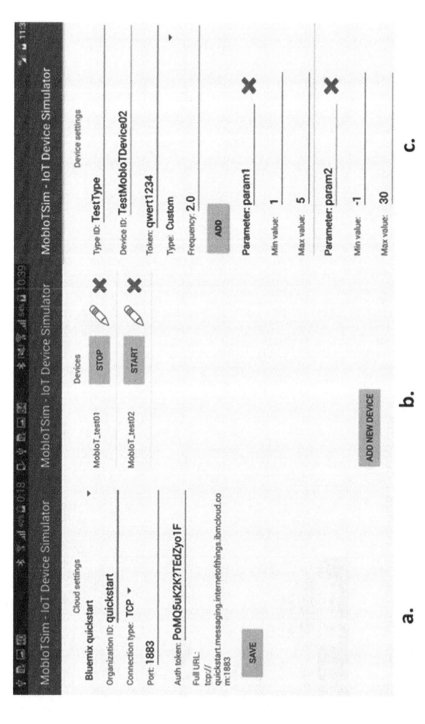

Fig. 6.1 Screenshots of the MobIoTSim Android application: (**a**) Cloud settings, (**b**) Devices, (**c**) Device settings

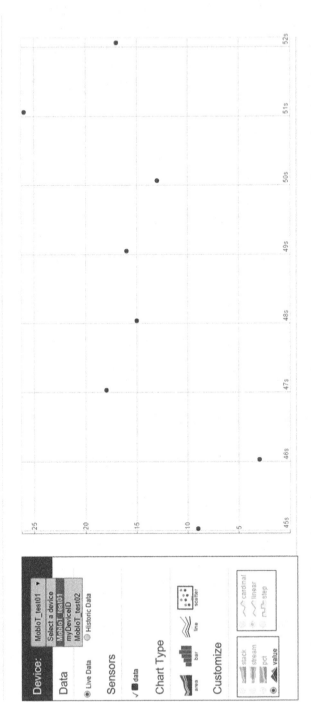

Fig. 6.2 Data visualization in the IBM IoT Foundation demo gateway

MobIoTSim device simulator by responding to critical sensor values. This gateway service is basically an extended version of the IoT visualization application [40] of the IBM Internet of Things Cloud. It has a web-based graphical interface to visualize sensor data coming from MobIoTSim. Messages (defined in JSON format) received from the simulated devices are managed by an MQTT server. It can also be used to send responses (or notifications) back to the simulated IoT devices in MobIoTSim.

Figure 6.3a shows how to connect the simulator to this gateway. Since it has a predefined template called Bluemix, we only need to specify an organization ID and the connection type (TCP or secure TLS) (the URL is given in the template) to enable connection to the MQTT server, while the application ID, the auth key, and token can be retrieved by registering to the gateway service (these parameters can be used later to sign in to the data visualization site of the gateway). The simulated devices also need to be registered to the MQTT server of the gateway service by specifying their device and type identifiers and sensor data thresholds, which replies with their token identifiers (to be used for device setting as shown in Fig. 6.1c).

a.   b.

Fig. 6.3 Screenshots for using an own gateway: (**a**) Cloud settings, (**b**) Devices screen showing a warning

Once these settings are made, simulated devices can be defined and started in the same way as shown previously for the demo gateway. With this own gateway, we can create advanced scenarios, such as managing more devices and responding to critical sensor data coming from the simulated devices. Figure 6.3b shows a situation in which a warning message is sent to a device (named MobIoT_test01 in MobIoTSim), when sensor data values are over/under a predefined threshold. Figure 6.4 shows the GUI of the own Bluemix gateway service by depicting the data received from a selected simulated device.

We have also created a gateway service in Azure IoT Hub [20] and connected MobIoTSim to it. In this way we can envision an inter-cloud scenario, in which simulated devices in MobIoTSim can send data to gateways in Bluemix and Azure clouds simultaneously. Figure 6.5 shows screenshots of the Azure IoT Hub, including the gateway service called SED-IoT-App and a MobIoTSim device called javadevice. We also included a screenshot on the usage tab, showing 23 received messages.

6.5.3   Evaluation of the Multiple Device Simulation Scalability

We created a refined android application to focus on the scalability testing of MobIoTSim. This application is a simplified version of MobIoTSim, containing only its device handling functionalities, by providing access to low-level configurations, e.g., specifying the number of threads for the simulated devices. It collects detailed statistical data regarding the simulation by measuring elapsed times for executing certain functions. It also connects to a Bluemix cloud IoT gateway and sends MQTT messages to it. When we performed the evaluations, the number of simulated devices was limited to 20 by the Bluemix platform.

There is a settings part of this application, where the number of devices, the message frequency, the number of used threads, and the message content type can be set. The content type can be a simple JSON object with one random parameter or an OpenWeatherMap structured JSON structure describing cities and their randomly generated weather values. Other settings are hardcoded to the application for this testing, like the address of the Bluemix IoT service MQTT broker. After starting the test, the statistics can be accessed by pressing the STAT button.

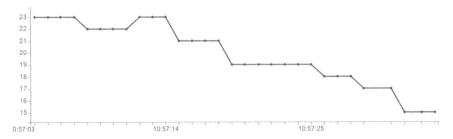

Fig. 6.4 Data visualization in an own gateway service in Bluemix

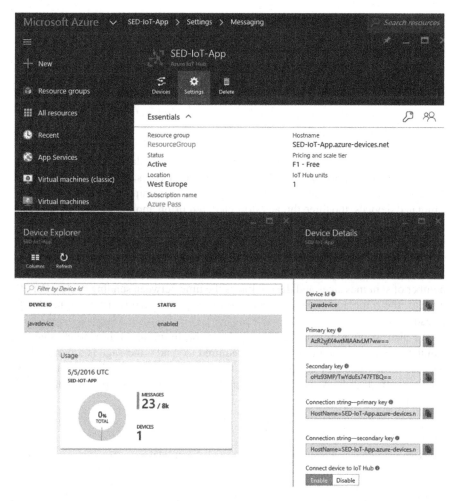

Fig. 6.5 Connection with an Azure gateway service

The statistical information has two main parts: the Settings and the actual Statistics part. In the Settings, we can find the number of used threads, the address of the MQTT broker, the number of simulated devices, the frequency of the messages, the generated clientID of one device, the MQTT topic where the messages were sent, the content type, and an example of JSON message. The Statistics part contains measured values like the duration of the simulation, the overall messages sent, and the total number of errors in the initialization, connection, or send process of the devices. The average times of the MQTT initialization, connection, and message send methods and the average overall time cost of a message exchange cycle. An important measure is regarding the real-time difference between the cycles of a device. If the message frequency is set to 1 s in the settings, we should know if it was achieved or not in the testing. It can happen that during the simulation the simulated device cannot start the message-sending method every second, because the other devices would not let it to get the required resources, like CPUs. The average required time of a random-generated message is measured, too.

The tests were made with a Samsung S5 smartphone and a node.js visualization application in Bluemix. The most informative tests were made with 1 s message frequency, simulating 10 to 20 devices and using 3 to 12 threads. The message contents were five random-generated values in a JSON object. The duration of each tests was 1 min.

The test results showed that the random data generalization consumes almost negligible time, so it does not interference with the simulation. First, we started using three threads, because the Samsung S5 has four cores, but from the results in Table 6.3, we can see that the number of threads is an important factor. With ten simulated devices, the three threads struggled, requiring approximately 1.5 s for the devices to start a message-sending cycle again, instead of the 1 s from the previous settings. With four threads the problem was solved. If the number of simulated devices grows, more threads are needed. For 15 devices, the threads are not enough, but 6 can manage the tasks. This can be seen in Fig. 6.6, where the blue line is the number of sent messages and the red line is the time between sending cycles. For 20 devices, the 6 threads look weak, and for the required performance, we needed 8 threads.

We also made additional tests to find out the limits of MobIoTSim using 20 simulated devices. The minimum time required to send a message is around 0.5 s, because if the frequency is 0.5 or 0.25 s, there is no difference in the measurements even with 16 threads. As a result, the simulator can send a total of 2300 messages per minute with 20 registered devices to Bluemix.

Table 6.3 MQTT device simulation

Used threads	Number of devices	Message count	Send time	Time between cycles
3	10	441	405	1374
4	10	588	403	1023
6	10	610	431	991
8	10	603	435	993
12	10	610	462	999
3	15	432	406	2078
4	15	593	402	1531
6	15	863	411	1048
8	15	908	425	988
12	15	915	420	997
3	20	433	402	2766
4	20	583	401	2054
6	20	843	407	1402
8	20	1153	404	1030
12	20	1219	433	993

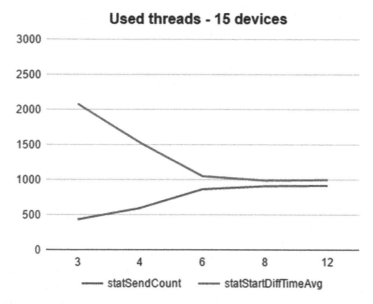

Fig. 6.6 Number of sent messages and time between send cycles

6.5.4 Future Extensions

We plan to extend MobIoTSim our research in several directions. First, we believe that gateway templates could provide useful means for experimenting with the simulator. Currently, the previously introduced gateway services for the IBM Bluemix platform and Azure IoT Hub are available, but we plan to support additional, popular cloud providers, e.g., Amazon and Google. A general, platform independent gateway would also be useful. It could be realized with a cloud visualization application consisting of three main parts: the data collection, the database, and the visualization part. We already started to design such a general solution, where data collection is managed by an MQTT broker and a REST server. The database could be excluded, if the data storage is not necessary and the data streaming is possible directly to the visualization part, but for advanced features like displaying data history or statistical reports it is useful. The visualization part will be supported by live charts showing the data coming from the IoT devices in real time, and statistical data will also be available.

We also plan to support larger, scalable experiments in the future. For this purpose, we will use a scripting language to be able to specify the devices and their properties and to schedule their activities. The bulk addition of devices future can be useful for larger tests, this way the user can add more than one instance of a device with one click. In the background, the application should register these devices to the gateway automatically, so the required authorization token cannot be a problem.

The network errors are common problems in real IoT systems, therefore we also plan to investigate this issue in more detail. The current version of MobIoTSim can only generate random errors upon request (with a static setting). However, more complex simulations can also model the IoT network more accurately by considering wireless interference and propagation models. Those networking conditions are typically considered by wireless network simulators such as NS-3 [41]. While such an extension makes the simulations more realistic, it will also significantly increase setup time and computation time of such simulations.

6.6   Conclusion

In this chapter, we presented our results toward developing a general purpose IoT device simulator. We overviewed the available IoT cloud providers and the most common IoT application scenarios. Then, we introduced the requirements and performed design steps of our mobile IoT simulator called MobIoTSim, which is capable of simulating more IoT devices by generating real-time sensor data. We have also developed private gateway services in the IBM Bluemix and Microsoft Azure platforms that can be connected to MobIoTSim to manage the simulated devices and to send notifications to the simulator by responding to critical sensor values. By using this tool, researchers and developers can examine the behavior of IoT systems and develop and evaluate IoT cloud applications more efficiently. Finally, we evaluated the scalability of the device management component of MobIoTSim.

Our future work will address the extension of MobIoTSim with predefined data generation templates and a basic propagation and loss model to simulate the network transmission. Further gateway developments for different cloud providers are also planned to ease integration with other clouds and foster inter-cloud deployments.

Acknowledgments This research was supported by the Hungarian Government and the European Regional Development Fund under the grant number GINOP-2.3.2-15-2016-00037 ("Internet of Living Things") and by the Janos Bolyai Research Scholarship of the Hungarian Academy of Sciences.

References

1. Sundmaeker H, Guillemin P, Friess P, Woelffle S (2010) Vision and challenges for realizing the internet of things. CERP IoT – cluster of European research projects on the internet of things, CN: KK-31-10-323-EN-C, March 2010
2. Mahoney J, LeHong H (2011) The internet of things is coming, Gartner report. Online: https://www.gartner.com/doc/1799626/internet-things-coming, September 2011
3. Buyya B, Yeo CS, Venugopal S, Broberg J, Brandic I (2009) Cloud computing and emerging it platforms: vision, hype, and reality for delivering computing as the 5th utility. Futur Gener Comput Syst 25(6):599–616
4. Gubbi J, Buyya R, Marusic S, Palaniswami M (2013) Internet of Things (IoT): a vision, architectural elements, and future directions. Futur Gener Comput Syst 29(7):1645–1660

5. Celesti A, Fazio M, Giacobbe M, Puliafito A, Villari M (2016) Characterizing cloud federation in IoT. In: IEEE 30th International conference on advanced information networking and applications workshops – workshop on cloud computing project and initiatives, 2016
6. Machado SG, Hausheer D, Stiller B (2009) Considerations on the interoperability of and between cloud computing standards. In: 27th Open Grid Forum (OGF27), G2CNet workshop: from grid to cloud networks, Banff, Canada, 2009
7. Botta A, de Donato W, Persico V, Pescape A (2014) On the integration of cloud computing and internet of things. The 2nd international conference on future internet of things and cloud (FiCloud-2014), August 2014
8. Nastic S, Sehic S., Le D, Truong H, Dustdar S (2014) Provisioning software-defined iot cloud systems. The 2nd International conference on future internet of things and cloud (FiCloud-2014), August 2014
9. Boson NetSim Network Simulator website. Online: http://www.boson.com/netsim-cisco-network-simulator. Accessed Feb 2017
10. QualNet communications simulation platform website. Online: http://web.scalable-networks.com/content/qualnet. Accessed Jan 2016
11. Varga A, Hornig R (2008) An overview of the OMNeT++ simulation environment. In: Proceedings of the 1st international conference on Simulation tools and techniques for communications, networks and systems & workshops (Simutools '08). 2008
12. Han SN, Lee GM, Crespi N, Luong NV, Heo K, Brut M, Gatellier P (2014) DPWSim: a simulation toolkit for IoT applications using devices profile for web services. In: proceedings of IEEE World Forum on Internet of Things (WF-IoT), pp 544–547, 6–8 March 2014
13. SimpleSoft SimpleIoTSimulator website. Online: http://www.smplsft.com/SimpleIoT-Simulator.html. Accessed Jan 2016
14. Atomiton IoT Simulator website. Online: http://atomiton.com/simulator.html. Accessed Feb 2017
15. LoRa Technology website. Online: https://www.lora-alliance.org/What-Is-LoRa/Technology. Accessed Jan 2016.
16. SIGFOX website. Online: http://www.sigfox.com/en/\#!/connected-world. Accessed Feb 2017
17. IBM Bluemix Platform website. Online: https://console.ng.bluemix.net/. Accessed Feb 2017
18. IBM Bluemix IoT Sensor website. Online: https://developer.ibm.com/recipes/tutorials/use-the-simulated-device-to-experience-the-iot-foundation/. Accessed Feb 2017
19. Google Cloud Platform website. Online: https://cloud.google.com/solutions/iot/. Accessed Feb 2017
20. Azure IoT Hub. Online: https://azure.microsoft.com/en-us/services/iot-hub/. Accessed Feb 2017
21. Perednia DA, Allen A (1995) Telemedicine technology and clinical applications. JAMA 273(6):483–488
22. Mimo website. Online: http://mimobaby.com/. Accessed Sept 2016
23. Vitality GlowPack website. Online: http://www.vitality.net/products.html. Accessed Sept 2016
24. AmSmart website. Online: http://www.amsmart.biz/. Accessed Feb 2017
25. Smart Outlets website. Online: http://www.postscapes.com/smart-outlets/. Accessed Sept 2016
26. Key Finder Tags website. Online: http://postscapes.com/wireless-key-locators. Accessed Sept 2016
27. Wireless Plant Sensors website. Online: http://postscapes.com/wireless-plant-sensors. Accessed Sept 2016
28. Bigbelly website. Online: http://bigbelly.com/solutions/stations/. Accessed Sept 2016
29. Echelon website. Online: http://www.echelon.com/applications/pl-rf-outdoor-lighting. Accessed Sept 2016
30. Open Source Lion Tracking Collars website. Online: http://home.groundlab.cc/lion-collars.html. Accessed Sept 2016

31. Smart Parking Sensor website. Online: http://www.save9.com/home/products-and-services/
    internet-and-wireless-networks/wireless-sensor-networks/. Accessed Sept 2016
32. Optoi Chemical Sensors website. Online: http://www.optoi.com/en/products/details/chemical-
    physical-sensors-mems. Accessed Sept 2016
33. Phenonet Project website. Online: http://www.csiro.au/en/Research/D61/Areas/Robotics-and-
    autonomous-systems/Internet-of-Things/Phenonet. Accessed Sept 2016
34. AquamatiX website. Online: http://www.aquamatix.net/. Accessed Sept 2016
35. Samsung refrigerator website. Online: http://www.samsung.com/us/explore/family-hub-
    refrigerator/. Accessed Sept 2016
36. GE Evolution Series Tier 4 Locomotive website. Online: http://www.getransportation.com/
    locomotives. Accessed Sept 2016
37. CleanGrow website. Online: http://www.cleangrow.com/. Accessed Sept 2016
38. IBM IoT Foundation message format. Online: https://docs.internetofthings.ibmcloud.com/
    gateways/mqtt.html#managed-gateways#managed-gateways. Accessed Feb 2017
39. IBM IoT Foundation Quickstart application. Online: https://quickstart.internetofthings.ibm-
    cloud.com. Accessed Feb 2017
40. IOT Visualization application. Online: https://github.com/ibm-messaging/iot-visualization/.
    Accessed Feb 2017
41. NS-3 website. Online: https://www.nsnam.org/. Accessed Mar 2016

Chapter 7
Managing Heterogeneous Communication Challenges in the Internet of Things Using Connector Variability

**Muhammed Cagri Kaya, Mahdi Saeedi Nikoo, Selma Suloglu,
Bedir Tekinerdogan, and Ali H. Dogru**

Abstract Internet of Things (IoT) comprises smart systems that embrace computational and physical elements. In these systems, physical and software components are often tightly coupled. They are used widely in today's technological systems, such as smart buildings, avionics, self-driving cars, etc. IoT systems are typically developed using hardware and software components with different interaction types. This chapter introduces an approach to manage hyper-connectivity in the IoT through connectors that are equipped with variability capability. Computational and physical elements in IoT-based systems are represented as components. Different types of communications among these components are abstracted and managed in the definition of connectors. XCOSEML is a modelling language that leverages the variability concept for the component-oriented development methodology. Variable connectors of XCOSEML are employed to address the hyper-connectivity challenges of the IoT domain. In our approach, systems are designed with XCOSEML constructs, and IoT domain needs are mapped to connector mechanisms. The heterogeneity in IoT communications is addressed by connector variability. The proposed approach is illustrated with a case study for proof of concept.

M.C. Kaya • M. Saeedi Nikoo • A.H. Dogru
Department of Computer Engineering, Middle East Technical University, Ankara, Turkey

S. Suloglu
SoSoft Information Technologies, Ankara, Turkey

B. Tekinerdogan (✉)
Information Technology Group, Wageningen University, Wageningen, The Netherlands
e-mail: bedir.tekinerdogan@wur.nl

© Springer International Publishing AG 2017   127
Z. Mahmood (ed.), *Connected Environments for the Internet of Things*,
Computer Communications and Networks,
https://doi.org/10.1007/978-3-319-70102-8_7

7.1   Introduction

Internet of Things (IoT) offers new capabilities to the distributed software intensive systems. Many devices are being connected to the Internet offering the availability of location-agnostic use: an already existing device that has been allocated somewhere in the physical world can be made a part of a new application, or its services can be utilized by different applications. Also, location-dependent services such as weather sensors in a specific city can be incorporated in various systems.

This kind of usage with widespread purposes is great; however, it comes with certain costs. There is no limit to types and capabilities of units that can be connected incorporating their own communication styles. They may be abiding with existing communication protocols or may have their own ways of sending and receiving data and commands. Consequently, a system's developer faces the problem of noncompatible devices trying to be integrated in a system. The scale of the diversity of what these units do and how they connect renders the job of the developer a difficult one. This problem is expressed as the heterogeneity in IoT and further, the multitude of communication techniques is expressed as hyper-connectivity.

Communication heterogeneity has been investigated in the literature to quite some extend. For example, heterogeneity among cooperating wireless sensor networks (WSNs) is referred in [1]. Device and protocol heterogeneity among different nodes of a WSN test bed are discussed in a survey on WSN test beds [2]. Different communication technologies in a smart home environment are investigated in [3]. Solutions to this problem are generally proposed through gateways handling different protocols at different levels of communication (such as application level or transport level) in some research [3–5]. However, they do not have the modular design perspective in terms of software components. Patel et al. [6] suggest development of IoT applications using software components without taking variability into consideration. In the work of Pradhan et al. [7], large-scale IoT applications are handled in a higher level of abstraction (like systems of systems), and the natural heterogeneity is considered as product line variability. However, they do not have explicit definition of connectors with the power of configurability.

This research is an effort towards offering a solution to such heterogeneity and hyper-connectivity. If a system integrated across a computer network such as the Internet can be visualized as nodes and links where procedural capabilities are modelled by the nodes and their connections modelled as links, naturally the architectural view "components and connectors" is associated. However, the goal in this chapter is not to use component-based modelling only for rigid definitions of different systems. Rather, a more flexible option is desired where a degree of variability in the "product" can be achieved through more flexible approaches: configuring or adapting a smaller number of more established constituents, namely, components. The variability concept has proven itself in the industry. Current trend, however, is applying variability to components that are mainly providing the functional units of a solution. Variability is also destined for connectors in this research, assuming different adaptation and communication tasks concerning the components.

The rest of the chapter includes a section on topic background that provides some brief information on IoT and Component-Based Software Engineering (CBSE). Then, a case study and problem description are explained before the section where heterogeneity and hyper-connectivity in IoT are explained. The XCOSEML language is explained, and hyper-connectivity and heterogeneity modelling in IoT are shown based on the case study. We discuss the applicability of our approach at the discussion section. After discussion and related work sections, the chapter ends with a conclusion.

7.2 Background

In this section, we provide the background that is required for the study. IoT and CBSE are included in the discussion.

7.2.1 Internet of Things

Nowadays, IoT has become a hot topic in the industry, but the concept is not new. It was in the early 2000s that Kevin Ashton was laying the foundation of the concept at Massachusetts Institute of Technology (MIT) that we call it as the IoT today. The idea was simply suggesting that if all objects in daily life were equipped with identifiers and wireless connectivity, they could communicate with each other. At the time, the vision required major technological advances. Today, many of the obstacles have been settled. The improvements in the communication medium include Internet Protocol version 6 (IPv6) and its support of billions of devices, improvements in mobile data coverage, advances in battery technology and low-cost electronic devices and sensors.

The building blocks of the IoT are smart objects that are cyber-physical or embedded systems that connect to the Internet. The idea of the IoT undoubtedly presents immense opportunities but it also involves several technical and social challenges [8, 9]. An IoT system makes computing truly ubiquitous – this is the idea proposed by Mark Weiser in the early 1990s [10]. Atzori et al. [11] identify the IoT as the realization of three paradigms: Internet-oriented (middleware), things-oriented (sensors) and semantic-oriented (knowledge). Although describing the IoT in this way is because of the interdisciplinary nature of it, the real power of IoT can be seen in the application domains with these paradigms meeting one another.

IoT basically describes a world in which devices and sensors are connected to the Internet via wired and wireless communication technologies. These sensors use different local connectivity such as Radio-Frequency Identification (RFID), Wi-Fi, Bluetooth and ZigBee. Also, they use wide-area connectivity such as General Packet

Radio Service (GPRS), Global System for Mobile Communications (GSM) and third-generation (3G) technologies. IoT presents connectivity for both living and nonliving things including people, places and objects. Sensors are the central part of IoT. Using the sensors attached to physical entities, new information is gained from the data produced by the sensors monitoring different conditions of the environment, such as temperature, light, location, motion, etc. Communication mostly was employed among people and machines in the past. IoT-enabled objects bring new aspects to this concept. It is expected in the future that objects will have identities and connectivity so that you will be able to track, identify or communicate with them.

7.2.2 Component-Based Software Engineering

CBSE emerged as a reuse paradigm in the late 1990s. Component-based systems are realizations of complex and large-scale software systems based on reusable building blocks, namely, components. CBSE offers processes and methodologies to define, model, implement and integrate loosely coupled and independent components. Starting from the 1990s, the core idea of Component-Based Software Development (CBSD) has been to integrate prebuilt software components for developing software systems rather than building them from scratch. Components have interfaces that indicate functionalities and behaviour whose implementation details are hidden. With specified interfaces, components can be integrated and deployed easily, even with third party components. As the demand for software systems grows for larger size and more complex requirements, component reusability and its management throughout the development process become an inevitable fundamental characteristic.

For handling connections by separating interaction and computation concerns in CBSD, there have been approaches defining connectors explicitly. In [12], by analysing existing component interactions, a connector taxonomy and classification are provided. They define service types and connector types. Some type of connectors deals with data communication among components (such as procedure call and events), and some others require additional processes to be done on data (such as unit conversion) or to coordinate the components in the system (such as arbitrators). These additional operations can be included into the definition of connectors.

There are very few studies in the IoT world that consider component-based application development. In [6], authors present an application development framework – a domain model for the IoT that captures the generic concepts and associations to represent IoT systems. This work does not specify any details about the paradigms concerning communication among software components. Pradhan et al. [7] propose UMRELA, which is an abstract feature model and uses product line concepts to represent commonalities and variation points in heterogeneous distributed applications. The work also presents Application Management Framework (AMF) as a system prototype that uses the UMRELA. However, the contribution does not discuss the communication interoperability.

7.3   Case Study and Problem Description

In this section, we describe the problem statement using an IoT case study on a smart office system that will be used throughout the chapter. We will use the case study for both explaining the problem and the solution.

7.3.1   Case Study: Smart Office

A smart office application is used as a case study to illustrate the heterogeneous communication needs and hyper-connectivity in an IoT system. This system is designed for providing employees a comfortable working place. It can also be extended with additional capabilities, such as security. Appliances and devices in this system can communicate with each other through different communication types and protocols. We describe a relatively small smart office system for the sake of simplicity. In our case, the smart office system can automatically or on demand make coffee and keep the temperature of the environment at a desired value. People can check the temperature, humidity and light level of the office by using their smart phones. They can request video or photo from the security camera that is connected to the local network. They can control the air conditioner and the coffee machine directly using their smart phones from the same office or from another room in the same building.

The smart office system is described in Fig. 7.1. A software-defined radio (SDR) connected to a personal computer (PC) is used to ease the communication with

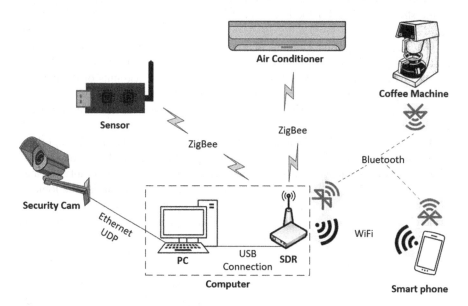

Fig. 7.1 Illustration of the example smart office system

other devices that use different communication protocols. This assembly is referred to as "computer" in the remaining part of the chapter. A security camera is connected to the computer via a wired connection and uses User Datagram Protocol (UDP) protocol to transmit data. A sensor that is capable of measuring the temperature (in Celsius), humidity and light level is placed in the office. It uses the ZigBee protocol to communicate with other devices. Another ZigBee-supported device is the air conditioner that can work autonomously and can be controlled by the user remotely. There is also a coffee machine in the office that can make coffee automatically if lights are turned on in the office or by receiving commands from users' smart phones. It can be reached only through Bluetooth communication. Smart phones can communicate through Wi-Fi and Bluetooth, and they are used by people to monitor the desired information and to interact with other devices in the office.

7.3.2 Problem Description

In the smart office environment, devices use different communication protocols. In our case study, users control air conditioner, use sensor to get measurements and use security camera through their smart phones. However smart phones do not contain a ZigBee unit. The security camera is only connected to the local network and it can be reached through wired connection. Also, the air conditioner and the coffee machine use the sensor in their automatic mode. Coffee machine also does not have a ZigBee unit, and the air conditioner cannot communicate with the sensor directly. Coffee machine can only be reached through Bluetooth. Smart phones can use Bluetooth to control the coffee machine if they are in the same office. However, due to the short range of Bluetooth, it cannot be used from other offices in the same building.

Using a generic protocol among all devices or producing devices capable of supporting all possible protocols at once is not realistic and feasible when different device characteristics, vendors, power and computation constraints of the devices and their purpose of usage are considered. Moreover, an IoT configuration is not static but dynamic, that is, new IoT devices may be added and removed from the configuration at different times.

To address the required various interactions, the components should adapt their communication channels with interacting parties which in turn bring the duty of multi interaction management to the component. This increases complexity and decreases reusability of both components and connectors as the interaction logic is hidden inside the communicating components. Following the separation of concerns principle, where components carry out their core functionality and connectors satisfy interaction needs, a highly reusable and dynamic infrastructure is needed.

7.4   Heterogeneity and Hyper-Connectivity in IoT

As a structure to enable integration of various applications and devices with diverse capabilities, IoT provides flexibility through a plug and play approach. Although IoT seems promising, the heterogeneity and the hyper-connectivity seriously impede the integration of different components. Its diversity shapes heterogeneous environments which interconnect different types of applications (software) and things (physical devices such as sensors and smart devices). In essence, the complexity of interconnectivity lies in the variability of interaction semantics and functionalities.

IoT is an architecture that comprises a set of components together with their properties and connections requirements (via connectors) [13]. Software (applications) and hardware parts (things/devices) are considered as components of IoT. This architecture also employs a set of design decisions with respect to different views and viewpoints. Basically, heterogeneity in IoT reflects architectural elements: components represented via their interfaces, connectors and behaviour. Besides, the IoT architectures can be analysed in data, function and process dimensions as detailed in the following paragraphs.

Data dimension comprises the information which resides in the components and is shared with the other ones. Within this dimension, heterogeneity occurs where interacting components try to exchange different types, structures or semantics of data. For instance, a temperature sensor sends its sensory data in Celsius to a SCADA (Supervisory Control and Data Acquisition) system which processes the data in Fahrenheit.

Function dimension indicates the tasks that the component achieves. Heterogeneity in this dimension leads to discrepancy at either the semantic or syntactic levels, while a mobile application requests the status of sensors as a single response where each sensor sends its status separately.

Process dimension includes the collaborative behaviour of the interacting components to achieve a goal which is realized by component composition. Processes can be analysed via interaction properties:

- Behaviour (Interaction Logic): The flow of the collaborative behaviour
- Connector (Interaction Type, Task and Protocol): The way components use to connect with others

Heterogeneity is handled in process sub-dimensions of behaviour and connector. Heterogeneity in behaviour occurs when interacting components follow different workflows or when application of a set of changes is required with inclusion/exclusion of a component. Heterogeneity at the connector level is a prominent one which leads to hyper-connectivity – multiple means of communication among IoT components. Multiple communication protocols and broad and short-range protocols are widely used introducing heterogeneity: RFID, ZigBee, Bluetooth (1.0, 2.0, 3.0 and 4.0, Bluetooth Low Energy), Wi-Fi, GSM (2G, 3G, 4G, 5G), Z-Wave, etc. Having these in mind, the needs to address hyper-connectivity in IoT are listed in

Table 7.1 Analysis of IoT heterogeneity

Architectural element	Sub-elements	Realized by	Heterogeneity dimension
1.Components	Functions	Component interfaces	Function
	Parameters of the functions		Data
2. Connectors	Type	Connectors	Function, data, process
	Task		
	Protocol		
3. Interaction	Behaviour	Composition	Process

Table 7.1 where architectural elements (with their sub-elements) are listed along with associated heterogeneity.

Concerning hyper-connectivity, components working with different protocols shall join/participate in component interaction. Constraints on interacting components shall be taken into consideration. Components which use different protocols such as Wi-Fi and Bluetooth shall seamlessly communicate with each other (compatibility) in all dimensions: function, data and process.

7.5 XCOSEML

XCOSEML [14] is a text-based domain-specific language with variability support for component-oriented development paradigm. It is named after a graphical modelling language – Component-Oriented Software Engineering Modelling Language (COSEML).

COSEML is proposed to be used with the Component-Oriented Software Engineering (COSE) approach [15]. The COSE approach emerged based on the idea of exploiting the component concept throughout all stages of development unlike CBSD. As a text-based version of its predecessor COSEML, XCOSEML is equipped with variability support. The primary target is to bring the advantages of component technology and benefits of using variability together. XCOSEML's variability approach is inspired from the Orthogonal Variability Model (OVM) [16] and Covamof [17]. It separates variability specifications from other specifications, to be associated by using mapping constructs.

There are six types of constructs defined in XCOSEML: package, component, interface, connector, configuration interface and composition specification. Package represents the logical organization of a system or a part of a system. It can be used to show system level entities and can be represented by a component. It can contain further packages, but there must be components at the leaf level. A component represents physical code. In component-oriented development, it is assumed that the code was implemented before. If the desired component cannot be found, it can be implemented from scratch as a final choice. Functionality of a component is shown through one or more interfaces.

XCOSEML did not have detailed connector definition when it was first defined, and the provided connector definition did not support variability. In a recent work [18], the language was enhanced with connector variability, and the definition of connector has been extended. In [18], the connector definition is enriched by adding connector's service type and connector type, as suggested by Oussalah et al. [19] based on the connector taxonomy of Mehta et al. [12]. Moreover, the interacting interfaces of components and their caller and responder methods are defined explicitly. As some connector types necessitate, connector operations are added to the connector definition. For example, unit conversion process between two components is done by a connector. This process is abstracted with the "operation" keyword and an identifier in the connector definition.

Connectors invoke the interface of a component for a desired functionality. An interface shows the methods that the component has with the classification of *provided* and *required*. Provided methods represent the functionality that the component performs itself. A component must have at least one provided method in its interface. The functionality that the component expects from other components is listed as required methods.

The configuration interface is where the variability specification of the system is defined. It contains variation points, variants and constraints among different variation points and variants. It defines high-level "Configuration" variation points that are able to resolve low-level variation points by mapping relations when they are bound to a specific variant or a set of variants. "External" variation points are shown to developers for customization purposes. Configuration variation points also can be tagged as external. "Internal" variation points are bound by other (generally configuration) variation points to hide the details from the developer. Packages and components can have configuration interfaces.

Composition specification is the process model of XCOSEML and shows interactions among the system components through connectors. In early versions of the language, messaging among components was explicitly shown in the composition. After a detailed connector definition in [18], connectors are employed to represent the messaging between two components (an atomic interaction) and connectors appear in the composition specification that is saved as the composition file. Composition specification also has composite interactions: *sequence, parallel* and *repeat*. As their names suggest, they are used to group atomic interactions to be executed in a sequence, in parallel and iteratively, respectively. Composition specifications can only be defined for the package level in XCOSEML.

System configuration is conducted through composition specification in XCOSEML. In other words, first variability is bound in the interaction model, and then other constructs are chosen according to this interaction selection. Variability options in the configuration interface are shown with tags in composition specification to choose a desired interaction. After desired variants are provided, corresponding interactions are included in the configured composition specification by using the variability tags. Then, interacting components and related connectors are allocated in the final system based on the chosen interactions. As connectors refer to the interacting component interfaces and their methods, these interfaces and methods are also included in the final product. Therefore, XCOSEML has variability support for system composition, components, interfaces and connectors.

Before system customization, i.e. configuring the models that contain variability to obtain a functioning system, model checking can be applied to domain models. The SNIP model checker [20] is employed for this purpose that is based on the featured transition system (FTS) [21] approach. This tool uses textual variability language (TVL) [22] and fPromela, an extended version of the process modelling language Promela of the SPIN model checker [23] with variability, as the input models. XCOSEML's configuration interface (variability model) and composition specification (process model that contains variability) can be transformed for verification to TVL and fPromela, respectively. Therefore, all possible products of the system family can be checked against errors and deadlocks. A semiautomated tool for this transformation and model checking process for XCOSEML models is introduced in [24].

After configured system models are obtained, components and connectors in the model are matched to the existing implemented ones. Our modelling language has an abstract modelling view and it encourages developers to visualize the system as decomposed units independent of implementation details. Therefore, it does not restrict the usage of different implementation languages and component models. If the desired components, connectors or interfaces cannot be found or they do not exist, they can be developed by choosing any programming paradigm.

In this chapter, XCOSEML connector definition is extended to meet heterogeneous communication challenges and hyper-connectivity in IoT. As we propose a solution for communication heterogeneity in the network protocol level, we extend the connector definition by showing the communication protocols of components explicitly.

7.6 Modelling Hyper-connectivity Using XCOSEML

In this section, we provide an approach to modelling heterogeneity and hyper-connectivity in the IoT environment using the XCOSEML language. We illustrate the approach using the case study presented in Sect. 7.3.

The proposed approach suggests variability-intensive component-oriented modelling of IoT systems. Our focus is on separating functioning units from communication concerns and solving heterogeneity and hyper-connectivity issues of the systems exploiting connectors.

The first step of the development is system decomposition. Figure 7.2 illustrates the decomposition for smart office system. The system itself is an abstract entity that is composed of physical and computational components and represented as a package. Air conditioner, smart phone, security camera, sensor and coffee machine are components of the smart office system and they are shown in Fig. 7.2 with "_comp"

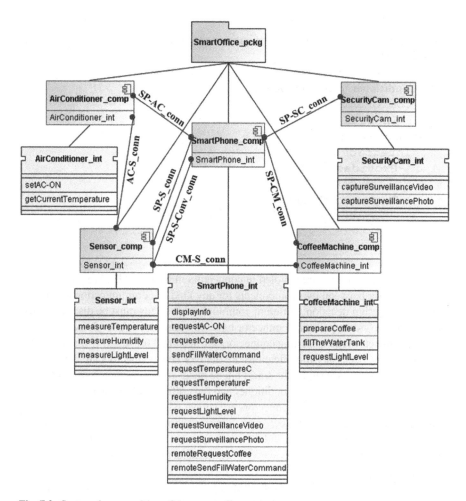

Fig. 7.2 System decomposition of the smart office system

suffix appended to their names. Functionalities of components are exposed through interfaces. In this system, we define one interface for each component. It is also possible to add more than one interface for each component according to the design and the system requirements. Along with interface symbols as shown in Fig. 7.2, we used the "_int" suffix appended to their names to indicate interfaces. Provided methods and required methods are shown in the separate sections of the interfaces. For example, "setAC-ON" is a provided method in the "AirConditioner_int" interface, and "getCurrentTemperature" is a method representing the required functionality for the system operation. Listing 7.1 represents XCOSEML model of the air conditioner component and its interface.

Listing 7.1 The Air Conditioner Component and Its Interface in XCOSEML

AirConditioner_comp component

```
1   Component AirConditioner_comp
2     Interface AirConditioner_int
```

AirConditioner_int interface

```
1   Interface Air Conditioner_int
2     Provided Methods
3       setAC-ON
4     Required Methods
5       getCurrentTemperature
```

Communication concerns are handled in connectors in XCOSEML. We place a single connector between two components for any kind of communication as an architectural design decision. Different communication needs must be discovered to identify the "service type" and "connector type" of connectors. After detecting system's connector types, existing connectors are searched for reuse. If they cannot be used directly, necessary modifications are done or new connectors are developed from scratch. In the case study, the smart phone needs to communicate with all other components. Moreover, the air conditioner and the coffee machine need to communicate with the sensor. Connectors are shown with blue lines between components. Their names contain "_conn" suffix as shown in Fig. 7.2. As can be seen in Fig. 7.2, the smart phone and the sensor communicate through two connectors: one of them is of service type "communication" and the other one is "conversion".

XCOSEML allows connector variability by directly choosing connectors and by configuring selected connectors. This capability leads designers to first think of a connector's service type and connector type. Also, similar communication concerns can be defined in the same connector. Then, the connector is customized considering purpose of usage.

Communication occurs between two components defining the two ends of a connector. Even if the communication is multicast or broadcast type, connectors have a source and a destination as we consider destinations individually at the modelling level. Both sides of the interacting components can have different communication protocols. Based on the heterogeneity of the communication protocols of IoT devices, XCOSEML connector definition is extended considering this two-sided structure. Listings 7.2 and 7.3 show the connectors "SP-CM_conn" and "SP-S-Conv_conn" of the smart office system. A connector definition starts with the name of the connector. Then service type and connector types are included.

Listing 7.2 An excerpt from the SP-CM_conn connector in XCOSEML

```
1    Connector SP-CM_conn
2    ServiceType communication
3    ConnectorType procedurecall
4    ConnectorMessage makeCoffee {
5        RequesterInterface SmartPhone_int
6        MethodOut requestCoffee
7        ResponderInterface CoffeeMachine_int
8        MethodIn prepareCoffee
9        RequesterProtocol Bluetooth
10       ResponderProtocol Bluetooth}
11       ...
12   ConnectorMessage makeCoffeeR {
13       RequesterInterface SmartPhone_int
14       MethodOut remoteMakeCoffee
15       ResponderInterface CoffeeMachine_int
16       MethodIn prepareCoffee
17       RequesterProtocol WiFi
18       ResponderProtocol Bluetooth}
```

Listing 7.3 The SP-S-Conv_conn connector in XCOSEML

```
1    Connector SP-S-Conv_conn
2    ServiceType conversion
3    ConnectorType adaptor
4    ConnectorMessage askTempF {
5        RequesterInterface SmartPhone_int
6        MethodOut requestTemperatureF
7        ResponderInterface Sensor_int
8        MethodIn measureTemperature
9        RequesterProtocol WiFi
10       ResponderProtocol ZigBee
11       Operation C2F}
```

Interacting component interfaces and their methods are inserted in a structure called "Connector Message". The communication protocols for the interacting components are defined as "Requester Protocol" and "Responder Protocol". The "source" side of the connector corresponds to the requester and "destination" to the responder. SP-CM_conn in Listing 7.2, connects the smart phone and the coffee machine components. Both of the devices can use Bluetooth. Therefore, SP-CM_ conn indicates both requester and responder protocols as Bluetooth in the "make-Coffee" message in Listing 7.2, lines 9 and 10. This message is used for short-range communication due to the limitation of Bluetooth. However, employees want to send commands to the machine from outside of the office in order not to waste time to wait for preparation. The "makeCoffeeR" message is used for this purpose (between lines 12 and 18). This time the connector uses the computer (PC + SDR) in the office as a communication medium. The connector uses Wi-Fi to send the request from the smart phone to the computer, and then the computer transmits this request to the coffee machine via Bluetooth.

Listing 7.4 shows the variability model of the system, "SmartOffice_conf" configuration specification. Here, an external variation point is defined with three alternative variants. Binding time of this variation point is "development time" as line 7 indicates. Variability is used in XCOSEML to select desired interactions in the process model. An example process model, "SmartOffice_ cmps" composition specification, is given in Listing 7.5. Variability is shown with tags that start and end with a "#" symbol before an interaction. A tag becomes active only when its condition holds and it affects only one interaction (atomic or composite). In Listing 7.5, all interactions are atomic, and there are no dependencies among the variants.

Listing 7.4 Configuration interface of smart office system in XCOSEML

```
1 Configuration SmartOffice_conf of Package SmartOffice_pckg
2       externalVP officeTypeChoice:
3           alternative
4               variant basic
5               variant standard
6               variant advanced
7           bindingTime devtime
```

Listing 7.5 The SmartOffice_cmps composition specification in XCOSEML

```
1    Composition SmartOffice_cmps
2    import configuration SmartOffice_conf
3    has component AirConditioner_comp Sensor_comp ...
4    has connector SP-S_conn SP-S-Conv_conn ...
5    Context Parameters
6       remoteConnection false
7       converter false
8    Method OfficeProcess:
9       SmartPhone_comp -> Sensor_comp {SP-S_conn.askTempC}
10      guard(converter == true)
11      #vp officeTypeChoice ifOneSelected(basic standard)#
        SmartPhone_comp -> Sensor_comp {SP-S-Conv_conn.askTempF}
12      #vp officeTypeChoice ifSelected(advanced)#
        SmartPhone_comp -> AirConditioner_comp {SP-AC_conn.turnOnAC}
13      guard(remoteConnection == true)
        AirConditioner_comp -> Sensor_comp {AC-S_conn.getTemp}
14      #vp officeTypeChoice ifSelected(advanced)#
        SmartPhone_comp -> CoffeeMachine_comp {SP-CM_conn.makeCoffeeR}
15      #vp officeTypeChoice ifSelected(standard)#
        CoffeeMachine_comp -> Sensor_comp {CM-S_conn.getLightLevel}
16      #vp officeTypeChoice ifSelected(advanced)#
        SmartPhone_comp -> SecurityCam_comp {SP-SC_conn.getPhoto}
        #vp officeTypeChoice ifSelected(advanced)#
        SmartPhone_comp -> SecurityCam_comp {SP-SC_conn.getVideo}
```

SmartOffice_cmps in Listing 7.5 starts with the name of the composition. The variability model, in the form of a configuration interface, is imported in line 2. Components and connectors that take part in the interactions are also imported in lines 3 and 4. Context parameters, between lines 5 and 7, are global variables that can be used in any interaction in the file. Their values are tracked with guard statements such as in line 10. Composition specifications include interactions after a "Method" keyword and an identifier (line 8). In this process, the first interaction appears in line 9. Interacting components are shown at the left-hand side and right-hand side of an arrow operator (−> or <−) that indicates the request direction of the interaction. The connector and its corresponding message, which are used for the interaction, are given in curly braces ({ }). The dot operator is used to separate the connector and its message. In this interaction, "SmartPhone_comp" requests temperature from "Sensor_comp". All communication details – which interfaces are used, which methods are invoked for this communication, protocols of requester and responder components – are embedded in the connector. Here, the smart phone uses Wi-Fi and the sensor responds with ZigBee. Computer is used for mediation.

The sensor is able to send the temperature in Celsius. For the users that need the Fahrenheit degree, the system should provide a solution. This unit conversion is not the job of either the requester or the responder component considering separation of concerns. Conversion must be done in the connector. For this purpose, "SP-S-Conv_conn" connector is defined with service type "conversion" and connector type "adaptor" (in Listing 7.3). In addition to different communication protocols, a connector needs to represent the conversion operation. This is modelled with the "operation" keyword in the connector message in Listing 7.3 line 11. Corresponding interaction is given in Listing 7.5 at line 10. When the guard condition holds, the interaction occurs. Context parameters in guards can be set at development time; they also can be changed at run time. In this case, it is just checked once in the sequence of execution. If the parameter "converter" is set to "true" at the system development, the interaction will be executed. XCOSEML has the "parallel" interaction type to model the creation of a thread that can keep track of the changes on the value of a context parameter at run time.

In line 11 of Listing 7.5, turning the air conditioner on by the smart phone is provided with a variability tag. When "basic" or "standard" variants are selected for the "officeTypeChoice" variation point, the smart phone sends the "AC-ON" message to the air conditioner in the configured composition specification. This communication requires combining two components that use Wi-Fi and ZigBee. If the "advanced" variant is selected (line 12), the air conditioner requests the temperature of the environment from the sensor to turn itself on automatically. Both the air conditioner and the sensor use ZigBee communication. Similarly, the coffee machine requests the light level of the environment to prepare coffee when the employees come to office and turn on the lights (line 14). This is also included in the "advanced" version and requires Bluetooth and ZigBee communication.

The language also allows the configuration inside of a connector for a particular communication. In Listing 7.5 at lines 15 and 16, the smart phone communicates with the security camera through the same connector (SP-SC_conn). However, the security camera provides only photo of the environment when "standard" variant is selected via the "getPhoto" message of the connector (line 15) and provides a video stream when the "advanced" variant is selected via the "getVideo" message (line 16). This communication is conducted through a wired UDP connection between the security camera and the computer and through Wi-Fi between the computer and the smart phone.

7.7 Discussion

A modelling perspective has been introduced to component-oriented development, especially addressing the issues related with the heterogeneity and hyper-connectivity in IoT-based systems. However, this scope is conforming to a broader study to allow more automated system development through a variability-centric approach. Previous work [25] has laid out the foundations for propagation of configuration actions from high-level models towards executability in a top-down manner that includes the processes and components of a software intensive system. For a future goal that assumes well-matured domain engineering, fundamentally specifications only relating to variability should lead to a well-automated production of executable systems. The outcome of this research can be utilized as a step towards such a goal.

For the broader context of the older work related with defining the adaptation among components and web services, there has been attempts to classify the operations in the data, function and control dimensions. This research allocates executable code in terms of "operations" inside "messages" in the connector that essentially are bringing in any kind of computational capability relating to those dimensions.

Traditionally, component-centric approaches have allocated the bulk of the tasks in the components and left the connectors as less complex items serving the component connections. However, this research increased the responsibility of the connector element, allocating important tasks such as those surfacing with the problems related to IoT hyper-connectivity. A similar concept, that is "adaptors", manifesting themselves previously as a component kind, or a design pattern, is now allocated in the connectors. It is observed through the experimentation that moving such tasks out of components to the connectors frees the components from noncohesive accommodations. Separation of concerns has been achieved to an extent. The "aspect" of adaptation is isolated and allocated in a more adept construct. A natural task allocation shapes up where more functional tasks are with components and communication-related tasks are within the connectors.

A decision has been made to only allow two-end connectors in adapting different protocols. A multiport connector involving more than two components was avoided that would almost function like an enterprise service bus, in a local scale. This decision offers better modularity to the component models for the solutions. Adaptations for one pair of components at a time result in a library of connectors that could be utilized by ease and at need. There is no limit to the number or type of connectors that can be employed among any number of components.

Where to deploy a connector will continue to be studied as different IoT applications will suggest optimized adaptations: software or hardware will be one related question. Our approach is emphasizing the modelling view and can accommodate different deployment alternatives at this abstraction level. Also the model-driven approaches in configuring variability solutions in different platforms have proven feasible. The distributed nature of component-based systems makes it possible to deploy a component at different nodes in a networked setting. Even, run-time allocations are potentially possible. The suggested connectors are similar to components in this regard – their allocation is just like that of components; connectors are also computational units that are prepared for reuse. After the correct allocation of a connector between the components in a decomposition model, its deployment can be decided based on implementation-level optimizations. XCOSEML is fundamentally serving the decomposition view of software architecture. A connector can be deployed together with one of the connected components or even at a separate platform that is along the connection path of the two components. Likewise, the implementation technology could be software or hardware, as the implementation decisions will suggest.

SDR is a promising solution at the implementation level to cope with communication heterogeneity in an IoT environment. With a broad frequency range (e.g. 70 MHz–6 GHz), it can handle many wireless communication protocols without a need for a new device per protocol. SDR and its hosting PC comprise a good medium to deploy our connector. However, we do not need to have a specific hardware to implement connectors or components as we have an abstract modelling view. For example, a PC equipped with Wi-Fi, ZigBee and Bluetooth capabilities and having a wired connection is enough to implement our case study without including an SDR.

There are limitations to the solutions offered in this research. Although effort has been exerted to provide a generic approach for addressing the variability and hyperconnectivity in IoT, solutions in this direction are yet young, and new research is being conducted by different teams around the world currently. There may be different requirements arising that could suggest some adaptation to our mechanisms. Also, there is a lack of industrial-level experience. The proposed approach works well in example problems and assignments conducted in academic settings. An analogy could be made to the "orchestration" facilities offered for the Service-Oriented Architecture (SOA) where the overall organization of multiparty services can be specified. A new unit with a different connection technology can be integrated through specifying its protocol for connection with the existing system. Therefore, new developments in the IoT technologies are expected to be contained within the framework of this approach by the specification of their adaptation mechanisms in corresponding connectors.

7.8   Related Work

In this section, we describe the related work about connector modelling and variability in connectors. Also hyper-connectivity and heterogeneity in IoT systems are covered.

A detailed connector definition is provided by Oussalah et al. [19]. Their connector specification includes nonfunctional properties, service and connector types based on the connector taxonomy provided in [12]. However, they do not propose a mechanism for variability support. There are also some approaches that consider connector as a variable asset, while not defining operations and detailed specification for connectors. For example, in [26], an approach is proposed to model component and connector view of software architecture based on OVM using UML annotations. With the same limitations, a hierarchical variability modelling is proposed that has mapping on connectors in the work of Haber et al. [27]. Guendouz et al. [28] propose an approach that integrates Software Product Line Engineering (SPLE) and CBSE whereby annotations are used to describe variability on architectural elements including connectors. Details on connectors, however, are not explicitly defined.

In the context of autonomic computing, Cetina et al. [29] introduce Model-Based Reconfiguration Engine (MoRE) focusing on adaptation to changes in context at run time. The dynamic reconfiguration of architectural elements is achieved through activation/deactivation of features following reconfiguration. Reconfiguration of communication channels is used as a way of incorporating variability in interaction among components through OSGi (Open Service Gateway Initiative) Wire class specifications. However, the variability logic of connectors is hidden in the feature model where the management of variability becomes difficult in large-scale systems.

In [30], an extension of LISA (Language for Integration Software Architecture) with variability is proposed where OVM is employed to configure architectural elements. Variability in connectors is achieved by specifications of variation points and variants that is linked with port definitions belonging to a specific component.

Desai et al. [5] suggest an IoT interoperability architecture based on services. Their work utilizes proxies and gateways, as constructs that associate with connectors, thus coming close to the approach offered in this chapter in terms of their association with the connector concept. However, their work does not leverage on variability.

In another approach, Issarny and Bennaceur [31] present a survey on state-of-the-art of interoperability in heterogeneous and distributed systems. They discuss multiple perspectives to be considered in this regard. They claim that consideration of only application-level interfaces to achieve interoperability among heterogeneous components is not enough, the middleware involved, plus the underlying network environments need to be taken into account as well. They argue that despite the large amount of research done on the topic, it still remains an open and challenging problem to be addressed.

Hallsteinsen et al. [32] consider connector variability through adaptation of middleware where one or more components and their connections are dynamically reconfigured with respect to the context. They utilize plans and utility functions by means of Quality of Service (QoS) properties. De Poorter et al. [33] introduce a solution to enable connectivity for heterogeneous objects in IoT through their IDRA architecture that connects units directly. However, this is not through component connectors or employing variability. Authors in [34] discuss the significance of communication heterogeneity among sensors which are using different communication platforms. They discuss the need for powerful devices that use different communication protocols to manage device communication.

Another valuable work was carried out regarding functional and nonfunctional interoperability of connectors under the Connect project which targets heterogeneous network systems [35]. By protocol interoperability, they offer a framework which figures out both functional and behavioural harmony of a set of components that are willing to achieve a goal. By fulfilling coordinator and mediator needs, the connector seamlessly glues components together relying on the sequences of messages visible at their interfaces.

The extension of the X-MAN component model with feature models, FX-MAN [36] incorporates features with logical architecture of the system which is modelled as a tree of interacting components. Product families are constructed by the use of variation operators and family connectors (F-Select and F-Sequencer) defined in the logical architecture. However, most of the connector variability logic is hidden in the logical architecture. The developer cannot configure different variations of a connector that glues two or more components.

Authors in [37] use two types of cyber connectors. For one-to-one communication, a call-return connector is used and for one-to-many communication, a publish-subscribe connector is used. They mention the extension possibilities for these connector types to support other communication and network specifications. Moreover, different types of connectors are used for a controller unit of a quadrotor in [38]. Communication from higher layers to lower layers is handled by the send-receive connector, whereas the publish-subscribe connector is used for the opposite direction.

7.9 Conclusion

To address the complexity related with the heterogeneity and hyper-connectivity in IoT-based systems, variability mechanisms have been allocated in the connector constituents of the component-based software development approaches. A smart office example is provided for the demonstration of a possible solution employing the new connector definition. Experimentations have pointed to an efficient modelling outcome that enables the developers to separate their concerns about component functionalities and their adaptation or communication needs.

This approach, if accepted by the industry, may develop with its specific engineering practices. The early experimentations resulted with some lessons learned. Our examples suggested the inclusion of only two-end connectors (those connecting not more than two components) where different adaptations and conversions for serving a variety of messages in two directions are included. Different connectors should be employed between any connected pairs of components. Different connectors should be deployed for even between the same pair of components for very different communication needs. Conforming to the existing connector types has also proven effective in our modelling assessments for different problems. Connectors to be defined should preferably be the suggested types, based on their assumed responsibilities.

Future work definitely will benefit from industrial applications. Our vision had been to offer solutions to the mentioned problem within the fast deployment of large-scale systems. To cater to this view, this research can be expanded by integration with variability-centric system development frameworks: building blocks for enabling the automated propagation of variability decisions and related configurations can be studied. Support for connector selection, configuration or even development can be provided through further tools to be developed that can guide intelligent and automated activities based on well-established domain knowledge.

References

1. Mainetti L, Patrono L, Vilei A (2011) Evolution of wireless sensor networks towards the internet of things: a survey. In: 19th International Conference on Software, Telecommunications and Computer Networks (SoftCOM), 15 Sept 2011
2. Horneber J, Hergenröder A (2014) A survey on testbeds and experimentation environments for wireless sensor networks. IEEE Commun Surv Tutorials 16(4):1820–1838
3. Chong G, Zhihao L, Yifeng Y (2011) The research and implement of smart home system based on internet of things. In: International Conference on Electronics, Communications and Control (ICECC), 9 Sept 2011
4. Bandyopadhyay S, Bhattacharyya A (2013) Lightweight internet protocols for web enablement of sensors using constrained gateway devices. In: International Conference on Computing, Networking and Communications (ICNC), 28 Jan 2013
5. Desai P, Sheth A, Anantharam P (2015) Semantic gateway as a service architecture for IoT interoperability. In: International conference on Mobile Services (MS), IEEE, 27 June 2015
6. Patel P, Pathak A, Teixeira T, Issarny V (2011), Towards Application Development for the Internet of Things. In: Proceedings of the 8th middleware doctoral symposium. ACM, Lisbon Portugal, 12 Dec 2011
7. Pradhan S, Dubey A, Otte WR, Karsai G, Gokhale A (2015) Towards a product line of heterogeneous distributed applications. Technical Report, ISIS-15-117, Apr 2015
8. Mattern F, Floerkemeier C (2010) From the internet of computers to the internet of things. Springer, Berlin/Heidelberg
9. Kopetz H (2011) Internet of things, real-time systems, design principles for distributed embedded applications. Springer US, Feb 2011
10. Weiser M (1999) The computer for the 21st century. ACM SIGMOBILE Mobile Comput Commun Rev 3:3–11

11. Atzori L, Iera A, Morabito G (2010) The internet of things: a survey. Comput Netw 54:2787–2805
12. Mehta NR, Medvidovic N, Phadke S (2000) Towards a taxonomy of software connectors. In: Proceedings of the 22nd International Conference on Software Engineering, ICSE '00, New York, 04–11 June 2000
13. Shaw M, Garlan D (1996) Software architecture: perspectives on an emerging discipline. Prentice Hall, Englewood Cliffs. 1 Apr 1996
14. Kaya MC, Suloglu S, Dogru AH (2014) Variability modeling in component oriented system engineering. In: Proceedings of SDPS the 19th international conference on transformative science and engineering, business and social innovation. Kuching Sarawak, Malaysia, 15–19 June 2014
15. Dogru AH, Tanik MM (2003) A process model for component-oriented software engineering. IEEE Softw 20:34–41
16. Pohl K, Bockle G, van Der Linden FJ (2005) Software product line engineering: foundations, principles and techniques. Springer Science & Business Media, 19 Sept 2005
17. Sinnema M, Deelstra S, Nijhuis J, Bosch J (2004) COVAMOF: a framework for modeling variability in software product families. In: 3rd International Conference on Software Product Lines (SPLC 2004). Springer, Berlin/Heidelberg, Aug 2004
18. Cetinkaya A, Kaya MC, Dogru AH (2016) Enhancing XCOSEML with connector variability for component oriented development. In: Proceedings of SDPS 21st international conference on emerging trends and technologies in designing healthcare systems. Orlando, FL, USA, 4–6 Dec 2016
19. Oussalah M, Smeda A, Khammaci T (2004) An explicit definition of connectors for component-based software architecture. In: Proceedings of 11th IEEE international conference and workshop on the engineering of computer based systems. Brno Czech Republic, 27–27 May 2004
20. Classen A, Cordy M, Heymans P, Legay A, Schobbens PY (2012) Model checking software product lines with SNIP. Int J Software Tools Technol Transfer (STTT) 14:589–612
21. Classen A, Cordy M, Schobbens PY, Heymans P, Legay A, Raskin JF (2013) Featured transition systems: foundations for verifying variability-intensive systems and their application to LTL model checking. IEEE Trans Softw Eng 39:1069–1089
22. Classen A, Boucher Q, Heymans P (2011) A text-based approach to feature modelling: syntax and semantics of TVL. Sci Comput Program 76:1130–1143
23. Holzmann GJ (2003) The spin model checker: primer and reference manual. Addison-Wesley, Reading, 4 Sept 2003
24. Kaya MC, Saeedi Nikoo M, Suloglu S, Dogru AH (2015) Towards verification of component compositions incorporating variability. In: Proceedings of SDPS the 20th international conference on transformative science and engineering, business and social innovation. Fort Worth Texas USA, 1–5 Nov 2015
25. Suloglu S (2013) Model-driven variability management in choreography specification. Ph.D. dissertation, Computer Engineering Department, Middle East Technical University, Sept 2013
26. Razavian M, Khosravi R (2008) Modeling variability in the component and connector view of architecture using UML. In: IEEE/ACS international conference on computer systems and applications, Mar 2008
27. Haber A, Rendel H, Rumpe B, Schaefer I, van der Linden F (2011) Hierarchical variability modeling for software architectures. In: 15th International Software Product Line Conference (SPLC), Aug 2011
28. Guendouz A, Bennouar D, Algeria B (2014) Component-based specification of software product line architecture. In: International Conference on Advanced Aspects of Software Engineering (ICAASE), 2–4 Nov 2014
29. Cetina C, Giner P, Fons J, Pelechano V (2009) Autonomic computing through reuse of variability models at runtime: the case of smart homes. Computer 42:37–43

30. Groher I, Weinreich R (2013) Supporting variability management in architecture design and implementation. In: 46th Hawaii International Conference on System Sciences (HICSS), IEEE, 7–10 Jan 2013
31. Issarny V, Bennaceur A (2012) Composing distributed systems: overcoming the interoperability challenge. In: International symposium on formal methods for components and objects. Springer, Berlin/Heidelberg, 24 Sept 2012
32. Hallsteinsen S, Geihs K, Paspallis N, Eliassen F, Horn G, Lorenzo J, Mamelli A, Papadopoulos GA (2012) A development framework and methodology for self-adapting applications in ubiquitous computing environments. J Syst Softw 85:2840–2859
33. De Poorter E, Moerman I, Demeester P (2011) Enabling direct connectivity between heterogeneous objects in the internet of things through a network-service-oriented architecture. EURASIP J Wirel Commun Netw 2011(1):1–14
34. Vicaire PA, Hoque E, Xie Z, Stankovic JA (2012) Bundle: a group-based programming abstraction for cyber-physical systems. IEEE Trans Ind Inform 8:379–392
35. Nostro N, Spalazzese R, Di Giandomenico F, Inverardi P (2016) Achieving functional and non functional interoperability through synthesized connectors. J Syst Softw 111:185–199
36. Di Cola S, Lau KK, Tran C, Qian C (2015) Towards defining families of systems in IoT: logical architectures with variation points, in internet of things, IoT infrastructures: second international summit, IoT 360°, Oct 2015
37. Rajhans A, Cheng SW, Schmerl B, Garlan D, Krogh BH, Agbi C, Bhave A (2009) An architectural approach to the design and analysis of cyber-physical systems. Electron Commun EASST 21
38. Rajhans A, Bhave A, Ruchkin I, Krogh BH, Garlan D, Platzer A, Schmerl B (2014) Supporting heterogeneity in cyber-physical systems architectures. IEEE Trans Autom Control 59(12):3178–3193

Chapter 8
Adopting the Essence Framework to Derive a Practice Library for the Development of IoT Systems

Görkem Giray, Bedir Tekinerdogan, and Eray Tüzün

Abstract The Internet of Things (IoT) is a global network of smart devices which enables these objects to collect and exchange data. Research in the IoT is still progressing, and it is now being applied in various domains. One of the key observations is that the development of IoT systems is not trivial and needs to be carefully managed to meet the required functional and quality concerns. Due to the heterogeneous aspects including software, hardware, and communication, developing the IoT systems implies various challenges that need to be explicitly considered in the development process and successfully resolved. Unfortunately, less focus has been provided so far on the development methods for the IoT systems. To address the particular IoT development concerns, we analyze and discuss the existing approaches that target the development of IoT systems. For this purpose, we use the Essence Framework, which has been recently developed as a framework for modeling various kinds of software development practices and methods. We propose an initial practice library, which can be used to develop and/or tailor project-specific IoT system development methods.

8.1 Introduction

The Internet of Things (IoT) is a global network of smart devices, which enables these objects to collect and exchange data. An IoT system consists of many different devices including software, hardware, and communication elements.

G. Giray
Independent Researcher, Izmir, Turkey

B. Tekinerdogan (✉)
Information Technology Group, Wageningen University, Wageningen, The Netherlands
e-mail: bedir.tekinerdogan@wur.nl

E. Tüzün
Technology and Academy Directorate, Havelsan, Ankara, Turkey

© Springer International Publishing AG 2017

Z. Mahmood (ed.), *Connected Environments for the Internet of Things*,
Computer Communications and Networks,
https://doi.org/10.1007/978-3-319-70102-8_8

Research in the IoT is progressing at various levels and from different perspectives [1]. In this context, various reference architectures have been proposed, different sensor and actuator technologies are being investigated, and different communication protocols have been proposed. In addition, IoT is being applied in different application domains, and the size as well as the complexity of IoT systems is growing rapidly. Similar to the development of other systems, it is important that IoT systems are developed in a systematic manner in order to achieve a proper system with respect to both the functional and nonfunctional requirements. So far, several IoT system development methods have been proposed in the literature, but a broader focus on development methods for IoT is still missing.

In this chapter, we explicitly focus on the development methods dedicated to IoT systems and environments. The development of IoT systems is not trivial and needs to be carefully managed to support the communication between the stakeholders, to support the analysis of the design decisions, and to derive the IoT system that meets the required functional and quality concerns. Unfortunately, not enough focus has been provided so far on the development methods for IoT systems. Due to the heterogeneous aspects including software, hardware, and communication, developing IoT systems implies various challenges that need to be explicitly considered in the development process. To address these concerns, we analyze and discuss the some of the existing approaches that focus on the development of IoT systems. For this purpose, we intend to use the Essence Framework, which has been recently developed as a framework for modeling various kinds of software development practices and methods. We also propose an initial practice library, which can be used to develop and/or tailor project-specific IoT system development methods. This practice library consists of generic practices from software engineering (such as use case), from project management (such as project initiation), and IoT-specific practices derived from two IoT system development methods [2, 3].

The remainder of the chapter is organized as follows. In Sect. 8.2, we present the background including IoT and the Essence Framework. In Sect. 8.3, we summarize the existing IoT system development methods in the literature. We propose a practice library for IoT system development based on the Essence Framework in Sect. 8.4. Section 8.5 provides the discussion. Section 8.6 includes the related work, and finally Sect. 8.7 concludes the chapter.

8.2   Background

In this section, we first provide a conceptual model for IoT systems. Subsequently, we present the Essence Framework in Sect. 8.2.2.

8.2.1 Internet of Things

Figure 8.1 illustrates a conceptual model for IoT systems, which is based on the AIOTI Domain Model [4]. Referring to this figure, an *Entity of Interest* (*EoI*) or *Thing* is an object (such as room, book, laptop, a sensing device) including attributes that describe it and its state that is relevant from a user or an application perspective. The *EoI* has an observable state (e.g., temperature) that is observed by a *Sensor* (e.g., thermometer or tag reader). An *Actuator* can make changes to the *EoI* through an action. The interaction between a *User* and *EoI* is mediated by an *IoT Service* which is associated with a *Virtual Entity*, a digital representation of the *EoI*. Different kinds of digital representations of *EoI*s can be used such as objects, 3D models, avatars, or even a social network account. Some *Virtual Entities* can also interact with other *Virtual Entities* to fulfill their goal. An important aspect in the IoT is that changes in the properties of a *Thing* and its corresponding *Virtual Entity* needs to be synchronized. This is usually realized by an *IoT Device* that is embedding into, attached to, or simply placed in close vicinity of the *Thing*. The *IoT Device* can interact with other devices and includes *software components* that implement the *IoT Services*.

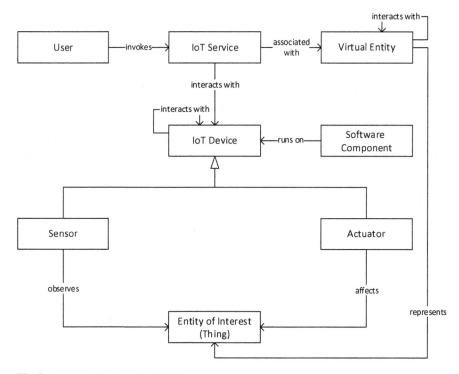

Fig. 8.1 A conceptual model for IoT systems

In the following subsection, we discuss the Essence Framework that was recently introduced by the SEMAT (Software Engineering Method and Theory) community [5] and published as a standard by the Object Management Group (OMG) [6].

8.2.2   The Essence Framework

The Essence Framework was introduced by the SEMAT [5] and published by OMG [6]. Its specification consists of an Essence Language and the Essence Kernel, as illustrated in Fig. 8.2. The Essence Language is basically a meta-model used to define practices and methods for system and software engineering. The Essence Kernel is a set of elements used to form a common ground for describing a software engineering endeavor and represented in terms of the Essence Language. These two components provide a common ground for understanding, comparing, and combining software development practices and methods.

As illustrated in Fig. 8.2, practices and methods can be represented using the Essence Language. A practice is defined as a systematic and repeatable way of achieving a predefined objective [7]. Practices can be seen as reusable ways of doing things in software development endeavors. Concretely, a method is composed of the Essence Kernel and a set of practices. The Essence Framework aims to set a ground for building a library of practices from which one can build methods respecting the actual needs of a specific software development project. This way, it can boost the reusability of best practices. Moreover, the Essence Kernel provides a base for starting with establishing a specific method. A library of practices has been launched recently [8].

The core elements of the Essence Language used in this work are shown in Fig. 8.3. An *Alpha* (Abstract-Level Progress Health Attribute) is defined as an important dimension whose state should be progressed and tracked during a project. *Work product*s are concrete representations of *Alpha*s and describe them by providing evidence for *state*s of *Alpha*s. Progress in *work product*s is tracked through *level*

Fig. 8.2 The essence
framework architecture

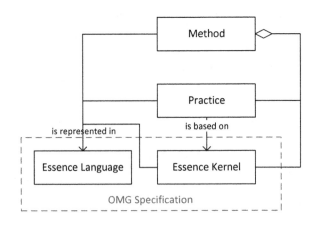

of details. Both *state* of *Alpha*s and *level of details* of *work product*s are checked against *checklist item*s. *Activities* update *level of details* of *work product*s and cause progress in s*tates* of *Alpha*s. *Activities* are organized into *activity space*s, which target changes in *Alpha states* through the *activities* they contain. *Pattern*s are used for defining complex concepts made up of practice or kernel elements. For instance, a role can be defined by a pattern involving required competencies, responsibility for *work product*s, and participation in *activities*.

The Essence Framework is based on Meta-Object Facility (MOF) architecture [9]. Figure 8.4 illustrates three layers with some sample concepts and neglects the fourth layer for the sake of simplicity. The Essence Language resides in layer 2 and provides a meta-model for method engineering. Practices and methods are defined in layer 1 by instantiating meta-model concepts. In Fig. 8.4, *Opportunity*, which is an instance of Alpha, is a part of the Essence Kernel. Business model is an instance

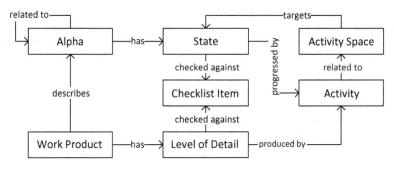

Fig. 8.3 Partial conceptual model of the essence language

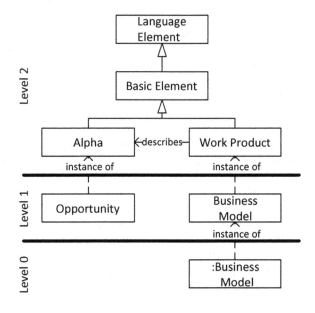

Fig. 8.4 A partial illustration of the essence framework meta-model architecture

Table 8.1 A partial illustration of the graphical syntax of the essence language

Alpha	Work Product	Activity space	Practice	Pattern
Alpha state	Level of detail	Activity	Kernel	

of work product and can be arbitrarily defined as part of a practice by a method engineer. The layer 0 includes the actual concepts in a specific software development project, for instance, a particular business model document written for a specific project.

The Essence Kernel, which resides in layer 1 in Fig. 8.4, provides a common basis for defining software engineering practices by instantiating three concepts of the Essence Language: Alpha, activity space, and competency. The Essence Kernel includes 7 Alphas, 15 activity spaces, and 6 competencies [6]. It defines states of all 7 Alphas along with their checklist items; on the other hand, it does not define any activity or work product.

The Essence specification provides a graphical syntax of its language elements. Table 8.1 illustrates the language elements used in this chapter along with their symbols.

The Essence Kernel provides seven Alphas along with their interrelationships (as illustrated in Fig. 8.5), which can be considered as a general, core domain model of software engineering. The Alphas are organized into three areas of concern, namely, *customer, solution,* and *endeavor* concerns [6]. *Customer* concern addresses the business perspective; *solution* concern examines the specification and development of software system; and *endeavor* concern scrutinizes the team and the way it performs its work.

The Essence Kernel also provides the states of each Alpha along with their initial checklists. As an example, the states of Opportunity Alpha and the checklist of its "identified" state are illustrated in the left and right sides of Fig. 8.6, respectively. The states of the seven Alphas and the items of the initial checklists cannot be changed, since these are forming the standard common ground. On the other hand, sub-Alphas can be defined to support seven Alphas. Moreover, the checklists of the seven Alphas can be extended by adding new checklist items (without changing the standard ones). In addition, the states of new sub-Alphas and their checklists should be defined by team according to specific needs of a particular project.

In summary, the Essence Language can be used to model the existing IoT system development methods or describe new methods. Moreover, the Essence Kernel can form a base to understand the portions of the methods addressing the development of software components of IoT systems.

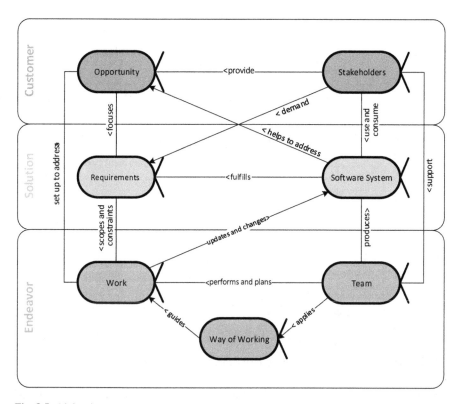

Fig. 8.5 Alphas in essence kernel and their interrelationships (Adopted from Ref. [6])

8.3 IoT System Development Methods

We identified six IoT system development methods in the literature after applying a thorough domain analysis process. Domain scoping and domain modeling are two basic activities in the domain analysis process. Defining the scope and selecting proper knowledge sources constitute domain scoping. In this case, the scope is made up of IoT system development methods in the literature. In the domain modeling activity, we modeled these methods using the Essence Framework as presented in the following sections.

8.3.1 The Ignite IoT Methodology

The Ignite IoT Methodology [2] (abbreviated as "Ignite" in this chapter) aims to provide guidelines for developing products (systems in this case) for the IoT. The methodology consists of best practices and deals with enterprise, product, and project levels and aimed at various IoT stakeholders including product managers,

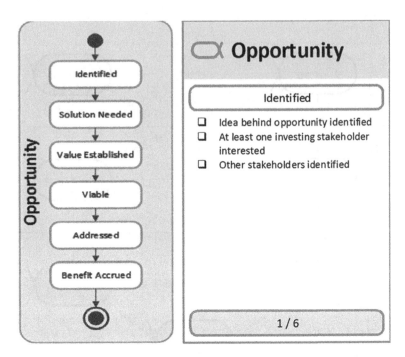

Fig. 8.6 The states of opportunity alpha and the checklist for the first state (Adopted from Ref. [6])

project managers, and solution architects. Ignite has two major groups of activities:

- IoT Strategy Execution encompasses defining an IoT strategy and a project portfolio (consisting of projects related to IoT) supporting this strategy. IoT Strategy Execution is about business perspective and involves identifying and managing opportunities, as well as making decisions on how to realize projects addressing these opportunities (such as internal project, external acquisition, spin-off, etc.).
- IoT Solution Delivery supports IoT system design and IoT project management along with some artifacts such as project templates, checklists, and solution architecture blueprints. IoT Solution Delivery is about realizing an IoT system, which is conceptually defined during IoT Strategy Execution, and has a life cycle consisting of planning, building, and running. Planning starts with project initiation, in which an initial system design and a project organization chart are delivered. Moreover, an analysis of stakeholders, environment, requirements, risks, and resources should be conducted. After the initiation, the tasks are managed under seven work streams: (1) project management, (2) cross-cutting tasks, (3) solution infrastructure and operations, (4) backend services, (5) communication services, (6) on-asset components, and (7) asset preparation.

These two groups of activities should be synchronized to keep the project portfolio in line with the strategy and revise the strategy according to the outcomes of the project portfolio.

8.3.2   The IoT Methodology

The IoT Methodology [3] (abbreviated as "IoT-Meth" in this chapter) is a generic, lightweight method built on iterative prototyping and lean start-up approaches. It consists of best practices, tried and tested tools, protocols, and solutions used in real-world projects. IoT-Meth comprises the following steps, which should be executed iteratively:

1. The first step named "cocreate" encompasses the identification of problem areas by communicating with stakeholders, especially end users. The result is some ideas on opportunities or potential problems to be refined in the next step.
2. In the second step named "ideate," some of the ideas identified in the former step are further elaborated to be communicated with project managers, designers, and implementers. An artifact named IoT Canvas can be used in brainstorming sessions with stakeholders to identify and validate high-level requirements.
3. The third step named "Q & A" involves analyzing refined ideas further to close the gap between idea and implementation. Further analysis of domain and requirements along with validation of requirements is performed.
4. The requirements are mapped to an architecture and infrastructure in the step named "IoT OSI." An artifact named as IoT-Architecture Reference Model can be used in this step.
5. "Prototyping" encompasses building prototypes and iterating toward minimal viable IoT systems. The forthcoming iteration plans are revised according to the assessments of prototypes.
6. The last step named "deploy" closes the feedback loop by deploying the IoT system. In most cases, feedbacks trigger improvements in the system.

8.3.3   IoT Application Development

This is an approach to IoT application development (abbreviated as "IoT-AD" in this chapter) that consists of a development methodology and a concrete development framework realizing this methodology [10]. IoT-AD treats the concerns of IoT domain in four areas, namely, domain, functional, deployment, and platform. IoT-AD proposes to specify the behavior of an IoT system using high-level abstractions and compile these abstractions to code. To this end, it provides a set of modeling languages and some automation techniques.

8.3.4   ELDAMeth

ELDAMeth (Event-driven Lightweight Distilled state charts-based Agents Methodology) is an agent-oriented methodology for developing smart objects (SO), which are considered as fundamental building blocks of IoT systems [11]. ELDAMeth has three main phases, namely, modeling, simulation, and implementation. In the modeling phase, a detailed design is produced to be translated into platform-independent code. Simulation phase encompasses the verification of platform-independent code against requirements through simulation. Platform-specific code is developed and tested in the implementation phase.

8.3.5   Software Product Line Process to Develop Agents for the IoT

Ayala et al. [12] applied software product line engineering (SPLE) approach to development of agents for IoT systems (abbreviated as "SPLP-IoT" in this chapter). What is borrowed from SPLE is identifying commonalities among software agents and developing a common reference architecture. To this end, the domain engineering phase is responsible for establishing a reusable platform and thus defining the commonality and variability of a multi-agent system. Two key work products, IoT multi-agent system variability model and IoT multi-agent system architecture, are produced in this phase. The application engineering part encompasses building agents, which meet specific application requirements, by exploiting variability model and leveraging IoT multi-agent system architecture.

8.3.6   A General Software Engineering Methodology for IoT

A general software engineering (SE) methodology for IoT (abbreviated as "GSEM-IoT" in this chapter) proposes some general guidelines for developing IoT systems [13]. GSEM-IoT involves three phases, namely, analysis, design, and implementation. In the analysis phase, actors, requirements, and existing infrastructure are identified and analyzed. Avatars, groups, and coalitions are designed in the design phase. The implementation phase is about implementing avatars and coordinators along with deployment.

8.4 Proposed IoT System Development Practice Library Based on the Essence Framework

Methods play an important role in developing quality systems. Therefore, many practices and methods have been proposed in system and software engineering, including six methods for IoT system development. All of these proposed methods are monolithic [14] and are hard to reuse in every IoT-related project. Moreover, extracting various practices from these methods and reusing them as a combined new method is another challenge. On the other hand, it is generally accepted that each project is unique and needs a tailored method to run it. Therefore, it makes sense to have a practice library consisting of reusable pieces validated in real-world projects.

In this chapter, we present the results of our initial analysis and modeling of the current IoT system development methods based on the Essence Framework. The process of modeling a practice or method based on the Essence Framework is called essentialization [15]. We used the approach proposed in [16] for essentialization. We worked through the practices, which address the Alphas in the customer concern illustrated in Fig. 8.5. Moreover, we present an initial practice library mainly derived from Ignite and IoT-Meth methods. The reason we have chosen these methods is that they are more appropriate to be broken down into reusable practices.

Ignite addresses the customer concern by two practices named IoT Opportunity Identification and IoT Opportunity Management, illustrated in Figs. 8.7 and 8.8, respectively. IoT Opportunity Identification practice is about generating and refining IoT Opportunities. Each opportunity can be progressed and tracked using a sub-Alpha named IoT Opportunity. The practice contains activities regarding generation, initial assessment, and refinement of IoT Opportunities. Structured and open idea generation approaches are two ways of generating IoT Opportunity ideas. St. Gallen Business Model Navigator and Innovation Project Canvas are work

Fig. 8.7 An Ignite practice: IoT Opportunity Identification

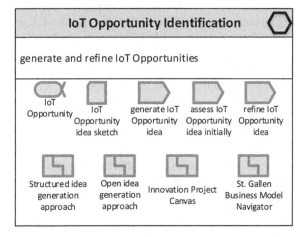

Fig. 8.8 An ignite
practice: IoT opportunity
management

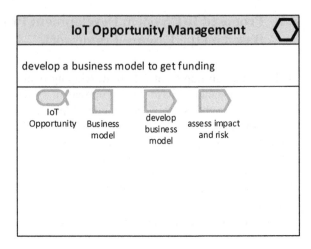

Fig. 8.9 An IoT-Meth
practice: cocreate

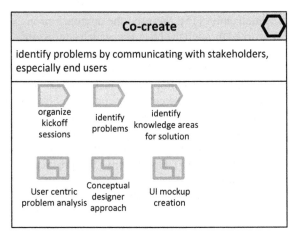

products, which can be used for refining IoT Opportunity idea. The output of refining an idea is an IoT Opportunity idea sketch work product.

As illustrated in Fig. 8.8, IoT Opportunity Management practice involves developing a business model to get funding. This practice can provide progress on IoT
Opportunity sub-Alpha. This progress is achieved by developing a business model.
An input for this business model work product is IoT Opportunity idea sketch,
which is produced within the scope of IoT Opportunity Identification. Another
important activity is assessing impact and risk.

The first two steps of IoT-Meth are directly related to the customer concern.
Cocreate practice (Fig. 8.9) is about identifying problems, which can be solved by
developing IoT systems. Since these problems can be identified through stakeholder
involvement, the practice has activities for eliciting information from stakeholders
using some approaches.

Fig. 8.10 An IoT-Meth
practice: ideate

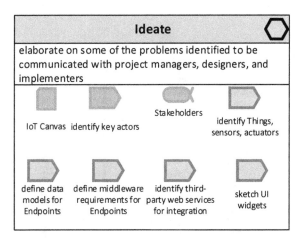

Fig. 8.10 An IoT-Meth
practice: ideate

The second step of IoT-Meth involves ideate practice (Fig. 8.10), in which problems are elaborated further to be communicated with project managers, designers, and implementers. IoT-Meth proposes to use a work product named IoT Canvas for brainstorming with various stakeholders. Therefore, IoT Canvas has information both for customer and solution areas of concern. Moreover, ideate practice has "identify key actors" activity for the customer concern and the rest of activities for the solution concern.

IoT-AD starts with modeling the domain in which an IoT system will be developed. It examines application architecture and logic according to the requirements along with deployment- and platform-specific concerns. As a result, IoT-AD proposes activities and work products for the solution concern. ELDAMeth expects requirements and high-level design model to begin developing an agent for an IoT system. It does not cover any activity regarding the customer concern. SPLP-IoT method takes domain and application requirements as an input. Therefore, it addresses the solution concern by proposing some activities and work products.

GSEM-IoT starts with identifying stakeholders in its analysis phase. It proposes three abstract classes of actors, namely, global managers, local managers, and users to address the different components of an IoT system. Apart from this, it does not contain any guideline regarding the customer concern. Therefore, we can conclude that GSEM-IoT does not contain any practice in the customer area of concern.

The practices of Ignite and IoT-Meth, which are modeled in this chapter, cause some state changes in stakeholders and Opportunity Alphas, as shown in Fig. 8.11. From this figure, we can infer that there are practices whose objectives are overlapping. GSEM-IoT mentions about identifying key actors, which partially addresses recognized state of stakeholders Alpha.

Figure 8.12 illustrates the idea of having a practice library for IoT system development projects. This vision is explained in [6, 7] in general terms and exemplified in [14, 15] for the IoT domain.

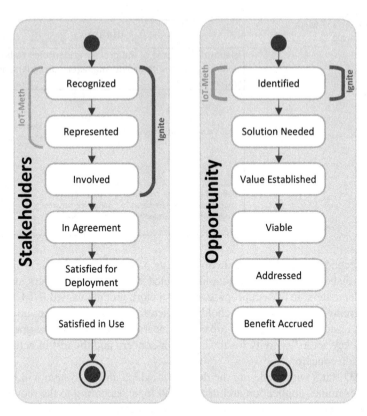

Fig. 8.11 Coverage of Ignite and IoT-Meth practices modeled in this chapter based on the essence framework

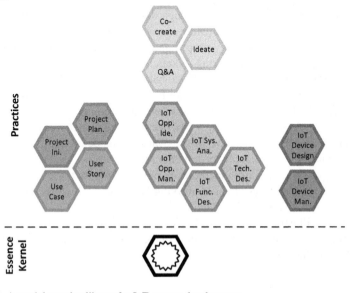

Fig. 8.12 A partial practice library for IoT system development

The practices shown in Fig. 8.12 have been obtained from different sources. Use case and user story practices are well-known in software engineering domain. They are also defined as practices in [8]. Some practices from project management domain are essential to every system/software development project. It is suggested that Ignite should be complemented with project management practices [2], preferably proposed by PMBOK [17]. Therefore, our practice library involves project initiation and project planning practices, which are defined in PMBOK (Project Management Body of Knowledge) as well. IoT Opportunity Identification (IoT Opp. Ide.), IoT Opportunity Management (IoT Opp. Man.), IoT System Analysis (IoT Sys. Ana.), IoT Functional Design (IoT Func. Des.), and IoT Technical Design (IoT Tech. Des.) have been derived from Ignite [2]. Cocreate, ideate, and Q&A practices have been derived from IoT-Meth [3]. As shown in Fig. 8.11, some of the practices proposed by Ignite and IoT-Meth are overlapping according to the Essence Framework. Therefore, some of the practices can be compared before using them as a building block of a tailored method. Ignite also states that it does not cover any practice regarding IoT device management. Therefore, we added two illustrative practices, namely, IoT device design and IoT device manufacturing. When IoT device manufacturing is needed for an IoT project, appropriate practices can be used to fulfill these needs.

8.5   Discussion

The use of a practice library is important for documenting, reusing, improving, and enhancing the body of knowledge in system and software engineering. The descriptions of some methods state the areas they do not cover. For instance, Scrum practice does not define how to specify requirements. Scrum practice should be complemented with a practice to specify requirements, such as use case, user story, or any other practice. As a second example, Ignite complements its content using PMBOK practices. Moreover, it explicitly states that it does not cover any practice on IoT device management. As a result, such a practice library, a language to define practices (the Essence Language), and a common ground (the Essence Kernel) are beneficial both for practitioners and method engineers. From method engineering perspective, we can also observe that there are overlapping activities in Ignite and IoT-Meth. This means that two separate efforts are put on achieving the same or similar objective. Such a library can direct method engineers' effort to the areas where new practices are needed.

In our case, the Essence Kernel constitutes the common ground for the practice library. On the other hand, the Essence Kernel is originally designed for software engineering. Therefore, it will not cover all parts of an IoT project, since such projects include IoT devices, sensors, actuators, etc. (as shown in Fig. 8.1). Having a system engineering kernel is an enhancement area, which is already identified in [18].

The book that describes Ignite [2] includes a semi-structured description of the method along with many project-specific details. While essentializing Ignite, we had difficulty in separating the description of the method, which is much more general, from project-specific details. A practice library makes it possible to define a method using the Essence Language by capturing the essentials and separating the details [7]. In addition, IoT-Meth is described only by a short presentation [3], which is far from guiding a team for an IoT system development project. The method engineers designing IoT-Meth may benefit from the Essence Language, the Essence Kernel, and a system engineering kernel (not in place yet) to structure more knowledge and experience from real-world projects and present these to system and software engineering body of knowledge in the form of a practice library.

Besides providing a practice library, the Essence Kernel also provides a medium to assess the status of a project (using Alphas and checklists) and decide on the next steps. This actionable nature of the Essence Kernel is also useful in complex projects. One of the challenges of IoT system development projects is the involvement of many stakeholders with different backgrounds [10]. Key stakeholders can extend the Essence Kernel at the initiation stage of an IoT system development project by defining sub-Alphas collaboratively. Such a tracking mechanism can constitute a common ground among the stakeholders during the project. For this purpose, as an example, Ignite proposes a work product named IoT Project Dimensions, which can be used to conduct project assessment and compare different IoT projects [2]. The Alpha concept of the Essence Language is more general, which can be applicable to all system and software development projects and cover IoT Project Dimensions as well.

8.6   Related Work

The Essence Framework specification includes some demonstrations of essentializing of some practices, such as Scrum, user story, Unified Process, and waterfall life cycle [6]. Essentialized version of Scrum is presented in [19]. In this study, the authors illustrate how the practices of Scrum, XP, and DevOps can be combined to establish a method. A partial essentialized version of Nexus is presented in [16]. References [14, 15] involve an introduction to the establishment of a practice library for IoT system development and the essentialization of Ignite. In this chapter, we use the same idea of having a practice library and propose an initial library after partially analyzing two IoT system development methods.

The Software and Systems Process Engineering Meta-model (SPEM) is a process engineering meta-model as well as a conceptual framework, which can provide the necessary concepts for modeling, documenting, presenting, managing, interchanging, and enacting development methods and processes [20]. Both the Essence Framework and the SPEM provide a language to define practices and methods. In addition to this, the Essence Framework also provides a generic domain model of software engineering, which is the Essence Kernel. As illustrated in Fig. 8.4, the Essence Framework provides a language at layer 2 and the Essence Kernel at layer 1, whereas SPEM provides only a meta-model, which resides at layer 2. The Essence Kernel forms a base to understand, compare, and combine practices and methods.

Moreover, the Essence Framework emphasizes the importance of tracking progress and health of a project using Alphas and sub-Alphas.

8.7   Conclusion

The IoT is a recent paradigm that has a pervasive impact on society. For many different application domains, IoT concepts will become an important innovation. Developing IoT-based systems however appears to be different from traditional software-intensive systems. In this chapter, we have discussed the application of the Essence Framework for building an initial practice library using practices derived from two different IoT system development methods, as well as more generic practices from software engineering and project management domains. In principle, it appears that the Essence Framework is to a large extent expressive to model software portion of IoT system development methods. An improvement area can be the development of a system engineering kernel to cover hardware and communication aspects of IoT systems. The application of the Essence Framework to the IoT methods also highlighted some of the shortcomings or incomplete aspects for developing IoT systems using the current IoT development comnet methods. Hence, we think that our study is of value for both providing insight in the Essence Framework and IoT methods. On the one hand, the results of our study can be used to enhance the Essence Framework; on the other hand, these results could be used to enhance existing IoT development methods or create even novel IoT methods. Our future work will indeed include the development of a novel IoT method based on the observations from this study. Further we will apply the IoT method for developing real IoT systems.

References

1. Atzori L, Iera A, Morabito G (2010) The internet of things: a survey. Comput Netw 54(15):2787–2805. https://doi.org/10.1016/j.comnet.2010.05.010
2. Slama D, Puhlmann F, Morrish J, Bhatnagar RM (2016) Enterprise IoT strategies & best practices for connected products & services. O'Reilly Media, Inc
3. Collins TA. Methodology for building the internet of things. http://www.iotmethodology.com. Accessed 24 Feb 2017
4. AIOTI (2016) High level architecture (HLA), Release 2.1. AIOTI WG03 – IoT Standardisation. http://www.aioti.org/wp-content/uploads/2016/10/AIOTI-WG3-IoT-High-Level-Architecture-Release_2_1.pdf. Accessed 23 Feb 2017
5. SEMAT web site. http://semat.org. Accessed 22 Feb 2017
6. Object Management Group (2015) Essence – kernel and language for software engineering methods, version 1.1. http://www.omg.org/spec/Essence. Accessed 22 Feb 2017
7. Jacobson I, Ng PW, McMahon PE, Spence I, Lidman S (2013) The essence of software engineering: applying the SEMAT kernel. Addison-Wesley Professional

8. Ivar Jacobson International. Practice Library. http://practicelibrary.ivarjacobson.com. Accessed 23 Feb 2017
9. Object Management Group (2016) Meta object facility, version 2.5.1. http://www.omg.org/spec/MOF. Accessed 23 Feb 2017
10. Patel P, Cassou D (2015) Enabling high-level application development for the internet of things. J Syst Softw 103(C):62–84. https://doi.org/10.1016/j.jss.2015.01.027
11. Fortino G, Russo W (2012) ELDAMeth: an agent-oriented methodology for simulation-based prototyping of distributed agent systems. Inf Softw Technol 54(6):608–624. https://doi.org/10.1016/j.infsof.2011.08.006
12. Ayala I, Amor M, Fuentes L, Troya JM (2015) A software product line process to develop agents for the IoT. Sensors 15(7):15640–15660. https://doi.org/10.3390/s150715640
13. Zambonelli F (2017) Key abstractions for IoT-oriented software engineering. IEEE Softw 34(1):38–45. https://doi.org/10.1109/MS.2017.3
14. Jacobson I (2016) What you need for IoT: smarter methods. IoT World Congress. https://www.ivarjacobson.com/videos/what-you-need-iot-smarter-methods. Accessed 23 Feb 2017
15. Jacobson I, Spence I, Seidewitz E (2016) Industrial scale agile – from Craft to engineering. acmqueue 14(5). https://doi.org/10.1145/3012426.3012428
16. Giray G, Tüzün E, Tekinerdogan B, Macit Y (2016) Systematic approach for mapping software development methods to the essence framework. In Proceedings of the 5th international workshop on theory-oriented software engineering (TOSE '16). ACM, New York, pp 26–32. doi: https://doi.org/10.1145/2897134.2897139
17. Project Management Institute (2013) A guide to the project management body of knowledge (PMBOK® Guide), 5th Edition. Project Management Institute
18. Jacobson I, Lawson HB, McMahon PE (2015) Towards a systems engineering essence. In: Jacobson I, Lawson HB (eds) Software engineering in the systems context. College Publications
19. Park JS, McMahon PE, Myburgh B (2016) Scrum powered by essence. SIGSOFT Softw Eng Notes 41(1):1–8. https://doi.org/10.1145/2853073.2853088
20. Object Management Group (2008) Software & systems process engineering meta-model specification, version 2. http://www.omg.org/spec/SPEM/2.0. Accessed 23 Feb 2017

Chapter 9
Integration of Buildings Information with Live Data from IoT Devices

Zohreh Pourzolfaghar and Markus Helfert

Abstract Information generated by smart buildings is a valuable asset that can be utilised by various groups of stakeholders in smart cities. These stakeholders can benefit from such information in order to provide additional valuable services. The added value is achievable if there is access to buildings information integrated with the live data being generated and collected from smart devices and sensors residing within the Internet of Things (IoT) environment. Notwithstanding the prominence of this combination, there are some barriers relating to the integration of buildings information with the live data. With the aim of examining such barriers, this chapter primarily focuses on information exchanges between various domains in smart cities. It also provides a vision on specific domains that can benefit from integration of buildings information with other live data. This can impact and improve the quality of various e-services. This chapter describes the barriers and suggests solutions to realise these visions. At the end of this chapter, a summary of the barriers is provided and discussed followed by proposals for future research topics to provide solutions to the inherent barriers.

9.1 Introduction

The concept of smart cities has emerged during the last few years to describe how investments in human and social capital and modern ICT infrastructure and e-services fuel sustainable growth and quality of life, being enabled by appropriate management of natural resources and through a participative government [1]. Smart buildings refer to a suite of technologies used to design, construct and operate the buildings more efficiently [2]. To enable smart buildings, Zhou [3] stated that a wide range of information needs to be available from varied sources. Baetens [4] suggested that the smart buildings include different smart features, analytics

Z. Pourzolfaghar (✉) • M. Helfert
Lero – The Irish Software Research Centre, School of Computing, Dublin City University, Dublin, Ireland
e-mail: z_pourzolfaghar@yahoo.com

© Springer International Publishing AG 2017
Z. Mahmood (ed.), *Connected Environments for the Internet of Things*,
Computer Communications and Networks,
https://doi.org/10.1007/978-3-319-70102-8_9

and sensors used to monitor and control the power supply through renewable energy, smart metering technologies and smart windows. Zhou [3] also expressed that most of the smart technologies exploit information about the buildings design and operation specifications at a later stage as far as smart buildings are concerned. This can be valuable, for example, to estimate energy consumptions for industrial or marketing purposes.

Smart buildings information can be utilised by various groups of stakeholders in smart cities. These diverse groups of stakeholders may take advantage of the information and add more values to their services. Some examples of these industries are facility management, utility companies and smart commerce. Maintenance companies can use buildings information to speed up the maintenance processes, as well as improving the efficiency of their services. Likewise, utility companies need to know the buildings specifications to estimate energy consumptions of the buildings. Moreover, actual over usage of energy consumption can be compared with estimated buildings energy consumption from the design phase. In this way, useful information can be provided on energy consumption to promote energy savings behaviours.

Similarly, related to smart commerce, traditional and online retailers can profit from accessing the buildings information. The retailers can manage the demands based on the specifications for the devices and materials used for the buildings in an urban area. In this way, they have the opportunity to advertise their products for the right potential customers. Moreover, integration of the buildings information with the live data (produced by the sensors embedded in installed equipment) can provide retailers with useful information about the faulty devices and potential future demands. Likewise, they will have the opportunity to inform the customers on the new products having advantages like lower energy consumption.

To achieve the above-mentioned goals, there is a need to integrate the buildings information with the live data from the Internet of Things (IoT) devices on the status of devices, energy consumption and devices specification in different spaces of buildings. However, integrating the buildings information with the live data is not easily accessible for the potential users. The problem is attributable to the difficulty in accessing the buildings information, as well as the challenge to integrate this information with the live data from heterogeneous sources.

In this chapter, first we explain how information sharing between various domains may transform a city to a smart city. Then we will have more concentration on smart buildings and potential users of the buildings information in the other smart domains. For this purpose, a number of potential smart industries which may take advantage of the combination of this valuable information are introduced. The remainder of this chapter presents and discusses the barriers preventing the integration of the live data with the buildings information.

9.2   Information Management in Smart Cities

As Wenge [5] expressed, successfully deploying smart systems alone is not enough to make an entire city smart. They emphasised that the city is not truly smart if only a single system can meet the citizens' needs. In other words, the intelligent city is different from a smart city, and the validity of any city's claim to be smart has to be based on something more than its use of information and communication technologies [6, 7]. Indeed, integration, information sharing and communication between many various domains can facilitate making a city smart (see Fig. 9.1). This implies that contrary to the traditional cities, the smart cities require to innovate and connect establish infrastructures for the citizens and organisations. Indeed, the ultimate goal of the smart cities is to improve the quality of life and sustainable economic growth. To achieve these goals, various drivers like efficient services, appropriate interactions with community and city infrastructure, monitoring and planning play pivotal roles.

On the other hand, a variety of IoT devices are producing a huge amount of information in each smart city domain. To realise the efficiency of the intended services, information systems infrastructures across different domains need to be able to interact with each other.

Bischof [8] discussed at length the challenges and issues arising from the nature of different smart city data sources, their various formats and often changing data quality. They lay emphasis on providing semantic interoperability as well as data integration. Anthopoulos [9] showed through examination of various use cases that the cities around the world encounter common challenges in areas such as information sharing and exchange. As a consequence, the effective information flow between the smart city stakeholders and also the provision of good quality information are the two critical issues of this era. In a smart city, the information is created and stored in different systems and services. However, there is a gap in their abilities

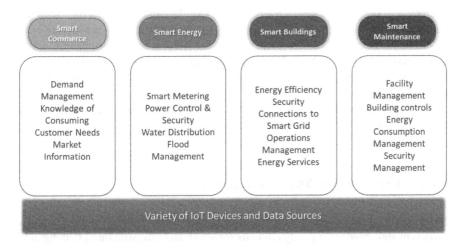

Fig. 9.1 Communication and integration of smart systems in smart cities

to transfer this information to the other smart domains and utilise it for the other areas in an efficient and effective way. Some researchers, e.g. Anthopoulos [9], have considered the information exchange as an upcoming challenge in the smart cities. It is also noteworthy that it is costly and non-secure for standalone services to exchange information. This is why most societies fail to exploit the potentials of this valuable property. In the next section, the merits associated with the information exchange are elucidated for some potential users in the smart city context.

9.2.1 Smart Buildings

With the advent of IoT technologies, cities inevitably move towards environments recognised by full integration and semantics. As Pan [10] pinpointed, diverse application areas of such technologies are often summarised with terms such as 'smart city', 'smart home', 'smart buildings' and lately smart commerce. As such, smart environments include smart objects, such as houses, buildings, sustainable urban infrastructure, cars, sensor technology and a lot more. Within these environments, through the application of semantic web technologies and intelligent applications, we are able to offer personalised, responsive and intuitive systems. According to Baetens [4], smart buildings are prominent examples of smart environments and include different smart features, analytics and sensors used to monitor and control the power supply through renewable energy, smart metering technologies, etc.

According to some researchers, smart buildings describe 'a suite of technologies used to make the design, construction, and operation of the buildings more efficient'. To realise the exact meaning of smartness in the smart buildings and gain full benefit from the IoT devices and technologies, it is inevitable to integrate the buildings information with the live data obtained from the IoT devices (see Fig. 9.2).

Smart buildings are embedded with large amounts of latent data from different sources, e.g. the IoT devices, sensors and the like. Integration of this data with the buildings information can highly impact the efficiency of services provided by various industries such as facility management companies, utility companies, smart commerce and so forth. Nonetheless, the potential users of this information, e.g. facility management companies, are still unable to fully derive benefit from the buildings information. This problem is attributable to some challenges in sharing the buildings information with the potential users from the other smart industries. In the following section, we introduce some potential users.

9.2.2 Users of Buildings Information

Smart buildings information is a valuable asset which can be utilised by various groups of stakeholders, e.g. city councils for urban and infrastructure planning, and maintenance/facility management companies to speed up their services and utility

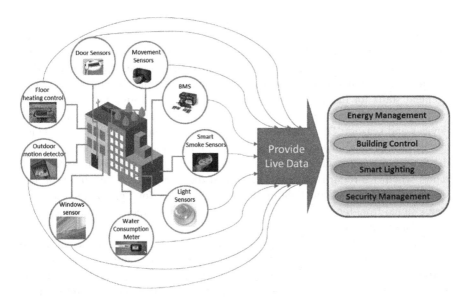

Fig. 9.2 Realisation of smart buildings by integration of buildings information with live data

companies to estimate energy consumption. In the following subsections, a number of potential users of the buildings information are discussed. Then, we describe their current approaches to provide their services. At the end of each subsection, we illustrate how they can provide more added values to their services by utilising the buildings information and the live captured data.

9.2.2.1 Buildings Maintenance

Facility management is a profession that encompasses multiple disciplines to ensure functionality of the built environment by integrating the people, the place, the process and the technology. Likewise, facility management organisations are responsible for providing and delivering timely, quality, professional facility management analysis and consulting support services for the customers [11]. According to Lavy and Jawadekar [12], facility management activities depend on the accuracy and accessibility of the information created in the design and the construction phases. This information is maintained throughout the operations and the maintenance phase. Referring to the General Service Administration (GSA) [13], lack of this information can result in cost overruns, inefficient buildings operations and untimely resolution of client requests. In order to provide efficient services, facility management departments should ensure that all the equipment installed in building spaces are in active status and work properly. Moreover, they are responsible for providing repair/replacement services at the earliest possible time.

The errors and failures are normally reported by the users of the building spaces. However, some common areas are used for special purposes such as meetings, seminars, lectures and all that. To ensure that all the devices in these common areas are working properly, it is indispensable to inspect these spaces on a timely basis. Normally, these types of inspections take a considerable time from the facility management staffs for the areas which even need no further action to be taken. This happens in the digital era when most of the buildings are equipped with the IoT devices and sensors. These devices provide huge amounts of valuable data which can be used in combination with the buildings information and add more values to the facility management services. For instance, movement sensors in a space can report whether a room is occupied or not. At the same time, light sensors in this space should switch off the light in case of inoccupation for a given time. The 'on' status signal from the light sensor besides an unoccupied report can raise a failure report on the light sensor.

Obviously, combination of the live data from the IoT devices and the embedded sensors can add more values by early replacement of the faulty device. For this purpose, there is a need to have a list of the installed devices integrated with the buildings spaces information. Moreover, the live part of this integrated information needs to be structured with the ability to be updated over time. To illustrate the usefulness of this combination, a list of faulty devices for buildings spaces and their costs can be prepared and reported to the senior managers. An immense number of similar cases can be exemplified and implemented, in case of having access to the buildings spaces information along with the live data from the IoT devices and sensors. Notwithstanding the importance of this combination, there are still some barriers to integrate the buildings information with the live captured data.

9.2.2.2 Smart Energy

A smart energy system is a cost-effective, sustainable and secure energy system in which renewable energy production, infrastructures and consumption are integrated and coordinated through energy services, active users and enabling technologies. Regarding the increased efforts for energy saving and energy cost reduction, utility companies attempt to find new ways to promote more effective ways of energy usage. Towards this, they need to evaluate energy consumption and estimate energy consumption costs.

For the purpose of estimating energy consumption for buildings, many researches have been conducted. In this regard, Capozzoli [14] proclaimed that it is exceedingly paramount to have the capability to quickly and reliably estimate the buildings' energy consumption, especially for the public authorities and institutions that own and manage large building stocks. For the purpose of predicting and estimating the energy consumption, some innovative techniques including machine learning, data mining, discovery in database [15] and regression models [16] have been developed and applied. Other researches, e.g. Asadi [17] emphasised that predicting building energy consumption depends on multiple variables such as buildings characteristics, energy systems characteristics, etc.

Likewise, Chai [18] expressed that the smart grid is regarded as the next-generation power system to fulfil the energy consumption challenges. Smart grids have been defined as the power grid systems that incorporate a smart metering infrastructure capable of sensing and measuring power consumption from consumers with the integration of advanced information and communication techniques [19]. In this relation, demand response management (DRM) has been introduced as one of the main features in smart grids. Mohsenian-Rad [20] and Zugno [2] explained that DRM refers to the routines implemented to control the energy consumption at the customer side and aims to improve the energy efficiency and reduce the costs. As such, Karnouskos [21] predicted that in the future, the heterogeneous devices will be able to measure and share their energy consumption and actively participate in house-wide or buildings-wide energy management systems.

Despite the plethora of research on using the mathematical methods to predict the energy consumption, still researchers believe that having access to the buildings information can highly impact the reliability of consumption prediction and estimation for the buildings. As the precedent researches have predicted, nowadays, many buildings are equipped with IoT and smart devices with sensing and measuring capabilities. Although this information is produced for building spaces, they are not accessible for the potential users in the domain of smart energy. In other words, still this valuable asset has not been thoroughly involved in energy management systems. Indeed, to estimate or predict the buildings energy consumption, there is an essential need to have sufficient technical information about building spaces, installed equipment as well as live data from IoT and smart devices.

9.2.2.3 Smart Commerce

Pan [10] introduced the smart commerce by means of using the information about consumption to improve the marketing affairs. Many small businesses can take advantage of this information and technical knowledge. Yan [22] elucidated that both kinds of traditional and online retailers can always gain profit from having information about customers' needs. As such, they concurred that the market information is vital for a firm's decision-making processes. In addition, Yan [22] laid emphasis on the forecast information accuracy effect on the profit of the traditional and online retailers. In this context, he expounded that major retailers such as Marks & Spencer, A&P grocery stores and Von's Supermarket have made substantial investment in the development of tracking information systems, while being engaged in ongoing marketing research to improve the information accuracy [23]. In the light of the studied literature on retailers' efforts, it is indispensable for these small business owners to inspect their customers' needs.

Many businesses and manufacturers providing services and products for buildings can similarly gain benefit from the consumers' information. This information can be related to the building components, e.g. windows, air conditions, pipes, bulbs, etc., or diverse types of IoT devices and sensor, e.g. light sensors, cameras, fire alarms, etc. Some recent researches have been conducted to specify the availability of building components in the market. For instance, Baetens [4] performed a survey on the types of smart windows which are currently available on the market. However, these types of researches have a concentration on the market side, and still there is a need to make the information from the customer side available to the businesses. For instance, in case of having access to the buildings information integrated with the live data, plenty of faulty reports for some devices can disclose performance issues and consequently fewer future demands for some products. As such, manufacturers can use this information to improve quality of their products.

9.3   Challenges and Barriers

With the advancement of technologies related to 'Internet of Things', we inevitably move towards environments characterised by full integration and semantics. Nonetheless, there are some barriers on the way of benefiting from this integration. Some of the barriers stem from various phases of the buildings life cycle, including the design, construction and operation. The design phase of the buildings is an imperative stage through which fundamental information is created. This information is preserved in various forms of plans, report, tables and so forth. In the next phase, i.e. the construction phase, due to variety of changes as a result of different reasons, some updates are produced. These updates are essential for the further steps of the buildings life cycle. In the operation phase, the IoT devices and sensors are responsible for providing information on the current status of the building spaces.

The main barrier originated from the buildings life cycle is that the buildings information is not available in a digital format. For the majority of the existing and even under-construction buildings, architectural, mechanical and all other plans are only available in nondigital formats. Likewise, despite using new emerging technologies, i.e. BIM, to transform the building plans and specifications into the digital format, still the digital buildings information is not available for the other industries. In other words, the users need to have professional skills to use the software associated with the BIM models to be able to access the buildings information.

Another aspect of the integration problem is related to the smart technologies and the IoT devices. These devices have been developed for the environmental monitoring applications [24] or for combinational usage of different context data from different sources [25]. The provided information by these technologies and devices scatters across the separated data storages and in heterogeneous formats. Integration of the data from variety of IoT devices with the digital buildings information is a daunting challenge by itself. All these barriers are the reasons to frustration as for fully benefiting from the buildings information integrated with the live data.

In the following subsections, more detail is provided about all the recognised barriers associated with the above-mentioned issues.

9.3.1 Barriers Associated with the Design Phase

Creation of the buildings information begins from the early design phase. The design process of a buildings is a tacit-dominated phase [26, 27], in which multidisciplinary professionals are sharing and exchanging their knowledge. As Ibrahim and Nissen [28] illuminated, the tacitness of the knowledge can augment the probability of the knowledge loss. As such, Pourzolfaghar [29] pinpointed that the knowledge created by the design professionals tends to reside in their minds as tacit knowledge when not explicitly documented during the design phase of the building projects. This knowledge is invaluable for later use which is why it should be persevered. Therefore, a fraction of the valuable building information is not available due to knowledge loss phenome. To overcome this challenge, Pourzolfaghar [30] developed a theoretical knowledge-based framework to explicate and preserve this knowledge. However, more research work was needed to put this framework into the practice.

Despite losing a fraction of the valuable knowledge, the rest of the buildings information is handed over to the further phases to develop the operational plans. The building plans are normally developed using professional software, e.g. AutoCad, Revitt and so on. All the details for the plans are available in these environments. However, accessing the details of the plans is only possible for the users who have the skills to use these professional environments. As well, for the construction phase, normally the paper version of the plans is used. Apparently, the digital version of the buildings information is not utilisable for the users who are not familiar with the software associated with building plans. In the best condition, the plans are stored in a portable document format (commonly referred to as PDF). As a result, the stored information in this format cannot be combined with digital information from the other sources.

The other issue is related to the overall information about buildings energy consumption and infrastructural estimations. This information is presented in the form of reports as the outcome of the conceptual design phase. The detailed design of the mechanical and electrical plans is based on the estimations reported in the early design phase. This information can play a pivotal role in providing overall energy consumption estimation for a building. Availability of this information for all the buildings in an urban area can be utilised for infrastructure planning in the cities. However, this information is not stored in a digital format along with the other buildings information.

9.3.2 Barriers Associated with the Construction Phase

The construction phase of the building projects is a vibrant phase in which many changes arise. The changes can be the results of various aspects, e.g. design modifications, differing site conditions and so on. These types of changes are norms in the construction phase. As Pettee [31] stressed, there is a need to document these changes as the updates on the buildings information and specifications. The updated version of the building plans is called 'as-built' plans used to show the final version of the implemented works. Updating the building plan is a tedious task for contractors; and providing the as-built plans is often overlooked until the end of the project. Obviously, the delay in the documentation activities can impact the accuracy of the updated information.

The process of updating the plans requires that any changes modifying the original design be incorporated into the plans. Nonetheless, the contractors are not interested in it because of various reasons, e.g. lack of staff, time, budget, commitment, etc. Outdated plans can cause many problems in the construction and operation phases. In principle, the main consequence of this problem leads to an informational gap between the two consequential phases of the construction and operation. Later, in the operation phase, the updated information is required for many different purposes, e.g. for refurbishment of the buildings, repairing or replacing the installed devices. Another consequence of the outdated plans can be attributed to the buildings information modelling technologies. By developing the models based on as-design plans, the accuracy of the models is not ensured. In Sect. 9.3.4, more details are provided on the challenges for buildings information models.

9.3.3   Barriers Associated with the Operations Phase

The technologies developed over the last years for smart environments are currently summarised as the 'Internet of Things'. These technologies produce invaluable information for security management, control management and many other managerial aspects during the buildings operation phase. Schaffers [32] stated that the application of the IoT paradigm to an urban context is of particular interest as it responds to the strong push of the governments to adopt ICT solutions in the management of public affairs to realise the smart city concept. The IoT devices are designed to support the smart city vision, which aims at exploiting the ICTs to provide added-value services for the administration of the city and for the citizens ([33]. As they stressed, by enabling an easy access and interaction with a wide variety of devices, the IoT will foster the development of a number of applications to provide new services to citizens, companies and public administrations.

As [34] emphasised, the IoT paradigm finds application in many different domains, such as home automation, industrial automation, medical aids, energy management and smart grids, facility management and many others. However, a significant challenge remains to design and maintain the connectivity of smart systems by an integrated information system being able to support business processes and interoperability between the systems. As an example, Pan [35] conducted a research to build a unique IoT experimental test-bed for energy efficiency and building intelligence. In their research, they encountered a challenge to organise and integrate heterogeneous IoT devices to work together as a coherent system.

Likewise, Al-Fuqaha [36] underscored that the heterogeneity of the IoT elements needs a thorough solution to make ubiquitous IoT services a reality. To overcome the existing challenges, many researchers have been conducted, e.g. on communication enabling the use of wireless sensor network (WSNs) [37], enabling technologies and application services using a centralised cloud vision [38], enabling technologies with emphasis on the RFID and its potential applications [39], etc. Simultaneously, some other researchers, e.g. Gluhak [40], presented the IoT challenges to bridge the gap between the research and practical aspects.

In summary, most research work has been conducted to overcome the heterogeneity challenges for the IoT devices and sensors. Consequently, many of these researches have proposed solutions to attenuate the recognised challenges. Nevertheless, we believe that there are more potential benefits to the smart cities as long as the live data is integrated with the buildings information. In other words, building environments are still unable to fully benefit from the integration of buildings information with the live data captured from the IoT devices and sensors. Moreover, it is fundamental to bridge the gaps between the research and practice. For instance, it would be worthy to explore and recognise the information required for any specific industry and concentrate on defining meaningful linkages between the buildings information and the live data. In the following section, some research topics are suggested for future studies in this field.

9.3.4 Barriers Associated with Buildings Information Models

Over the last decade, buildings information modelling (BIM) technologies have been developed to manage the buildings information [41]. The BIM models contain valuable information about the building spaces and the installed devices in the buildings. However, the buildings information in BIM models are only available through the developed BIM models for the buildings. Moreover, still a large number of challenges are faced by BIM models, e.g. a pertinent semantic format for the maintenance stage [42], computerised facility management system integration [43] and updated data for as-built BIM models [41].

As further explanation for the latter challenge, the BIM models are mostly developed based on the existing plans for the buildings and are not incorporated with the IoT devices and sensors specifications which have been installed later for management purposes (e.g. for security management, energy consumption, etc.). In this condition, there is no possibility to update the buildings information regarding the new installed devices. Therefore, there is a high risk when there is a lack of updated information on the new devices for BIM models. Moreover, Mikučionienė [44] reported that the data required for the maintenance stage and the usable format are not necessarily stored in BIM. Maintenance companies need a specific type of information for the processes. For instance, they need to receive some information like the warranty of the device, technical information and building space as soon as a fault occurs. This can happen in case of the existence of a linkage between BIM models and all the installed IoT devices ad sensors. Similarly, Construction Operations Building Information Exchange (COBie) has been criticised for its inability to ensure comprehensive semantic data for the maintenance stage [14].

Similarly, several researchers have reported challenges for the maintenance stage. As Winch [45] and Shen [42] stated, some identified challenges relate to interoperability, interfaces with other systems as well as integration of wired and wireless sensor networks to enhance the live data collection during the construction phase and controlling the access to the project information. In line with this, Motawa and Almarshad [46] proclaimed that the building maintenance requires a comprehensive information system that captures/retrieves the information on the building maintenance components and all its related building components. Although they proposed an integrated information/knowledge system, this system was limited to capturing and retrieving data during the maintenance phase. Obviously, many researches have proposed methods and models to integrate the buildings information with the captured data to facilitate the building maintenance. However, inadequate data integration is a current challenge faced by building information models which stems from differences in the data syntax, schema or semantics [44]. Cohen [47] defined data integration as 'the combination of data from different sources with unified access to the data for its users'. Regarding the above-mentioned points, integration of data from diverse sources has been introduced as a challenge which prevents the potential users from taking advantage of the values of the integrated data.

9.3.5 Summary of the Challenges

Based on the reviewed literature, some barriers have been recognised as hampering the benefits gained from the valuable buildings information integrated with the live captured data in the building environments. What follows is a summary of these obstacles. First, no digital buildings information is accessible for the potential users in the smart cities, e.g. for facility management, utility companies, etc. The other barrier is related to the data captured form the IoT devices and sensors. This information scatters across the separated data storages and in heterogeneous formats. Consequently, integration of the buildings information with the live captured data has been recognised as the third barrier.

Although, during the last decades, BIM technologies have emerged for digitalising buildings information, this digital information needs to be available to other domains. Difficulty of extracting the buildings information from BIM models and making it accessible to the potential users is another barrier. A summary of the recognised barriers and their associated origins is provided in Table 9.1.

By reviewing the information provided in Table 9.1, it is evident that the recognised barriers are associated with three various aspects. The first group of the barriers arises from the design phase of the building projects. More details in the second column of Table 9.1 are to describe the origins of the barriers. The barriers for the design phase are mostly related to lack of explication on the fraction of the buildings

Table 9.1 Summary of the challenges to integrate the buildings information and the live data

Challenges associated with	Recognised challenges
Design phase	Tacitness of knowledge during the design phase of the buildings leads to loss of some parts of valuable buildings information
	The buildings information is stored in the form of architectural, mechanical plans or other plans (e.g. DWG format or reports) and is not accessible for the users of the other industries
	The general information about energy consumption is not available in the digital format (e.g. for authorities or utility companies)
	The information about the installed devices is not available for commercial purposes (e.g. for demand management purpose)
Construction phase	High risk of missing the updated buildings information
	High risk of handing over not updated plans to the operation phase
	Due to delays on documenting the changes, accuracy of the updates is not ensured
Operation phase	To organise and integrate heterogeneous IoT devices to work together
	Various applications and software store the live data in various formats
	Aggregation of the live data captured by various devices is a challenge
	Integration of the data from the IoT devices and sensors with the buildings information
BIM models	In BIM models, the buildings information is not available in digital format for the other industries
	Extraction of the buildings information from BIM models
	High risk of not updated information on the new devices for BIM models
	Accessing the buildings information is possible by using the BIM environment and needs professional skills
	The data required for potential users and the usable format are not necessarily stored in BIM

information which can be useful for the construction industry, as well as the other industries in the smart cities.

The second group of barriers are mostly associated with the IoT devices and their challenges for interoperability and integrity issues. Many researches have been conducted to propose solutions to provide communications between various IoT systems. Nonetheless, there is a need to investigate the applicability of these communications between the IoT devices applications and systems in the construction industry. Then, the next step would be to deal with the integration of the outcomes of these applications and systems with the digital buildings information.

The last group of barriers is related to the sematic and the format of the digitalised version of the buildings information through BIM technologies. Although huge efforts have been exerted in favour of developing these technologies, still there is long journey ahead to make the digital buildings information available for other smart domains. For this purpose, it is vital to recognise and extract the required information for various industries.

9.4   Conclusion

Various industries in smart cities can benefit from information from other domains to provide more effective services for the citizens. The buildings information is one of the essential sources of information in smart cities which can be utilised by many industries, e.g. facility management, smart grid, smart commerce, etc. Buildings information is created during various phases of a building life cycle. Live data is a dynamic part of the building information which is produced by IoT devices during the operation phase. Integration of the building information with the live data can assist many industries in providing more efficient services to the smart cities' citizens. However, there are barriers which disallow the potential users to take advantage from aggregation of the building information and the live data. In this chapter, we introduced some potential users of the building information. Simultaneously, we discussed the ways they may improve their services utilising the buildings information.

Then, the origins of the barriers were explored and explained thoroughly. Based on the studied literature, two main areas associated with these challenges were recognised, including (1) the barriers stemming from different phases of the building life cycle including the design, construction and operations and (2) the barriers associated with BIM models for the buildings. By bearing these studies and findings in mind, this chapter culminates by suggesting some areas for future research to remove the recognised barriers. The suggested areas are stated as follows:

- Development of a method to digitalise the buildings information created during the design phase
- Development of a method to use the data captured from the IoT devices to update the building plans during the construction phase
- Development of a method to integrate the buildings information with the live captured data from IoT devices during the operation phase
- Development of a method to extract the required buildings information from BIM models
- Development of a framework to recognise the required buildings information for the targeted smart industries
- Establishment of an open storage to preserve the integrated information in an appropriate format consistent with the construction industry standards with the ability of being shared with the other industries for improving their services

The proposed areas of the research can be put together to help integrate the buildings information with the live data available to the industries in the smart cities.

Acknowledgement This work was supported, in part, by Science Foundation Ireland grant 13/RC/2094 and co-funded under the European Regional Development Fund through the Southern and Eastern Regional Operational Programme to Lero – the Irish Software Research Centre (www.lero.ie).

References

1. Schaffers H, Ratti C, Komninos N (2012) Special issue on smart applications for smart cities-new approaches to innovation: guest editors' introduction. J Theor Appl Electron Commerce Res 7(3):ii–iv
2. Zugno M, Morales JM, Pinson P, Madsen H (2013) A bilevel model for electricity retailers' participation in a demand response market environment. Energy Econ 36:182–197
3. Zhou Z, Zhao F, Wang J (2011) Agent-based electricity market simulation with demand response from commercial buildings. IEEE Trans SMART Grid 2(4):580–588
4. Baetens R, PetterJelle B, Gustavsen A (2010) Properties, requirements and possibilities of smart windows for dynamic daylight and solar energy control in buildings: a state-of-the-art review. Solar Energy Mater Solar Cells 94:87–105
5. Wenge R, Zhang X, Dave C, Chao L, Hao S (2014) Smart city architecture: a technology guide for implementation and design challenges. China Commun 11(3):56–69
6. Hollands RG (2008) Will the real smart city please stand up? Intelligent, progressive or entrepreneurial? City 12(3):303–320
7. Komninos N (2008) Intelligent cities and globalisation of innovation networks. Routledge, London
8. Bischof S, Karapantelakis A, Nechifor CS, Sheth A P, Mileo A, Barnaghi P (2014) Semantic modelling of smart city data
9. Anthopoulos L, Fitsilis P (2010) From digital to ubiquitous cities: defining a common architecture for urban development. In: Intelligent environments (IE), 2010 sixth international conference on IEEE, 301–306
10. Pan G, Qi G, Zhang W, Li S, Wu Z, Yang LT (2013) Trace analysis and mining for smart cities: issues, methods, and applications. IEEE Commun Mag 51(6):120–126
11. Rondeau EP, Brown RK, Lapides PD (2012) Facility management. Wiley, Hoboken
12. Lavy S, Jawadekar S (2014) A case study of using BIM and COBie for facility management. Int J Facility Manag 5(2)
13. General Services Administration (GSA) (2011) GSA building information modeling guide series: 08 – GSA BIM guide for facility management, version 1 – December 2011, U.S. General Services Administration, Public Buildings Service, Office of Design and Construction
14. Capozzoli A, Grassi D, Causone F (2015) Estimation models of heating energy consumption in schools for local authorities planning. Energy Build 105:302–313
15. Yu Z, Haghighat F, Fung BCM, Yoshino H (2010) A decision tree method for building energy demand modeling. Energy Build 42:1637–1646
16. Korolija I, Zhang Y, Marjanovic-Halburd L, Hanby VI (2013) Regression models for predicting UK office building energy consumption from heating and cooling demands. Energy Build 59:214–227
17. Asadi S, Shams Amiri S, Mottahed M (2014) On the development of multi-linear regression analysis to assess energy consumption in the early stages of building design. Energy Build 85:246–255
18. Chai B, Chen J, Yang Z, Zhang Y (2014) Demand response management with multiple utility companies: a two-level game approach. IEEE Trans Smart Grid 5(2):722–731
19. Farhangi H (2010) The path of the smart grid. IEEE Power Energy Mag 8(1):18–28
20. Mohsenian-Rad AH, Leon-Garcia A (2010) Optimal residential load control with price prediction in real-time electricity pricing environments. IEEE Trans Smart Grid 1(2):120–133
21. Karnouskos S (2010) The cooperative internet of things enabled smart grid. In: Proceedings of the 14th IEEE International Symposium on Consumer Electronics (ISCE 2010)
22. Yan R, Ghose S (2010) Forecast information and traditional retailer performance in a dual-channel competitive market. J Bus Res 63:77–83
23. He C, Marklund J, Vossen T (2008) Vertical information sharing in a volatile market. Mark Sci 27(3):513–530

24. Szewczyk R, Mainwaring A, Polastre J, Anderson J, Culler D (2004) An analysis of a large scale habitat monitoring application. In: Proceedings of the 2nd international conference on embedded networked sensor systems, pp 214–226
25. D'Elia A, Roffia L, Zamagni G, Vergari F, Bellavista P, Toninelli A, Mattarozzi S (2010) Smart applications for the maintenance of large buildings: how to achieve ontology-based interoperability at the information level. In: Computers and communications (ISCC), 2010 IEEE symposium, pp 1077–1082
26. Ibrahim R, Fay R (2006) Enhancing cognition by understanding knowledge flow characteristics during design collaboration. ALAM CIPTA Int J Sustain Trop Des Res Pract 1(1):9–16
27. Ibrahim R, Paulson B (2008) Discontinuity in organisations: identifying business environments affecting efficiency of knowledge flows in product lifecycle management. Int J Prod Lifecycle Manag 3(1):21–36
28. Ibrahim R, Nissen M (2007) Discontinuity in organizations: developing a knowledge-based organizational performance model for discontinuous membership. Int J Knowl Manag 3(1):18–36
29. Pourzolfaghar Z (2012) Improving tacit knowledge capture during conceptual design phase of building projects, UK, UMI Thesis Publications, ProQuest LLC
30. Pourzolfaghar Z, Ibrahim R, Abdullah R, Adam NM, Abang Ali AA (2013) Improving dynamic knowledge movements with a knowledge-based framework during conceptual design of a green building project. Int J Knowl Manag 9(2):62–79
31. Pettee S (2005) As-builts-problems & proposed solutions. CM eJournal
32. Schaffers H, Komninos N, Pallot M, Trousse B, Nilsson M, Oliveira A (2011) Smart cities and the future internet: towards cooperation frameworks for open innovation, the future internet. Lect Notes Comput Sci 6656:431–446
33. Zanella A, Bui N, Castellani A, Vangelista L, Zorzi M (2014) Internet of things for smart cities. IEEE Internet Things J 1(1):22–32
34. Bellavista P, Cardone G, Corradi A, Foschini L (2013) Convergence of MANET and WSN in IoT urban scenarios. IEEE Sens J 13(10):3558–3567
35. Pan J, Jain R, Paul S, Vu T, Saifullah A, Sha M (2015) An internet of things framework for smart energy in buildings: designs, prototype, and experiments. IEEE Internet Things J 2(6):527–537
36. Al-Fuqaha A, Guizani M, Mohammadi M, Aledhari M, Ayyash M (2015) Internet of things: a survey on enabling technologies, protocols, and applications. IEEE Commun Surv Tutor 17(4):2347–2376
37. Atzori L, Iera A, Morabito G (2010) The internet of things: A survey. Comput Netw 54(15):2787–2805
38. Gubbi J, Buyya R, Marusic S, Palaniswami M (2013) Internet of Things (IoT): a vision, architectural elements, and future directions. Future Generation Comput Syst 29(7):1645–1660
39. Yang DL, Liu F, Liang YD (2010) A survey of the internet of things. In: Proceedings of the 1st international conference on E-Business Intelligence (ICEBI2010), Atlantis Press
40. Gluhak A, Krco S, Nati M, Pfisterer D, Mitton N, Razafindralambo T (2011) A survey on facilities for experimental internet of things research. IEEE Commun Mag 49(11):58–67
41. Gu N, Singh V, London K, Brankovic L, Taylor C (2008) Adopting building information modeling (BIM) as collaboration platform in the design industry. In: CAADRIA 2008: Beyond computer-aided design, proceedings of the 13th conference on Computer Aided Architectural Design Research in Asia, The Association for Computer Aided Architectural Design Research in Asia (CAADRIA)
42. Shen W, Hao Q, Mak H, Neelamkavil J, Xie H, Dickinson J, Xue H (2010) Systems integration and collaboration in architecture, engineering, construction, and facilities management: a review. Adv Eng Inform 24(2):196–207
43. Becerik-Gerber B, Jazizadeh F, Li N, Calis G (2011) Application areas and data requirements for BIM-enabled facilities management. J Constr Eng Manag 138(3):431–442

44. Mikučionienė R, Martinaitis V, Keras E (2014) Evaluation of energy efficiency measures sustainability by decision tree method. Energy Build 76:64–71
45. Winch GM (2010) Managing construction projects. Wiley, Chichester
46. Motawa I, Almarshad A (2013) A knowledge-based BIM system for building maintenance. Autom Constr 29:173–182
47. Cohen B (2012) What exactly is a smart city? www.fastcoexist.com/1680538/what-exactly-is-a-smart-cityIntelligence. Collective intelligence handbook

Part III
Advances and Latest Research

Chapter 10
Interoperability in the Internet of Things with Asymmetric Schema Matching

José Carlos Martins Delgado

Abstract Interoperability is one of the main challenges of the Internet of Things environments, given the huge number of interconnected devices and the wide range of manufacturers and models. The classical solution, symmetric interoperability, in which both interacting devices share the same data schema, usually leads to a coupling problem, since a device cannot change its schema without changing it as well in the devices with which it interacts. This chapter proposes asymmetric interoperability mechanism, in which the schema used to produce a message does not need to be identical to the schema of the messages expected by the receiver. This leads to a lower coupling level and allows a device to interact with others, which send or receive messages with different schemas, and to replace another one with a new schema without impairing existing interactions. This asymmetry in interoperability is based on the concept of structural compliance and conformance, which state that schemas need only be compatible in the message components that are actually used and not in the full message schema. A simple interoperability framework and a model of coupling, adaptability and changeability are presented to illustrate the impact of these concepts. A few implementation examples are also provided.

10.1 Introduction

The Internet of Things (IoT) paradigm is currently experiencing an explosive growth. Gartner [1] estimated that, by the end of 2016, around 6.4 billion IoT devices were in use, with a forecast of 20.8 billion for 2020. Other analysts predict much higher numbers [2]. Independently of the numbers, the fact is that there will be a huge number of devices, from a large number of manufacturers with a wide variety of models, all needing to interact. Interoperability is thus one of the main challenges of the IoT environments [3]. The obvious solution is to define standard

J.C.M. Delgado (✉)
Instituto Superior Técnico, Universidade de Lisboa, Porto Salvo, Portugal
e-mail: jose.delgado@tecnico.ulisboa.pt

© Springer International Publishing AG 2017
Z. Mahmood (ed.), *Connected Environments for the Internet of Things*,
Computer Communications and Networks,
https://doi.org/10.1007/978-3-319-70102-8_10

APIs that all devices should implement, thereby making interaction between devices an achievable goal. In practice, however, several issues conspire to make this a hard problem to overcome:

- De jure standards require time for technology to settle down, something unlikely to readily occur in such a young and vigorous field as IoT.
- De facto standards can only be imposed by a giant provider, such as Amazon or Microsoft. Again, this is not easy to achieve, given the enormous variability of manufacturers, devices and applications.
- Even if a standard is successful, its main usefulness rests with the consumers, by reducing the vendor lock-in. For providers, it can be a straitjacket that hampers differentiation from competition and added value from additional, vendor-specific features (which leads to vendor lock-in). This expresses the conflicting nature of standards.

Without standard application programming interfaces (APIs), interoperability is possible if interacting devices agree on data and/or service schemas, typically based on data description languages such as Extensible Markup Language (XML) [4] and JavaScript Object Notation (JSON) [5] and on service models such as Service-Oriented Architecture (SOA) [6] and Representational State Transfer (REST) [7]. These technologies were not conceived for small devices requiring weak computing power, such as those typically found in the IoT, but their main disadvantage is that they are symmetric, in the sense that both the sender and receiver of a message must use the same schema. This means that:

- Sharing a schema description, such as an XML Schema file or a Web Services Description Language (WSDL) file
- Agreeing, prior to interaction, on a fixed schema (typical of JSON-based data)

This entails more coupling than actually needed, because the interacting devices need to support all the data values valid for the schema, even if they use only a fraction of these values. Worse, they do not even allow variations on the schema, which means that a sender can only interact with the specific receiver for which it was designed. To solve this problem, we propose to use asymmetric interoperability, based on the concepts of compliance and conformance, as follows:

- The schema of the sender must comply with that of the receiver. This means that the schema of the sender needs to include all the mandatory features of the schema of the receiver but may or may not include the optional features (if not specified, the receiver may use default values) and may include any additional feature, not present in the schema of the receiver, which will ignore it.
- The schema of the receiver needs to conform to the schema that the sender requires. This means that the receiver needs to implement at least all the features that the sender expects that the receiver supports but can also implement others that the sender does not know about.

Compliance allows a sender to meaningfully transmit a message to many receivers, not just to one that implements the same schema as the sender.

Conformance allows a receiver to meaningfully receive messages from many senders, not just from those that implement the same schema. Both are ways to reduce coupling between the interacting devices and to increase the interoperability range. Taking a basic API (standard or not) as a starting point, variations to that API are allowed at both the sender and the receiver, as long as compliance and conformance hold. There is no longer the need to stick to a fixed API. It should be noted that interacting devices can reverse the roles of sender and receiver during a message-based transaction (request and response) or by changing the device that takes the initiative to start a transaction.

This chapter is structured as follows. Section 10.2 describes some of the existing technologies relevant to the context of this chapter. Section 10.3 describes what device interaction involves, whereas Sects. 10.4, 10.5 and 10.6 detail some of the interoperability, coupling and adaptability and changeability aspects, respectively. Section 10.7 discusses the importance of the architectural style used for device interaction. Section 10.8 lays out the main proposal of this chapter, asymmetric interoperability, and Sects. 10.9 and 10.10 discuss the underlying data model and asymmetric interoperability concepts (compliance and conformance), respectively. Finally, Sect. 10.11 provides some illustrative examples.

10.2   Background

The Internet of Things (IoT) has definitely become mainstream [8] and is now the subject of active research [9, 10]. The Internet World Stats (http://www.internetworldstats.com/stats.htm) estimates the number of Internet human users to be around 3.7 billion in 2017, almost half the worldwide population of roughly 7.5 billion people. By 2050, the worldwide population is expected to grow to around 9.5 billion.

This contrasts with the conservative Gartner predictions [1]; according to which, in 2017, the number of IoT devices will be comparable to the worldwide human population, whereas in 2020 that number will have roughly tripled, and it is almost impossible to predict what that number will be by 2050!

The number of Internet-enabled devices is thus clearly growing much faster than the number of Internet human users, which means that the Internet is no longer dominated by humans but rather by smart devices that are small computers and require technologies suitable to them, instead of those conventionally used in Internet browsers. The sheer number and diversity of IoT devices entail an enormous problem in interconnecting the applications running on the devices. The Internet is global, distributed and huge, while still requiring that any device, subject to specific interoperability requirements, be able to interact with any other device.

Distributed interoperability is not specific of the IoT context. It has been studied in domains such as enterprise cooperation [11], e-government services [12], cloud computing [13] and healthcare applications [14]. Most of these domains involve applications running on full-fledged servers, not on the much simpler IoT devices, such as those involved in sensor networks [15] and vehicular [16] networks. The two main technological solutions for distributed interoperability, Web Services [17] and RESTful APIs [18], are based on data description languages such as XML and JSON.

SOA [19] is the architectural style underlying Web Services and models real-world entities by the behaviour (services) they can offer. REST [7] is the architectural style underlying RESTful APIs and models real-world entities by the structural state (resources) they can exhibit. A continuing debate has been going on over the past years about which architectural style – SOA or REST – is more adequate to specific classes of applications. The literature comparing these styles is vast [20, 21], usually with arguments more on technological issues than on conceptual and modelling arguments. [22] have made proposals to integrate SOA and RESTful services.

Although, these architectural styles and technologies have been able to connect distributed, independent and heterogeneous applications, they entail a significant level of coupling, in the sense that interacting applications need to share the same data description schema. A change in one application will most likely imply a change in the other.

Many metrics have been proposed to assess the maintainability of distributed systems, based essentially on structural features. Babu and Darsi [23] present an extensive set of metrics for service coupling, cohesion and complexity. Other authors focus on dynamic, rather than static, coupling. The authors of [24] present a survey of metrics for assessing coupling during program execution. Although centred on object-oriented programming, many of these metrics can also apply to distributed systems. There are also approaches trying to combine structural coupling with other levels of coupling, such as semantics [25].

We are also interested in compliance [26] and conformance [27] as the foundational mechanisms to ensure partial interoperability and thus minimize coupling. These mechanisms have also been studied in specific contexts, such as choreography [28], modelling [29], programming [30] and standards [31].

Searching for an interoperable device can be done in the conventional way, by schema matching with similarity algorithms [32] and ontology matching and mapping [33]. However, this does not ensure that interoperability and manual adaptations are usually unavoidable. Requiring that names of corresponding components be the same, when matching schemas, is limitative. An ontology matching and mapping [33] can be performed, but it is not easy to map different things. Compliance and conformance can come to the rescue, if ontology concepts are defined structurally in terms of more basic concepts that define an upper ontology [34]. Then, ontology mapping is just a question of checking compliance and conformance between concepts in two different ontologies.

10.3   Interaction Between Devices

As in most distributed systems, IoT devices interact by sending each other messages. When a given device needs to make some request or notification to another
device, the former plays the role of *consumer* of the functionality provided by the
latter, which plays the role of *provider*. A typical interaction is initiated by the consumer, which sends a request message to the provider, through some interconnecting network, which may cause the provider, upon executing the request, to answer
with a response message, as illustrated by Fig. 10.1.

This interaction makes sense only if the provider is able to understand what the
consumer is requesting and reacts and responds accordingly to what the consumer
expects. If the consumer and the provider were modules within the same application,
this would be a simple task. The network would simply be a reliable pointer, and the
module compatibility would be checked by a type system that relies on shared type
names and inheritance hierarchies.

In a distributed environment, however, type sharing is not guaranteed, since
devices and their applications evolve independently, and messages cannot be
assumed to be correct. The goal of achieving such a simple interaction can be
decomposed into the following objectives:

1. The request message reaches the provider, through a network.
2. The provider is willing to accept and to process the request.
3. The provider validates the request, according to its requirements for requests.
4. The provider understands what the consumer is requesting.
5. The reaction of the provider and the corresponding effects, as a consequence of
   executing the request message, fulfil the expectations of the consumer regarding
   that reaction.
6. The response message reaches the consumer.
7. The consumer is willing to accept and to process the response.
8. The consumer validates the response, according to its requirements for the
   response.
9. The consumer understands what the provider is responding.
10. The consumer reacts appropriately to the response, fulfilling the purpose of the
    provider in sending that response.

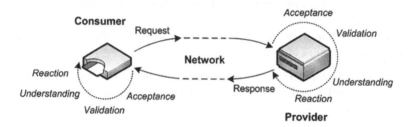

Fig. 10.1 Details of a message-based interaction between two IoT devices

What this means is that it is not enough for a device to send a request to another one and hope that everything goes well. Both request and response need to be validated and understood by the device that receives it. In general, meaningfully sending a message (the response reverses the roles of the consumer and the producer as sender and receiver, with regard to the request) entails the following aspects:

- *Willingness* (objectives 2 and 7). Both sender and receiver are devices that need to interact and, by definition, are willing to accept requests and responses, by running applications that expose services. However, non-functional aspects such as response times or security requirements can impose constraints.
- *Intent* (objectives 4 and 9). Sending a message must have a given intent, inherent to the interaction to which it belongs. This is related to the motivation to interact and the goals to achieve with that interaction.
- *Content* (objectives 3 and 8). This concerns the generation and interpretation of the content of a message by the sender, expressed by some representation, in such a way that the receiver is also able to interpret it.
- *Transfer* (objectives 1 and 6). The message content needs to be successfully transferred from the context of the sender to the context of the receiver.
- *Reaction* (objectives 5 and 10). This concerns the reaction of the receiver upon reception of a message, which should produce effects according to the expectations of the sender.

Device interaction is a complex issue with many factors, such as:

- *Interoperability* – Guaranteeing that one device understands the requests of another and reacts according to what is expected.
- *Coupling* – Mutual dependencies between devices, with the goal of reducing them as much as possible, to avoid unnecessary constraints to the evolution and variability of devices.
- *Adaptability* – Maintaining interoperability, even when interacting devices change some of their characteristics.
- *Architectural style* – Choosing how devices are modelled has a relevant impact on how devices interact.
- *Reliability* – Maintaining interoperability, even in the presence of unanticipated failures.
- *Security* – Ensuring interoperability is allowed only intentionally and with authorized and certified devices.
- *Performance* – Ensuring that interactions complete faster than agreed response times.
- *Scalability* – Ensuring that performance levels do not decrease substantially when the number of interacting devices increases.

To limit its breadth and scope, this chapter concentrates on the first three of the above, which deal with the basic aspects of device interaction. These are detailed in the following sections.

10.4   Interoperability

There is no universally accepted definition of interoperability, since its meaning can vary accordingly to the perspective, context and domain under consideration. Although limited to information, the 24765 standard [35] provides the probably most cited definition of interoperability as "the ability of two or more systems or components to exchange information and to use the information that has been exchanged".

Inspired by Fig. 10.1 in the context of IoT, we interpret this definition as "the ability of two or more devices to exchange messages and to react to them according to some pattern or contract that fulfils the constraints and expectations of all devices involved". What this really means cannot be taken as a whole but rather needs to be detailed, as the previous section has already hinted with the various aspects involved in an interaction, namely, intent, content, reaction and transfer.

Interoperability involves several abstraction layers, from low-level networking issues to high-level aspects reflecting the purpose of the interaction. Layering is an abstraction mechanism useful to deal with complexity. One early example is the Open Systems Interconnection (OSI) reference model [36], with seven layers, although it concentrates on the networking issues. This chapter proposes a different layering mechanism, detailing higher-level issues, as described in Table 10.1.

Using the Category column as the top organizing feature, Table 10.1 can be briefly described in the following way:

- *Symbiotic*. This category expresses the interaction nature of two interacting devices in a mutually beneficial agreement. This can be a tight coordination under a common governance, if the devices are controlled by the same entity, a joint-venture agreement, if there are two substantially aligned clusters of devices or a mere collaboration involving a partnership agreement and if some goals are shared.
- *Pragmatic*. The interaction between a consumer and a provider is done in the context of a contract, which is implemented by a choreography that coordinates processes, which in turn implement workflow behaviour by orchestrating service invocations.
- *Semantic*. Interacting devices must be able to understand the meaning of the content of the messages exchanged, both requests and responses. This implies compatibility in rules, knowledge and ontologies, so that meaning is not lost when transferring a message from the context of the sender to that of the receiver.
- *Syntactic*. This category deals mainly with form, rather than content. Each message has a structure, composed by data (primitive objects) according to some structural definition (its schema). The data in messages need to be serialized to be sent over the channel, using formats such as XML or JSON.
- *Connective*. The main objective in this category is to transfer a message from one device to another, regardless of its content. This usually involves enclosing that content in another message with control information and implementing a message protocol over a communications network protocol and possibly involving routing gateways.

Table 10.1 Layers of interoperability between IoT devices

Category	Layer	Main concern	Description
Symbiotic (purpose and intent)	Coordination	Governance	Motivations to have the interaction, with varying levels of mutual knowledge of governance, strategy and goals
	Alignment	Joint venture	
	Collaboration	Partnership	
Pragmatic (reaction and effects)	Contract	Choreography	Management of the effects of the interaction at the levels of choreography, process and service
	Workflow	Process	
	Interface	Service	
Semantic (meaning of content)	Inference	Rule base	Interpretation of a message in context, at the levels of rule, known application components and relations and definition of concepts
	Knowledge	Knowledge base	
	Ontology	Concept	
Syntactic (notation of representation)	Structure	Schema	Representation of application components, in terms of composition, primitive components and their serialization format in messages
	Predefined type	Primitive object	
	Serialization	Message format	
Connective (transfer protocol)	Messaging	Message protocol	Lower-level formats and network protocols involved in transferring a message from the context of the sender to that of the receiver
	Routing	Gateway	
	Communication	Network protocol	
	Physics	Media protocol	

This is a maximalist model, in the sense that all layers are involved in every interaction. Even the simplest interaction has a purpose, is part of a choreography, involves meaning, has a structure and needs a network to send the messages. However, in practice most of these layers are dealt with *tacitly* (based on unverified assumptions that are supported by documentation at best) or *empirically* (based on verified assumptions but hidden by already existing specifications or tools).

The most relevant layers are typically the structure (schema), those below it, and interface (service). The ontology layer (concept) has gained relevance in the last few years [37], given the high variability of devices in the IoT context and the need to resort to semantics to clarify the meaning of the schemas and of the services' interface.

10.5 Coupling

All these interoperability layers, as mentioned above, constitute an expression of device coupling, leading to two conflicting aspects:

- *Coupling* – Decoupled devices (with no interactions or dependencies between them) can evolve freely and independently, which favours adaptability, change-ability and even reliability (if one fails, there is no impact on the other). Therefore, coupling should be avoided as much as possible.
- *Interoperability* – Devices need to interact to cooperate towards common or complementary objectives, which implies that some degree of previously agreed mutual knowledge is indispensable.

The more feature devices make known to others, the easier it is to provide interoperability but the greater coupling it can get. Therefore, the fundamental problem of device interaction is to provide the maximum decoupling possible (exposing the minimum possible number of features) while ensuring the minimum interoperability requirements. In other words, the main goal is to ensure that each device knows just enough about others to be able to interoperate with them but no more than that, to avoid unnecessary dependencies and constraints. This is an instance of the *principle of least knowledge* [38].

The usefulness of Table 10.1 lies in providing a framework that allows coupling details to be better understood, namely, at which interoperability layers they occur and what is involved in each layer, instead of having just a blurry notion of dependency. In this respect, it constitutes a tool to analyse and to compare different coupling models and technologies. Reducing the coupling increases the following:

- The probability of finding suitable alternatives or replacements for a given device
- The set of devices with which some device is compatible, as a consumer or as a provider

Figure 10.2 depicts the scenario of a device immersed in its environment, in which it acts as a provider for a set of devices (its consumers), from which it receives requests or event notifications and, as a consumer of another set of devices (its providers), to which it sends requests or event notifications. Coupling between this device and others expresses not only how much it depends on its providers but also how much its consumers depend on it.

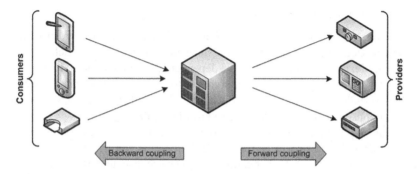

Fig. 10.2 Coupling between a device and its consumers and providers

Dependency on a device can be assessed by the fraction of its features that impose constraints on other devices. Two coupling metrics can be defined from the point of view of a given device (Fig. 10.2):

- C_F (*forward coupling*), which expresses how much a device is dependent on its providers, is defined as:

$$C_F = \frac{\sum_{i \in P} \frac{Up_i}{Tp_i \cdot N_i}}{|P|} \tag{10.1}$$

where:

P is the set of providers that this device uses.
$|P|$ denotes the cardinality of P.
Up_i is the number of features that this device uses in provider i.
Tp_i is the total number of features that provider i exposes.
N_i is the number of providers with which this device is compatible as a consumer, in all uses of features of provider i by this device.

- C_B (*backward coupling*), which expresses how much impact a device has on its consumers, is defined as:

$$C_B = \frac{\sum_{i \in C} \frac{Uc_i}{Tc \cdot M}}{|C|} \tag{10.2}$$

where:

C is the set of consumers that use this device as provider.
$|C|$ denotes the cardinality of C.
Uc_i is the number of features of this device that consumer i uses.
Tc is the total number of features that this device exposes.
M is the number of known devices that are compatible with this application and can replace it, as a provider.

The conclusion from metric 10.1 is that the existence of alternative providers to a device reduces its forward coupling C_F, since more devices (with which this device is compatible, as a consumer) dilute the dependency. Similarly, the conclusion from metric 10.2 is that the existence of alternatives to a device as a provider reduces the system dependency on it, thereby reducing the impact that device may have on its potential consumers and therefore its backward coupling C_B.

In either case, increasing the number of compatible alternatives implies reducing the number of features required for compatibility. Less constraints generally mean more compatible devices. Lower coupling is the basic tenet underlying this chapter. Section 10.10 shows how this can be done.

10.6   Adaptability and Changeability

An *adaptation* of a device is a set of changes made to that device due to a new specification. This implicitly assumes that the device already exists and that the changes made correspond to a solution to bridge the differences between the previous and the new specification. We assume that devices can be atomic (not composed of others) or structured (composed of other devices, recursively until atomic devices are reached). There must be a finite set of atomic resource types, upon which a device ontology can be built. We consider only the structural aspects and assume that adaptations and changes to atomic devices are also atomic.

The *similarity* between a device after adaptation and its previous specification is defined recursively in terms of the similarities of its components as:

$$S = \begin{cases} 0 & changed\ atomic\ device \\ 1 & unchanged\ atomic\ device \\ \dfrac{\sum_{i \in T} S_i}{|T|} & structured\ device \end{cases} \quad (10.3)$$

where:

T is the set of components of this device.
S_i is the similarity of component i (recursively) of the device.

A similarity of 1 means that nothing has changed, whereas a similarity of 0 means that all components of a device have changed.

The *adaptability* of a device expresses how easily it can suffer a given adaptation. As a metric, a value of 0 in adaptability means that the device cannot be adapted and is unable to support the new intended specification, due to some limitation, and a value of 1 means that the cost or effort of adaptation is zero. It depends essentially on two factors:

- The *forward decoupling* D_F, the decoupling between the device and its provider. We use decoupling instead of coupling to reflect what we want to achieve.

$$D_F = 1 - C_F \quad (10.4)$$

- The *similarity* S between the specification of the device before and after the adaptation.

Adaptability A is directly proportional to these two factors:

$$A = D_F \cdot S \quad (10.5)$$

Adaptability does not depend on which devices use the device being adapted and reflects only the ability (*can* it be adapted?) and the cost/effort to adapt it. Many changes (low S) or a high dependency on other devices (low D_F) reduces adaptability. The complementary adaptation question (*may* it be adapted?) is included in its *changeability* property Ch [39], defined here as:

$$Ch = D_B \cdot D_F \cdot S \tag{10.6}$$

or

$$Ch = D_B \cdot A \tag{10.7}$$

in which

$$D_B = 1 - C_B \tag{10.8}$$

D_B is the *backward decoupling* between the device being adapted and its consumers, expressing the impact of the adaptation of the device. If many consumer devices are affected (low D_B), changeability becomes lower than desirable. All the factors in Eq. 10.6 vary between 0 and 1. Any low value becomes dominant and imposes a low value on the changeability, which translates to a poor device architecture or implementation.

The conclusion from this equation is that a device is more changeable (impacts less its consumers and its use of providers) for a given similarity (which expresses the degree of changes made) if it has a higher forward and backward decoupling (lower coupling). This is in line with the conclusion of the previous section.

10.7   Architectural Style

An architectural style can be defined as a collection of design patterns, guidelines and best practices to design the architecture of a system [40]. SOA [6] and REST [7] are the main architectural styles in use today for distributed system interoperability.

In SOA, each problem-domain entity should be modelled as closely as possible, in a one-to-one mapping. A small change in the problem should yield a small change in the SOA model. Each entity has its own interface, which means that a consumer using the functionality of a provider needs to know the operations and semantics of the interface of the latter. The REST proponents contend that this is an unacceptable coupling, hampering scalability and changeability. A consumer should only know the provider's link (Uniform Resource Identifier – URI – in Web terms), obtain a representation of it (an universal operation) and from then onwards follow the links contained in that representation by using only a fixed set of universal operations, supported by all the devices [41].

Fielding, the creator of REST, designated this as "hypermedia as the engine of application state" (HATEOAS) [42]. The basic idea is that the client (consumer) needs to know very little about the server (provider), since it only follows the links that the server provides, and that the server needs to know nothing about the client, which has the responsibility to decide which link to follow. The intended goal is to minimize coupling (both in terms of interface and of choreography) and to maximize scalability. However, this is an elusive goal.

Apparently, if the server changes the links it sends in the responses, the client will follow this change automatically by using the new links. The problem, however, is that this is not as general as it may seem, since the client must be able to understand the structure of the responses. It is not merely a question of blindly following all the links in a response. To achieve this, REST imposes the constraint that the schema of returned representations is shared with the client. Moreover, just stating the data syntax (using languages such as XML or JSON) is not enough. The semantics and the actual set of names used (the schema, in fact) must be known by both client and server [43].

This is no different from what happens with SOA, in which the schema of the service interface must be shared between consumer and provider. SOA is guided by services (behaviour), whereas REST is guided by resources (state). REST uses schemas of resources instead of services, but the coupling is still there.

What REST indeed does is to trade interface variability for structure variability, something that SOA lacks. REST cleanly separates the mechanism of traversing the graph of possible interaction states from the processing of individual graph nodes (interaction states) [44]. Therefore, varying the structure allows changing the overall behaviour without affecting the traversal mechanism. However, this requires that all nodes are treated alike, which means that all nodes must have the same interface. This implies decomposing the SOA-style objects into their most elementary components and treats them all as first-class resources, which in turn leads to a state diagram (instead of a class diagram) programming style.

The main problem with this is that the model is no longer guided by the static entities of the problem, in an object-oriented fashion, but rather by state, as an automaton. Most people will find it harder to model state transitions than static entities (classes). This is not a problem for simpler applications that can be organized in a CRUD (Create, Read, Update and Delete) approach, a natural method when structured state is the guiding concept. However, for more complex applications in which behaviour and information hiding (including state) are fundamental factors, it becomes a relevant issue.

It turns out that many applications are simple and the technologies typically used to implement REST are simpler, lighter and in many cases cheaper than those used to implement SOA (viz. SOAP-based Web Services), which justifies the growing popularity of RESTful applications and their APIs. The level of resource coupling in REST, however, is not lower than that of service coupling in SOA, since both require that the schemas used are known by both interacting devices.

It should also be noted that SOA lacks support for structured resources. Services (the set of operations supported by a resource) have just one level, offering operations but hiding any internal structured state. Structure is a natural occurrence in most problem domains, and, in this respect, REST is a better match.

10.8 Asymmetric Interoperability

Independently of whether IoT devices are modelled as services or as resources, their interaction is message based. Messages are serialized data structures described by schemas, and the typical interoperability solution used in distributed systems is to share the message's schema between the sender and the receiver of that message, as illustrated by Fig. 10.3.

This is designated *symmetric interoperability*, since both sender and receiver need to have the same knowledge about the message. The sender can produce any structured value allowed by the message schema, and therefore the receiver needs to be able to read any of these values as well. Both sender and receiver work on the same message, with the same schema.

This is reminiscent of the document-based interoperability, using data description languages such as XML or JSON, in which a writer produces a document according to some schema and the reader uses the same schema to validate and to read the contents of the document. The document is now replaced by the message, but the principle is the same. This has the following main drawbacks:

- The receiver needs to deal with the message using the schema of the sender, which produced the message. This usually implies endowing the receiver with a stub (interface code) that knows the schema and how to access the message components (data binding).
- The receiver needs to deal with the message using the ontology (viz. message component names) of the sender, which produced the message. An ontology mapping, between the message and the receiver, is required for the receiver to be able to interpret the message's semantics.

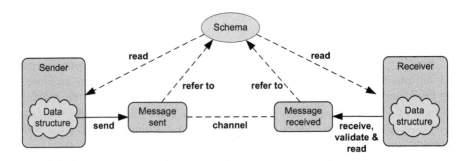

Fig. 10.3 Symmetric message-based interaction

- The sender and the receiver are coupled for the entire range of values supported by the schema, even if only a fraction of that range is actually used in the interactions. When this happens, coupling is higher than the interacting devices actually require.

The first step towards solving these problems is to recognize that device interaction is inherently asymmetric:

- The roles of sender and receiver (or consumer and provider) are different. One requests, and the other provides.
- The ontologies of the two are most likely different, particularly when we consider the enormous variability of devices and respective manufacturers.
- The set of message values that the sender can generate does not have to match the set of message values that the receiver can accept.

Nevertheless, in most cases, interaction is made symmetric artificially by design, i.e. sender and receiver are designed together, to work together, under some common specification. However, this hampers decoupling and changeability, which constitutes one of the main criticisms to the SOA architectural style.

This chapter contends that device interaction should assume its inherent asymmetry, replacing Fig. 10.3 by Fig. 10.4.

Figure 10.4 can be described in the following way:

- The message sent by the sender includes a self-description but only about the message's concrete value (which may be structured), designated here *value schema*, since it is valid only for this value, not a range of values.
- The receiver specifies and exposes a *type schema*, in line with what schema description languages support (schemas that are satisfied by a range of values). This schema specifies the range of message values that the receiver is willing to accept.
- When the message arrives at the receiver, the message's value schema is compared with the type schema of the receiver, in the *compliance checker*. If the former *complies* with the latter, the message is accepted, which in practice means that the value of the message is one of those that satisfy the receiver's type schema.

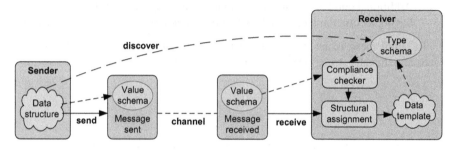

Fig. 10.4 Asymmetric message-based interaction, with compliance

- Prior to sending messages, the sender can use the type schemas exposed by potential receivers to check compliance and thus discover suitable receivers.
- If compliance of a received message holds, the message's value is *structurally assigned* to the *data template*, which is a data structure that satisfies the type schema and is partly filled in with default values for the components in the type schema that are optional, i.e. their minimum cardinality (number of occurrences) is zero.
- Structural assignment involves mapping the value schema of the message to the type schema, by assigning the message to the data template, component by component (not as a whole value), according to the following basic rules:

  - Components in the message that do not comply with any component in the data template are ignored (not assigned).
  - Optional components in the data template with no counterpart in the message keep their default value.
  - Components in the data template that have counterparts in the message have their values set to the corresponding message's component values.
  - Structured components are assigned by recursive application of these rules.

- After this, the components of the data template are completely populated and ready to be accessed by the receiver. Each message received populates a new instance of the data template.

  The main advantages of asymmetric interoperability are the following:

- The receiver deals only with a schema it already knows, the one for which it was designed. There is no need for a stub to deal with the schema shared with the sender.
- The mapping between the message and the data template is done in a universal manner, by the message-based platform, and does not depend on the receiver's schema.
- The structural assignment rules mean that coupling is reduced by comparison with symmetric interoperability, since:

  - Only the actually involved components are used in the structural assignment.
  - Only one message value, instead of all satisfying a schema, is involved in the compliance check between the message and the schema of the receiver.
  - Additional and less stringent component matching rules are possible besides having a common name, such as by position and by type.

To detail these issues, we need a data model that specifies the primitive data types and the data structuring mechanisms.

10.9 A Foundational Data Model

A common baseline, universally agreed and known by all interacting devices, is needed to act as a foundation for interoperability, much in the same way as XML and XML Schema support XML-based interactions. Basically, what is needed is as follows:

- A set of built-in data types and the respective values, considered atomic (not composed of other values)
- A set of structuring mechanisms that enable the construction of arbitrarily complex structured (non-atomic) types and the respective values

The actual choice of these sets is not important in the context of this chapter. The conclusions will be the same whichever these sets are, since we reason at a generic level. For illustration purposes, Table 10.2 provides possible sets of built-in types and structuring mechanisms, loosely based on those of XML.

The Union types are simply sets of types, each of which may be any of those in Table 10.2. Values belong to (satisfy) a Union type if they belong to at least one of its member types. It is important to note that, contrary to many type systems, a value does not actually belong to just one type but to all that it satisfies. What satisfaction means is explained in Sect. 10.10.

The Record and List structured types consist of a set of components (not necessarily belonging to the same type), each of which has the attributes described in Table 10.3. Attribute letters are used in Sect. 10.10.

In Fig. 10.4, we notice that:

- A value schema is a data type in which the type attribute of each component has been reduced to a single value and its cardinality has been fixed (the minimum and maximum cardinalities are identical). Therefore, it corresponds to the data structure of the message with self-description.
- A type schema corresponds to what Tables 10.2 and 10.3 describe.
- A data template is a type schema that additionally specifies, for each component with a minimum cardinality of zero (therefore optional in a message that satisfies the type schema), a default minimum cardinality and the corresponding values.

Table 10.2 Possible sets of built-in and structured data types

Data type category	Data type	Description
Built-in types	Integer	Integer numbers
	Float	Real numbers
	Boolean	True or false
	String	Strings
Structured types	Record	An unordered set of components
	List	An ordered set of components
Choice type	Union	A set of data types, any of which can be chosen

Table 10.3 Attributes specified for each component of the structured types

Attribute	Letter	Description
Name	N	Name of the component, possibly qualified by some ontology (just on Records)
Position	P	Ordering number of the component (on Records, position is the order by which components appear in the specification)
Type	T	Type of the component (any of the types of Table 10.2)
Minimum cardinality	m	Minimum number of occurrences of components with this name
Maximum cardinality	M	Maximum number of occurrences of components with this name

If the message includes a matching component, it is assigned to the corresponding component of the data template; if the message does not include such a component, the default information is used. In any case, the data template becomes fully populated after the structural assignment, even if the message lacks some components. This does not work for mandatory components (those with a minimum cardinality greater than zero).

10.10   Compliance and Conformance

Asymmetric interoperability (Fig. 10.4) assumes that, unlike symmetric interoperability (Fig. 10.3), the schema of a message does not have to be the same as the schema the receiver is expecting. This decreases coupling, since the message's value schema just needs to comply with the minimum requirements (mandatory components) of the receiver's type schema.

In other words, the two schemas (of the message and of the receiver) have only to match *partially*. This enables the receiver to receive messages from different senders, as long as they match the relevant part of the receiver's schema. In the same vein, we can consider the case of replacing the receiver with another one, with a different schema, as an alternative to the first one. This can occur due to evolution of the receiver (replaced by a new version) or by resorting to a new receiver altogether.

Allowing a receiver to be able to interpret messages from different senders, and a sender to be able to send messages to different receivers, is just what is needed to decrease coupling, as Eqs. 10.1 and 10.2 show. Note that a sender/receiver pair deals with one message, whereas a consumer/provider pair may require two sender/receiver pairs, for the request and response messages, but the considerations are valid for each of these messages.

These *use* and *replace* relationships lead to two important schema relations, which are central to asymmetric interoperability:

- *Compliance* [26]. The sender must satisfy (*comply with*) the *minimum* set of requirements established by the receiver to accept requests sent to it.
- *Conformance* [27]. The alternative receiver must satisfy the *maximum* set of requirements established by the original receiver to accept requests sent to it. Therefore, the alternative receiver is able to take the form of (*conform to*) the original receiver and to continue to support any existing sender.

These relations are not symmetric (e.g. if X complies with Y, Y does not necessarily comply with X) but are transitive (e.g. if X complies with Y and Y complies with Z, then X complies with Z).

Figure 10.5 illustrates these relations between several IoT devices, from the point of view of a request message.

In semantic terms:

- Compliance means that the set of possible message values sent by a sender is a *subset* of the set of values that satisfy the type schema of the receiver.
- Conformance means that the set of values that satisfy the type schema of an alternative receiver is a *superset* of the set of values that satisfy the type schema of the original receiver.

This means that, as long as compliance and conformance hold, the receiver can accept messages from different senders and that a sender can start using an alternative receiver without noticing the difference with respect to the original receiver. The compliance and conformance relations obey the following rules (denoting compliance and conformance between types X and Y by $X \blacktriangleleft Y$ and $X \blacktriangleright Y$, respectively):

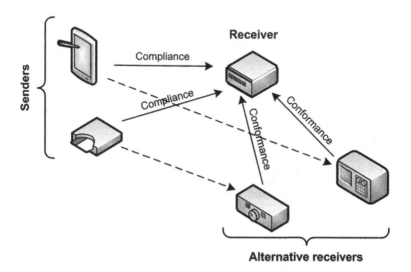

Fig. 10.5 Illustration of the compliance and conformance relations

- Each built-in type complies with and conforms to just itself, with the exception that Integer complies with Float (subset) and Float conforms to Integer (superset).
- A Union type U complies with a built-in type B only if each member type of U complies with type B.
- A Union type V conforms to a built-in type C only if at least one member type of V conforms to type C.
- Tables 10.4 and 10.5, respectively, describe compliance and conformance between the more complex types, structured and choice.

Note that, in a type W conformant to a type Z, any additional components (not in Z) need to be optional, so that values that complied with Z still comply with W. This means that a receiver with data template (Fig. 10.4) of type Z can be replaced by a receiver with data template of type W, without impairing interoperability.

Table 10.4 Rules for compliance of a type X with another type Y

◀	Type Y		
Type X	Record	List	Union
Record	If, for each Y_i, there is a X_j such that $X_{jN} = Y_{iN}$, $X_{jT} \blacktriangleleft Y_{iT}$, $X_{jm} \geq Y_{im}$ and $X_{jM} \leq Y_{iM}$	If, for each Y_i, there is a X_j such that $X_{jP} = Y_{iP}$, $X_{jT} \blacktriangleleft Y_{iT}$, $X_{jm} \geq Y_{im}$ and $X_{jM} \leq Y_{iM}$	If X complies with at least one Y_i
List	If, for each Y_i, there is a X_j such that $X_{jP} = Y_{iP}$, $X_{jT} \blacktriangleleft Y_{iT}$, $X_{jm} \geq Y_{im}$ and $X_{jM} \leq Y_{iM}$	If, for each Y_i, there is a X_j such that $X_{jP} = Y_{iP}$, $X_{jT} \blacktriangleleft Y_{iT}$, $X_{jm} \geq Y_{im}$ and $X_{jM} \leq Y_{iM}$	If X complies with at least one Y_i
Union	If all X_j comply with Y_i	If all X_i comply with Y_i	If each X_j complies with at least one Y_i

The subscripts i and j designate component/member type, and the letters designate component attributes (Table 10.3)

Table 10.5 Rules for conformance of a type W to another type Z

▶	Type Z		
Type W	Record	List	Union
Record	If, for each Z_i, there is a W_j such that $W_{jN} = Z_{iN}$, $W_{jT} \blacktriangleright Z_{iT}$, $W_{jm} \leq Z_{im}$ and $W_{jM} \geq Z_{iM}$, and for all remaining W_j, $W_{jm} = 0$	If, for each Z_i, there is a W_j such that $W_{jP} = Z_{iP}$, $W_{jT} \blacktriangleright Z_{iT}$, $W_{jm} \leq Z_{im}$ and $W_{jM} \geq Z_{iM}$, and for all remaining W_j, $W_{jm} = 0$	If W conforms to all Z_i
List	If, for each Z_i, there is a W_j such that $W_{jP} = Z_{iP}$, $W_{jT} \blacktriangleright Z_{iT}$, $W_{jm} \leq Z_{im}$ and $W_{jM} \geq Z_{iM}$, and for all remaining W_j, $W_{jm} = 0$	If, for each Z_i, there is a W_j such that $W_{jP} = Z_{iP}$, $W_{jT} \blacktriangleright Z_{iT}$, $W_{jm} \leq Z_{im}$ and $W_{jM} \geq Z_{iM}$, and for all remaining W_j, $W_{jm} = 0$	If W conforms to all Z_i
Union	If at least one of W_j conforms to Z	If at least one W_j conforms to Z	If, for each Z_i, there is at least one W_j that conforms to it

The subscripts i and j designate component/member type, and the letters designate component attributes (Table 10.3)

Mapping Records to Lists and Lists to Records allow structural assignment by position instead by name, considering the position of each named component in Records as the position it occupies in its definition or declaration.

There is still another possibility, mapping by component type. In this case, components are assigned to those that comply with (or conform to) the other type. The advantage of this is to avoid needing to have exactly the same name in corresponding components. This cannot always be used, since different components can have the same type but different semantics. These rules can lead to ambiguities, i.e. matching solutions that are not unique, in particular when unions are involved. In this case, the solution adopted can depend on the implementation. Types should be chosen to avoid ambiguities, or a compiler can check for them and generate an error if it is the case.

Extending the compliance and conformance concepts to services, at the interface layer (Table 10.1), is straightforward. Consider a service C (the consumer) and a service P (the provider). C can invoke some of the operations of P. For each invoked operation, we consider:

- Crq – The type of the request message, sent by the consumer
- Prq – The type of the request message, expected by the provider
- Prp – The type of the response message, sent by the provider
- Crp – The type of the response message, expected by the consumer

A consumer C is compliant with (can *use*) a provider P ($C \blacktriangleleft P$) if, for all operations i of P that C invokes, $Crq_i \blacktriangleleft Prq_i$ and $Prp_i \blacktriangleleft Crp_i$. Structural assignment is used to assign a message received (either request or response) to the data template of the receiver (Fig. 10.4).

In a similar way, a provider S is conformant to (can *replace*) a provider P ($S \blacktriangleright P$) if, for all operations i of P, $Srq_i \blacktriangleright Prq_i$ and $Prp_i \blacktriangleright Srp_i$.

10.11 Examples

Compliance and conformance, as described in this chapter, apply to data types and can be used directly in RESTful APIs, by a client that receives a resource representation from a server. Compliance means that the schema of that representation just needs to comply with the schema that the client expects, not actually be the latter. Conformance means that the client can be replaced by another one that conforms to the original one but can include different features. This lowers coupling with respect to the current RESTful platforms.

To illustrate these concepts, suppose that we have an IoT device that implements a weather sensor with a RESTful API. Upon reception of a GET request, it returns a representation of itself according to the JSON data shown in Listing 10.1.

```
{
 "temperature": 20,
 "temperature_unit": "Celsius",
 "average_temperature": 16.3,
 "humidity": 72.5
}
```

Listing 10.1 A representation of a weather sensor, in JSON.

The actual JSON Schema used to produce these data is irrelevant for asymmetric interoperability. It could be one of many. The receiver should assume that the message's schema has just one value (no variability) and is precisely what the message states, with its components, names, types and values.

Now, suppose that we have a simple client, which just reads the temperature and expects data with the schema shown in Listing 10.2.

```
{
 "$schema": "http://json-schema.org/schema#",
 "type": "object",
 "required": ["temperature", "temperature_unit"],
 "properties": {
 "temperature": { "type": "number" },
 "temperature_unit": { "enum": ["Celsius", "Fahrenheit"] },
 }
}
```

Listing 10.2 A JSON Schema describing data expected by a simple client

The weather sensor's schema *complies* with the client's schema. The temperature property accepts any number, which includes the 20 stated by the weather sensor's representation. The weather sensor uses just the Celsius scale in temperature_unit, which is also a subset of the scales supported by the client. The client ignores the average_temperature and humidity properties of the weather sensor's representation.

Compliance means that the representation of the weather sensor can be structurally assigned to the client's data template (see Fig. 10.4). The client's code will only have access to the properties it has declared in its own schema and will never know that the representation returned by the weather sensor had additional properties.

This is mapping by component names and requires the same ontology (same component names on both schemas). This can be avoided by mapping by position, as shown in Listing 10.3, in which component names are different, but the relative positions are the same, and the component types match. In this case, the temperature component is assigned to the temp component, and the temperature_unit component is assigned to the unit component.

```
{
  "$schema": "http://json-schema.org/schema#",
  "type": "object",
  "required": ["temp", "unit"],
  "properties": {
  "temp": { "type": "number" },
  "unit": { "enum": ["Celsius", "Fahrenheit"] },
  }
}
```

Listing 10.3 A JSON Schema describing the data expected by a client with a compatible but different ontology

Finally, mapping can still be done by type (without component names), which can even support components in different positions, as long as the mapping of component types is unambiguous, as shown in Listing 10.4. In this case, components have to be specified in a JSON array, since they have no name, but the rules of Table 10.4 support this. Note that the order of the components is not the same as in the previous listings, to show that the order is not relevant in mapping by type. However, the first component to match a type is used, and the data returned by the weather sensor has three components that match the type number, which means that mapping by type should be used with care and only when there is no ambiguity.

```
{
  "$schema": "http://json-schema.org/schema#",
  "type": "array",
  "minItems": 2,
  "maxItems": 2,
  "items": [
  { "enum": ["Celsius", "Fahrenheit"] },
  { "type": "number" }
  ]
}
```

Listing 10.4 A JSON Schema describing the data expected by a client, without component names

Current technologies support only mapping by name, which means that Listings 10.3 and 10.4 are illustrative only.

Now, suppose that we replace the client of Listing 10.2 with a new version that is now able to make use of the average_temperature and humidity properties of the weather sensor's representation. Its schema is represented in Listing 10.5.

```
{
 "$schema": "http://json-schema.org/schema#",
 "type": "object",
 "required": ["temperature", "temperature_unit"],
 "properties": {
 "temperature": { "type": "number" },
 "temperature_unit": { "enum": ["Celsius", "Fahrenheit"] },
 "average_temperature": { "type": "number" },
 "humidity": { "type": "number" }
 }
}
```

Listing 10.5 A JSON Schema describing a new client, conformant to the previous one

This new client *conforms* to the old one, since it includes the properties of the latter and the additional properties are optional (not required). The reason for this is that, for a transparent client replacement, the new client must also accept all the weather sensor representations that the old client could accept, which means that properties ignored by the old client cannot be mandatory in the new client. Similar examples could be provided using XML Schema, but these would be more verbose.

Compliance and conformance can also be defined for services, in particular for Web Services, using XML, with the rules described in the previous section. Due to space limitations, service compliance and conformance are not illustrated here, and the reader is referred to [45] for an example.

Using symmetric interoperability, the communications interface with general-purpose programming languages, at either side of the interacting devices, is usually done with stubs, with code generated automatically from the shared schema, typically resorting to annotations. If the schema changes, the stubs have to be generated again, on both sides of the interaction. With asymmetric interoperability, the schemas of the sender and of the receiver become independent. They just need to comply, and as long as compliance is not impaired, one can be changed without impact on the other.

As an example, consider that the weather sensor is implemented by a C# application, which includes a class to describe the representation returned by the weather sensor in a RESTful API, such as the one shown in Listing 10.6. This C# class is simply composed of the data components in Listing 10.1, using auto-implemented properties as a concise way to define private data fields with public get and set accessors.

```
public class WeatherSensorRepresentation
{
  public int temperature { get; set; }
  public string temperature_unit { get; set; }
  public double average_temperature { get; set; }
  public double humidity { get; set; }
}
```

Listing 10.6 C# class used to generate the representation of the weather sensor

The weather sensor application either includes a JSON generator method in this class or has a general method that produces JSON from data fields, by reflection. There is no JSON Schema involved, only straight serialization to JSON. Assuming that the client application is written in Java (just to have another programming language), it needs to specify a data template (Fig. 10.4), against which the compliance of the weather sensor representation will be checked.

A Java class needs to be programmed for this, but, unlike the C# class, which represents just one structured value, it needs to include the variability allowed by the client's schema. This can be done by using Java annotations, as illustrated by Listing 10.7, which implements the data template of the client with the schema described by Listing 10.5, more complete than the one of Listing 10.2.

```
@Record
public class ClientDataTemplate
{
  private temperature double;

  @Union("Celsius")
  @Union("Fahrenheit")
  private temperature_unit String;

  @Optional
  private average_temperature double = 0;

  @Optional
  private humidity double = 0;

  . . . /* getters and setters */
}
```

Listing 10.7 Simplified implementation of the client's data template

The @Record annotation indicates that this data template is a record (Table 10.2). All data members will be exposed for compliance matching. Those annotated with @Optional may be missing from the received message. The @Union annotation (which can be repeated) indicates the allowed values for the data member they apply to. Listing 10.8 illustrates the declaration of repeated annotations in Java. We need to define not only the Union annotation itself but also a containing annotation UnionSet, which will enable to collect the various alternatives for the union into an array.

```
@Repeatable(UnionSet.class)
@interface Union { String name() }

@Retention(RetentionPolicy.RUNTIME)
@interface UnionSet { Union[] value() }
```

Listing 10.8 Simplified example of declaration of the @Union annotation

When a message is received, at runtime, the platform's endpoint creates an instance of the ClientDataTemplate class, gets its annotations, parses the message and, by reflection, tries to match (using the compliance rules described in the previous section) and structurally assign each component of the message to a component in the data template. The annotations indicate the structural type of the template (record, in this example) and its variability (optional components and unions). Extra components in the message are ignored, missing components that are optional in the data template (otherwise there is no compliance) use default values, and the values of matching components are assigned to the corresponding values of the data template. After this, the complete data template can be processed by the receiver's application.

The most relevant aspect of this mechanism is that the receiving application does not deal with the message, only with the data template and the components for which it has been designed. The assignment of relevant parts of the message to the data template is done in a universal way, independently of the types of the actual message or data template. These types have become decoupled, except for the components that are really needed for the interaction (minimum coupling possible).

In addition, it should be noted that the serialization format (text such as XML and JSON or binary such as Concise Binary Object Representation – CBOR [46] – and Efficient XML Interchange, EXI [47]) is not relevant in the context of this chapter. As long as they can be parsed and the semantic information (viz. component names) is present, this mechanism can be implemented. Naturally, both sender and receiver need to use the same serialization format.

10.12   Conclusion

The fundamental problem of device interaction is to provide the maximum decoupling possible (exposing the minimum possible number of features) while ensuring the minimum interoperability requirements, without which interaction is not possible. This ensures that each device knows just enough about others to be able to interoperate with them but no more than that, to avoid unnecessary dependencies and constraints.

Symmetric interoperability, in which both interacting devices share the same data schema, usually leads to a coupling problem, since a device cannot change its schema without changing it in the other(s) device(s) as well. Interacting devices are locked into each other, coupled for all the message values allowed by the schema, even if not all are actually used. *Asymmetric interoperability*, on the other hand, assumes that the schema used to produce a message does not have to be identical to the schema of the messages expected by the receiver.

This chapter has shown that the above discussion:

- Leads to a lower coupling level
- Allows a device:

  – To send messages to different devices (each expecting a different message schema)
  – To receive messages from different devices (each with its own message schema)
  – To replace another one, now with a changed schema, as long as the new schema can support all the characteristics of the old one

In this context, asymmetry entails the following ideas:

- *Compliance* – At the receiver, instead of validating an incoming message against a schema shared with the sender, check whether the message fulfils the minimum requirements of the receiver's schema.
- *Conformance* – A receiver device can be changed or replaced by another one, without impact on those sending messages to it, if the schema of the new receiver includes all the features of the old one and does not mandatorily require new ones. In this way, a device can send messages to the new receiver without noticing that it has been changed.
- *Universal reception mechanism* – The receiver does not see the message's schema. Compliance checking and the assignment of the compliant parts of the message to the receiver's data template (the receiver's view of the message) are done in a universal manner by the message-based platform, independently of the actual schemas used.

These interoperability features contribute to reduce coupling and to increase the range of devices that can interact with a given device. This is especially relevant in the Internet of Things, in which devices interact in huge numbers and with a wide range of characteristics, and therefore reducing the interoperability problems is of paramount importance.

References

1. van der Meulen R (2015) Gartner says 6.4 billion connected "Things" will be in use in 2016, Up 30 percent from 2015. https://www.gartner.com/newsroom/id/3165317. Accessed 28 Feb 2017
2. Nordrum A (2016) Popular internet of things forecast of 50 billion devices by 2020 is outdated. http://spectrum.ieee.org/tech-talk/telecom/internet/popular-internet-of-things-forecast-of-50-billion-devices-by-2020-is-outdated. Accessed 28 Feb 2017
3. Fortino G, Ganzha M, Palau C, Paprzycki M (2016) Interoperability in the internet of things. Comput now (special issue December) https://www.computer.org/web/computingnow/archive/interoperability-in-the-internet-of-things-december-2016-introduction. Accessed 28 Feb 2017
4. Fawcett J, Ayers D, Quin L (2012) Beginning XML. Wiley, Hoboken
5. Bassett L (2015) Introduction to JavaScript Object Notation: a to-the-point guide to JSON. O'Reilly media, Inc, Sebastopol
6. Erl T, Gee C, Chelliah P, Kress J, Normann H, Maier B, Wik P (2014) Next generation SOA: a concise introduction to service technology & service-orientation. Pearson Education, Upper Saddle River
7. Pautasso C, Wilde E, Alarcon R (eds) (2014) REST: advanced research topics and practical applications. Springer, New York
8. Feki M, Kawsar F, Boussard M, Trappeniers L (2013) The internet of things: the next technological revolution. IEEE Comp 46(2):24–25
9. Al-Fuqaha A, Guizani M, Mohammadi M, Aledhari M, Ayyash M (2015) Internet of things: a survey on enabling technologies, protocols, and applications. IEEE Commun Surv Tutor 17(4):2347–2376
10. Whitmore A, Agarwal A, Da Xu L (2015) The Internet of things – a survey of topics and trends. Inf Sys Front 17(2):261–274
11. Popplewell K (2014) Enterprise interoperability science base structure. In: Mertins K, Bénaben F, Poler R, Bourrières J (eds) Enterprise interoperability VI: interoperability for agility, resilience and plasticity of collaborations. Springer International Publishing, Switzerland, pp 417–427
12. Sharma R, Panigrahi P (2015) Developing a roadmap for planning and implementation of interoperability capability in e-government. Transform Gov: People, Process Policy 9(4):426–447
13. Zhang Z, Wu C, Cheung D (2013) A survey on cloud interoperability: taxonomies, standards, and practice. ACM SIGMETRICS Perform Evaluation Rev 40(4):13–22
14. Robkin M, Weininger S, Preciado B, Goldman J (2015) Levels of conceptual interoperability model for healthcare framework for safe medical device interoperability. In: Proceedings of the symposium on product compliance engineering. IEEE Computer Society Press, Piscataway, pp 1–8
15. Potdar V, Sharif A, Chang E (2009) Wireless sensor networks: a survey. In: Proceedings of the international conference on advanced information networking and applications workshops, pp 636–641
16. Hartenstein H, Laberteaux K (eds) (2010) VANET: vehicular applications and inter-networking technologies. Wiley, Chichester
17. Zimmermann O, Tomlinson M, Peuser S (2012) Perspectives on web services: applying SOAP, WSDL and UDDI to real-world projects. Springer Science & Business Media, New York
18. Pautasso C (2014) RESTful web services: principles, patterns, emerging technologies. In: Bouguettaya A, Sheng Q, Daniel F (eds) Web services foundations. Springer, New York, pp 31–51
19. Erl T (2016) Service-oriented architecture: concepts, technology, and design, 2nd edn. Prentice Hall, Upper Saddle River

20. Bora A, Bezboruah T (2015) A comparative investigation on implementation of RESTful versus SOAP based web services. Int J Database Theory Appl 8(3):297–312
21. Kumari S, Rath S (2015) Performance comparison of SOAP and REST based web services for enterprise application integration. In: Proceedings of the international conference on advances in computing, communications and informatics. IEEE Computer Society Press, Piscataway, pp 1656–1660
22. Sungkur R, Daiboo S (2015) SOREST, a novel framework combining SOAP and REST for implementing web services. In: Proceedings of the second international conference on data mining, internet computing, and big data. The Society of Digital Information and Wireless Communications, Wilmington, pp 22–34
23. Babu D, Darsi M (2013) A survey on service oriented architecture and metrics to measure coupling. Int J Comp Scie Eng 5(8):726–733
24. Geetika R, Singh P (2014) Dynamic coupling metrics for object oriented software systems: a survey. ACM SIGSOFT Softw Eng Notes 39(2):1–8
25. Alenezi M, Magel K (2014) Empirical evaluation of a new coupling metric: combining structural and semantic coupling. Int J Comp Appl 36(1):34–44
26. Tran H, Zdun U, Oberortner E, Mulo E, Dustdar S (2012) Compliance in service-oriented architectures: a model-driven and view-based approach. Inf Softw Technol 54(6):531–552. https://doi.org/10.1016/j.infsof.2012.01.001
27. Khalfallah M, Figay N, Barhamgi M, Ghodous P (2014) Model driven conformance testing for standardized services. In: Proceedings of the IEEE international conference on services computing. IEEE Computer Society Press, Piscataway, pp 400–407
28. Capel M, Mendoza L (2014) Choreography modeling compliance for timed business models. In: Proceedings of the workshop on enterprise and organizational modeling and simulation. Springer, Berlin, pp 202–218
29. Brandt C, Hermann F (2013) Conformance analysis of organizational models: a new enterprise modeling framework using algebraic graph transformation. Int J Info Sys Model Des 4(1):42–78
30. Preidel C, Borrmann A (2016) Towards code compliance checking on the basis of a visual programming language. J Inf Technol Constr 21(25):402–421
31. Graydon P, Habli I, Hawkins R, Kelly T, Knight J (2012) Arguing conformance. IEEE Softw 29(3):50–57
32. Rachad T, Boutahar J (2014) A new efficient method for calculating similarity between web services. Int J Adv Comp Sci Appl 5(8):60–67
33. Otero-Cerdeira L, Rodríguez-Martínez F, Gómez-Rodríguez A (2015) Ontology matching: a literature review. Expert Sys Appl 42(2):949–971
34. Ma M, Wang P, Chu C (2014) Ontology-based semantic modeling and evaluation for internet of things applications. In: Proceedings of the IEEE international conference on internet of things. IEEE Computer Society Press, Piscataway, pp 24–30
35. ISO/IEC/IEEE (2010) Systems and software engineering – vocabulary. International standard ISO/IEC/IEEE 24765:2010(E), 1st edn. International Standards Office, Geneva, p 186
36. ISO/IEC (1994) ISO/IEC 7498-1, information technology – open systems interconnection – basic reference model: the basic model, 2nd edn. International Standards Office, Geneva. http://standards.iso.org/ittf/PubliclyAvailableStandards/index.html. Accessed 28 Feb 2017
37. Wang W, De S, Toenjes R, Reetz E, Moessner K (2012) A comprehensive ontology for knowledge representation in the internet of things. In: Proceedings of the IEEE 11th international conference on trust, security and privacy in computing and communications. IEEE Computer Society Press, Piscataway, pp 1793–1798
38. Palm J, Anderson K, Lieberherr K (2003) Investigating the relationship between violations of the law of demeter and software maintainability. In: proceedings of workshop on software-engineering properties of languages for aspect technologies. http://www.daimi.au.dk/~eernst/splat03/papers/Jeffrey_Palm.pdf. Accessed 28 Feb 2017

39. Ross A, Rhodes D, Hastings D (2008) Defining changeability: reconciling flexibility, adaptability, scalability, modifiability, and robustness for maintaining system lifecycle value. Syst Engineer 11(3):246–262. https://doi.org/10.1002/sys.20098
40. Dillon T, Wu C, Chang E (2007) Reference architectural styles for service-oriented computing. In: Li K et al (eds) Proceedings of the IFIP international conference on network and parallel computing. Springer, Berlin, pp 543–555
41. Bloomberg J, Schmelzer R (2013) Deep interoperability: getting REST right (finally!). In: The agile architecture revolution: how cloud computing, rest-based SOA, and mobile computing are changing enterprise it. Wiley, Hoboken
42. Fielding R (2000) Architectural styles and the design of network-based software architectures. Doctoral dissertation, University of California at Irvine. http://www.ics.uci.edu/~fielding/pubs/dissertation/fielding_dissertation_2up.pdf. Accessed 28 Feb 2017
43. Palavalli A, Karri D, Pasupuleti S (2016) Semantic internet of things. In: Proceedings of the IEEE tenth international conference on semantic computing. IEEE Computer Society Press, Piscataway, pp 91–95
44. Meyer B (2000) Object-oriented software construction. Prentice Hall, Upper Saddle River
45. Delgado J (2015) Decreasing service coupling to increase enterprise agility. In: Achieving enterprise agility through innovative software development. IGI Global, Hershey, pp 225–261
46. Bormann C, Hoffman P (2013) Concise Binary Object Representation (CBOR). https://tools.ietf.org/html/rfc7049. Accessed 28 Feb 2017
47. Schneider J, Kamiya T, Peintner D, Kyusakov R (ed) (2014) Efficient XML interchange (EXI) format 1.0 (second edition). W3C. http://www.w3.org/TR/exi/. Accessed 28 Feb 2017

Chapter 11
Automatic Big Data Provenance Capture at Middleware Level in Advanced Big Data Frameworks

Anu Mary Chacko, Alfredo Cuzzocrea, and S.D. Madhu Kumar

Abstract Huge amounts of data are being generated by Internet of Things (IoT) devices. Termed as Big Data, this data needs to be reliably stored, extracted, and analyzed. Capturing provenance of such data provides a mechanism to explain the result of data analytics and provides greater trustworthiness to the insights gathered from data analytics. Capturing the provenance of the data stored in NoSQL databases can help to understand how the data reached its current state. A holistic explanation of the results of data analytics can be achieved through the combination of provenance information of the data with results of analytics. This chapter explores the challenges of automatic provenance capture at the middleware level in three different contexts: in an analytics framework like MapReduce, in NoSQL data stores with MapReduce analytic framework, and in NoSQL stores with SQL front ends. The chapter also portrays how the provenance captured in the MapReduce framework is useful for improving the future executions of job reruns and anomaly detection, apart from its use in debugging.

11.1 Introduction

With the rise in usage of the Internet and social media websites, digital data is now treated as an asset and is used to derive insights or meaningful information. With the advent of the Internet of Things (IoT), the amount of data has increased exponentially. Most of the data generated are unstructured and are of different file types. As data are generated in large volumes, they are termed as "Big Data." Big Data can contain information generated by sensors, chatter in the social media like Twitter or

A.M. Chacko (✉) • S.D. Madhu Kumar
National Institute of Technology Calicut, Kozhikode, Kerala, India
e-mail: anu.chacko@nitc.ac.in

A. Cuzzocrea
University of Trieste and ICAR-CNR, Trieste, Italy

© Springer International Publishing AG 2017   219
Z. Mahmood (ed.), *Connected Environments for the Internet of Things*,
Computer Communications and Networks,
https://doi.org/10.1007/978-3-319-70102-8_11

Facebook, or loads of information collected for user profiling. This data can act as powerful trend predictors if they can be reliably analyzed and mined. The reliability of the analytic results depends on how "good" the data used for analysis is, which in turn depends on the source of the data and transformations that the data underwent. Data provenance is the metadata that captures the history of data from its creation to how it reached its current state. In our day-to-day activities, different levels/types of provenance are collected by audit trails, logs, and change tracking software. All such data gives information that contributes to the history of data or provenance. Provenance metadata focuses on isolating all relevant details of history in one metadata in a systematic way, such that the advantages of verifiability and querying are obtained.

With the increase in complexity of data management, data provenance research is gaining a lot of attention. Every aspect of provenance handling, starting from capture and storage to representation, security, and querying, needs efficient schemes so that provenance can be seamlessly used. In the literature, there are schemes for applications to disclose provenance explicitly and schemes to capture provenance automatically at operating system and middleware level. Making all applications provenance aware is not a feasible solution, and so automatic capture of provenance is needed. Automatic capture can be done at operating system or at middleware layer. At the operating system level, the system is not able to understand the context in which data is used, and so if provenance is collected at this level, it is very fine grained, making it difficult to query and use the provenance collected. Automatically capturing provenance at middleware level gives the application designers the flexibility to focus on logic of application without worrying about provenance disclosure. Especially, in the context of Big Data, where a large number of Big Data applications are being deployed every day, automatic provenance capture at middleware layer is a feasible option for provenance capture.

This chapter focuses on processing of IoT data on the Big Data analytic frameworks. The next section provides a background to the work done in provenance research, and the rest of the chapter discusses approaches to capture provenance of analytics done on MapReduce framework and data stored and analyzed in NoSQL data stores.

11.2   Background

In eScience, many tools like *Chimera, myGrid*, and *CMCS* [1] were developed for provenance capture of scientific workflows. The primary focus for collecting provenance in workflows was to ensure reproducibility of experiments and providing provisions for debugging. Provenance was very interesting to the database community as it provided explanation for the results obtained. Tools like *DBNotes* [2], *Trio* [3], and *PERM* [4] focused on database provenance. Automatic provenance capture was explored in the construction of *PASS* [5], a modified Linux kernel that captured provenance of all operations happening in the kernel by observing the read/write system calls. Similar approach was used in *SPADE* [6] where provenance capture scheme was instrumented into the application to capture intra-provenance at compile time. Most of the works except *PASS* and *SPADE* described in the literature followed a disclosed provenance approach where specific applications were made provenance aware for domain-specific requirements.

Provenance is of interest in the area of Big Data, as provenance provides a mechanism to explain the results and provide proofs for the validity of data. The main focus areas of Big Data provenance is in storage, analytics, and data stores. Munniswamy et al. [7] developed *PASS* to work for cloud storage. They provided different versions that store provenance along with data in SimpleDB or Amazon S3. Another work in this area is by Sletzer et.al. [8] who proposed techniques to instrument Xen hypervisor to capture provenance of operations on the virtual hypervisors. In Big Data analytics, a major work was done to develop the analytic framework MapReduce provenance aware. *RAMP* (Reduce and Map Provenance) [9] captures provenance of MapReduce workflows while the job executes. The provenance is generated at the end of job execution resulting in a performance overhead of 20–70% as reported by the authors. *HadoopProv* [10] attempts to improve the performance of job execution of MapReduce jobs while capturing provenance by deferring the generation of provenance to the time when it is needed. *Lipstick* [11] tool enables database style workflow provenance to be captured for jobs written in Pig script. *Titian* [12] is a library that has been created for provenance support for jobs running in Apache Spark, and the authors claim that observed overhead for job execution is below 30%.

The early works in data provenance were mainly domain specific and consisted of making particular applications provenance aware. Through this approach, rich provenance information is obtained, as the semantics of the applications is an integral part of the provenance capture system. But in Big Data scenario, retrofitting all applications to make them provenance aware is not practical. On the other hand, capturing provenance at the operating system level, e.g., *PASS* [5], x being captured. The main issue here is the large size of provenance and false dependencies. Hence there is a need for schemes to capture provenance automatically at middleware layer.

Typically, the applications or software that acts as glue between operating system and applications are categorized as middleware [12]. Semantically, the middleware layer is placed between the operating system and application layers. Middleware caters to multiple applications at a time. Creating middleware to make a set of applications provenance aware provides the developer with the option of capturing provenance of multiple applications/data in applications in one go. In the Big Data landscape, where the number of applications for processing data is as well big, retrofitting provenance into all applications is not a practical solution.

In the literature, there are scientific experiments that followed this approach, where the workflow middleware was adapted to capture provenance of all workflows running on top of it e.g., *MyGrid* [13]. By making the workflow queue provenance aware, all the jobs running on it become automatically provenance aware. In the big data scenario, provenance capture contexts can be broadly divided into two: in the context of analytic tools and in case of Big Data stores. The following sections explain the techniques proposed for capturing provenance using middleware approach, in analytic tool like MapReduce and NoSQL store like MongoDB.

11.3   Provenance in MapReduce Workflows

In the context of Big Data applications, the collected data is useful only if it is amenable to analytics. The result of the analytics can be confidently used if and only if it is verifiable. So capturing provenance for analytic frameworks is a must. The major challenge with provenance capture is the high performance overhead caused to the job during provenance capture. The provenance collected is usually used for debugging results. This section explores a different approach for capturing provenance of MapReduce workflows and explores the use of provenance collected for improving the execution of MapReduce jobs during incremental runs and anomaly detection.

11.3.1   Provenance Capture

In the context of MapReduce, three types of provenance can be collected – job provenance (coarsely grained), data provenance (finely grained), and transformation provenance (process provenance):

- *Job provenance* is an example of coarsely grained provenance and captures the signature of job.
- *Data provenance* captures relation between the output data and the input data of a MapReduce job.
- *Transformation provenance* goes beyond the job execution and tries to capture details of job execution.

A lazy approach of generating provenance after the completion of job execution is adopted in our approach so that results of job are available for the user for review, while provenance is being generated. In this approach, provenance is captured by writing a wrapper code to the classes like Mapper and Reducer so as to capture details important for provenance into temporary files. At the completion of the job, a background MapReduce job is executed to consolidate the temporary files and generate provenance. Provenance thus generated constitutes the fine-grained data provenance. This provenance is useful for debugging the result or to understand flow of data from input to output.

Job provenance is the coarsely grained provenance captured by modified MapReduce framework so as to create signature of a particular run of a job. The details captured as part of job provenance are details of input-output, file names, input-output key types and input-output file formats, Mapper, Reducer and Combiner class names, MD5 hash of jar files, and offsets to which data is read in the current job run.

Fig. 11.1 Comparison of performance (job completion time) in word count problem

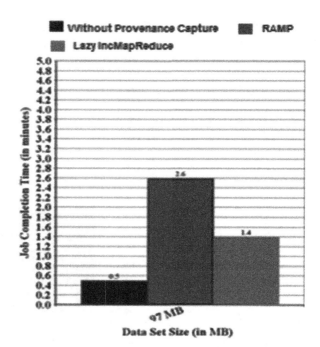

Modified MapReduce (*Lazy IncMapReduce*) was tested on a cluster of nine DataNodes and a NameNode for Hadoop. The HBase cluster consisted of nine region servers and a master server. Each system was configured with 4GB RAM and 500 GB hard drive. The results of experiment by running the above jobs are discussed next.

Provenance collection showed a performance and storage improvement for word count problem as shown in Figs. 11.1 and 11.2, respectively. For the word count problem, proposed method showed an average 50% improvement in the job completion time and an average 70% storage optimization over RAMP. This storage optimization is obtained as provenance collected is preprocessed and stored in HBase.

Another experiment was conducted to filter random *Apache WebLog* [14] data. A sample of 1 lakh weblogs was used to filter good weblogs out of ill-typed weblogs. Around 1 lakh logs were analyzed in Lazy IncMapReduce, and performance analysis is shown in Figs. 11.3 and 11.4. HBase storage required 186% more memory than RAMP as shown in Fig. 11.4.

In case of WebLog filtering, for each output record, a corresponding provenance record is written. As the number of output records increases, the number of write operations increases, and hence the storage requirement becomes larger, and job execution time degrades. These experiments indicate that significant storage and performance improvements are obtained in *Lazy IncMapReduce* for jobs where the number of output keys is less than the number of input keys.

Fig. 11.2 Comparison of storage requirement – word count problem

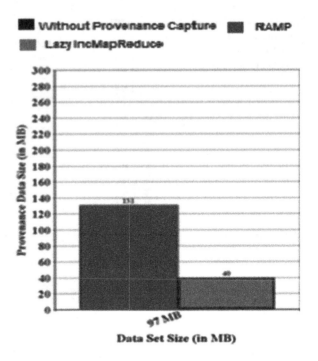

Fig. 11.3 Comparison of performance (job completion time) in WebLog filtering problem – MapReduce without provenance vs RAMP vs Lazy IncMapReduce

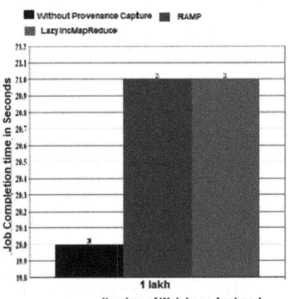

Fig. 11.4 Comparison of storage requirement: WebLog filtering problem – RAMP vs Lazy IncMapReduce

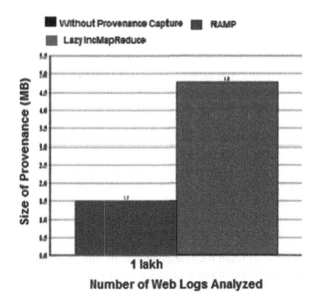

Transformation provenance consists of details of job execution. This can be extracted from the various logs created as part of the job execution. Once the job execution is over, the logs from the different nodes are consolidated, and transformation provenance can be mined from the logs using a rule-based execution framework. This is done by identifying patterns in the logs and defining rules to extract the information from log to deduce provenance. This provenance captures information on MapReduce execution, like details of task and job execution, split creation, dataset access, etc. Here, there is no change made to the MapReduce framework, but provenance is deduced from the preexisting logs.

Hadoop generates detailed log for all the services running in the cluster like *NameNode*, *DataNode*, *JobTracker*, and *TaskTracker*. The details of job extracted from the logs are used to generate a transformation provenance profile for the job. Provenance profile is captured as XML file so as to enable easy querying. The provenance profile contains complete information about the execution of the job run, cluster configuration information, as well as ERROR and WARNING messages generated.

The three provenances together provide the holistic picture about the MapReduce job execution and its results. In the literature the use of provenance collected has been demonstrated mainly for debugging of results. In the rest of this section, two novel uses of provenance collected are discussed: (1) the use of data and job provenance to improve the workflow execution of subsequent runs of MapReduce jobs and (2) the use of transformation provenance for anomaly detection.

11.3.2 Incremental MapReduce Using Provenance

In the literature, there are schemes like Incoop [15] and Itchy [16] that implement incremental MapReduce. *Incoop* [15] uses the concept of memoization and needs modified HDFS to implement incremental MapReduce. *Itchy* [15] uses the term provenance, but the provenance used is not conventional but a mapping between intermediate map result and input. Proposed approach, *Lazy IncMapReduce*, aims to reuse the provenance generated as part of workflow execution to improve the execution of job reruns.

In many MapReduce applications, the input data is of *append* only variety. For such MapReduce jobs, the old results can be reused, and computation can be restricted to the new appended input values alone. This will result in significant reduction in execution time. The following cases were evaluated as part of this work. Input file is considered to be *append* only:

- Case 1: Input file is appended with data or when input files are added.
- Case 2: Input file is processed as a sliding window of data.

The following section describes how *Lazy IncMapReduce* works for the two different cases described above.

Case 1: Jobs Rerun with Additional Data Appended to Input File or with Additional Files

When a MapReduce job is submitted by the user, its coarse-grained provenance is captured, and provenance store is queried to see if it is the first run of the job or rerun. It is considered as an incremental run if the provenance store returns a job with the following conditions satisfied:

- Jar file with same MD5 hash as current job
- Same Mapper, Reducer and Combiner classes as current job
- Same input files as current job
- Same type of output key and values as current job
- Same input format as current job

After verification, the current job submitted is classified as:

- *New run*: if no matching job is found in the provenance store, in this case, the job is run as a single MapReduce job with provenance capture.
- *Incremental run*: if a previous run of the same job is found, the input file is checked to see whether it is a case of new data appended to existing input files or new input files added. In both cases, MapReduce program runs only on the new data that was not processed in earlier run. Output of this job is combined with the output of old job by executing MapReduce job with *Identity Mapper*. This is the default Mapper class provided by Hadoop that writes all input key value pairs into output. This is diagrammatically illustrated in Fig. 11.5.

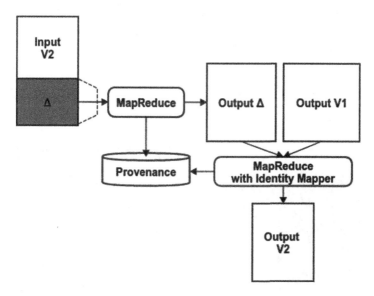

Fig. 11.5 Incremental MapReduce when new data is appended to input file

Case 2: Job Rerun on Sliding Window of Input Data

Frequently there are cases where MapReduce jobs are run for a window of data (e.g., last 30 days data). Every consecutive day, the window slides, deleting a day's information and adding a new day's information. *LazyIncMapReduce* is designed to handle incremental runs for such MapReduce jobs that process window of input data using tuple level fine-grained provenance. The first run of the job processes the window selected with provenance capture. In the next run of the job, the window has some new data appended and some old data removed. The data can be considered as having three sections as shown in Fig. 11.6:

- *Old data*: Data which is part of the old window but not included in the current job's window
- *Common data*: Data which is common to both old job and current job
- *New data*: Data which is newly added in the file and not part of old job.

The strategy for job reruns is as follows:

- Perform MapReduce on the *new data*.
- Refresh the previous job output file to reflect the removal of *old data* from input file. This is achieved by doing selective refresh of the output file of the previous run. The fine-grained provenance captured in the previous job run is used here to trace back the input for each output element. Depending on which part of the input file the input records lie, the following strategies are opted to prepare the refreshed output file:

    - Scenario 1: If inputs fall completely in common data, no refresh is done, and output file is used as such.

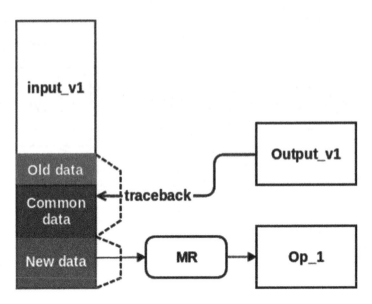

Fig. 11.6 Rerun of job in incremental MapReduce for the sliding window case

- Scenario 2: If dependent inputs fall in both common data and old data, then a selective refresh needs to be done for those input offsets using a MapReduce job.
- Scenario 3: If the dependent inputs are completely in old data, then the records in the old file can be discarded.
- Combine all the results by running a MapReduce job with Identity Mapper.

11.3.2.1 Experimental Results

For the evaluation of incremental MapReduce, two jobs whose number of output keys is less than number of input keys were considered: *word count* job and *grep* job. In these two cases, input file was appended with data, and sliding window of data approach was tested. Performance for the incremental run was analyzed.

Case 1: Input File Appended with 500 MB Data for Incremental Run
Performance analysis was done for incremental run when an input file (4.4GB) is appended with additional 500 MB data for both word count job and grep job. In the first run, a small run time overhead of 5 s was observed. But in the incremental run, our prototype outperforms the traditional MapReduce with 50% of run time improvement. Figure 11.7 shows a reduction of 50% in execution time of incremental run of word count job, and Fig. 11.8 shows a 98% reduction in execution time of incremental run of grep job.

Thus, there is a significant performance improvement for job reruns in *Lazy IncMapReduce* when jobs are rerun with additional data appended in the file, as the

Fig. 11.7 Job execution time (word count problem) when 500 MB data is appended

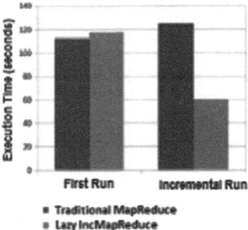

Fig. 11.8 Job execution time (grep problem) when 500 MB data is appended

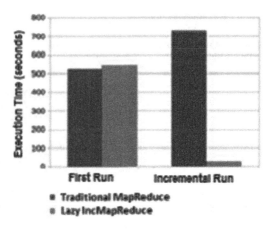

data in the previous run is not processed but output of the previous run is merged with MapReduce output of new data.

Case 2: Processing Input File with a Sliding Window of 500 MB Data for Incremental Run

To evaluate the performance of *Lazy IncMapReduce* in such cases, incremental MapReduce job was executed by moving the processing window by 500 MB. Performance analysis of incremental MapReduce was done for both *word count* Job and *grep* Job. The results obtained for the *word count* problem is shown in Fig. 11.9 and for *grep* problem, in Fig. 11.10.

In the case of experimental run of sliding window *word count* problem, a performance overhead of 400% was found. On analysis, it was found that this overhead was because of the bottleneck caused by *NameNode* during selective refresh. The inherent design of MapReduce gives *NameNode* the task of preparation of splits

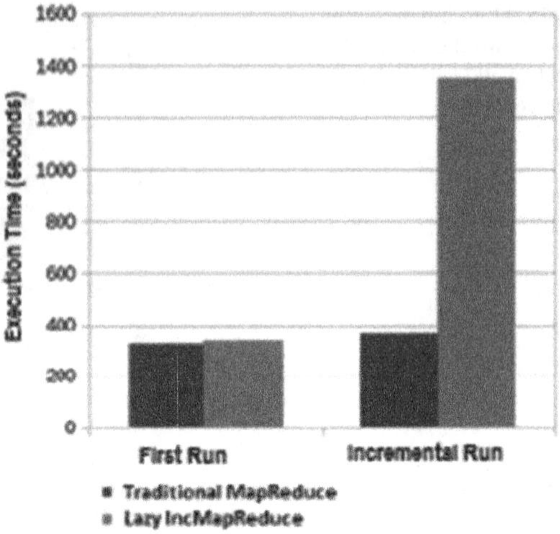

Fig. 11.9 Job execution time (word count problem) when window of processing is "slided" by 500 MB

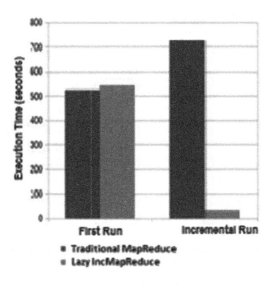

Fig. 11.10 Job execution time (Grep problem) when window of processing is "slided" by 500 MB

during selective refresh. When there are lots of output records that need refreshing, many splits have to be generated for facilitating selective refresh. Out of 1352 s of the incremental run, 1155 s were taken for selective refresh. The preparation of files for selective refresh was the main cause of the overhead. In the case of *grep* job, provenance query provided very few records for selective refresh, and so the time for preparing splits was greatly reduced. Thus, in the case of *grep*, incremental run in *Lazy IncMapReduce* gives a better performance over traditional MapReduce.

11.3.3 Anomaly Detection Using Transformation Provenance

Execution of MapReduce is handled transparently by Hadoop. Hadoop is an open source project designed to optimize handling massive amount of data through parallelism using inexpensive commodity hardware. The earlier versions of Hadoop concentrated on task distribution, and very little attention was given to security. In later versions, various techniques like mutual authentication, enforcement of HDFS file permission, using tokens for authorization, etc. were provided to enhance security. But Hadoop has a serious lack in detection of anomalous behavior. Hadoop does the data processing and scheduling in a way which is transparent to the user. There is a possibility that a compromised user or compromised node could do some malicious activity to gain additional resource usage and obstruct services to the other nodes for its purposes. An attacker could perform some attacks to slow down the data processing and create a denial of service situation in the cluster. Currently, any such anomalous activity would go unnoticed despite having security features enabled in Hadoop. Transformation provenance captured can throw light on many such malicious activities happening during MapReduce workflow.

After job execution, a provenance file is generated, and this provenance profile is used to detect anomalous behavior. The tool developed performs the set of checks as listed below:

- Check if input to all the tasks are valid.
- Check if output is stored in proper location.
- Total number of tasks performed.
- Status of nodes in cluster.
- Analyze task execution times.

Checking input and output file locations from the configuration files and actual execution log can throw light if any malicious user has made changes for leaking confidential data. The check on total number of tasks performed helps to identify any skipped computations. Logs provide information on the status of cluster. As job allocation is handled transparently by the framework, the user does not know whether the resources are properly utilized. The task execution times on different nodes can further throw light on the efficiency of nodes. This was verified by simulating a SYN flood attack on a slave machine in the cluster of three machines to make the slave system less responsive. The run times of all the map tasks were collected with and without attack. The mean and standard deviation for both the set of values were calculated. When there is an attack, the deviation is high (approx 50%) from the mean indicating that the run times of map tasks vary. Figure 11.11 describes a sample output of anomaly detection using provenance profile.

This section described the capture of data, job, and transformation provenance for jobs executing in MapReduce framework and the uses of provenance captured. The provenance collected is not only useful for error debugging but also for improving incremental runs of jobs. Transformation provenance captured is useful in

```
Check-1 : Input to all the tasks are valid inputs.

INFO: Tasks taking input from the correct directories
-------------------------------------------------------------
Check-2 : Output are stored in proper locations

INFO: Task is storing output to the correct directories
-------------------------------------------------------------
Check-3 : Checking Number of tasks performed

There are  10 map attempts and  10 map tasks and  1 reduce tasks
-------------------------------------------------------------
Check-4 : Status of nodes in cluster

INFO : No Anamalous Behaviour from the nodes in the cluster. ['hmaster', 'scl', 'sc2']   nodes performed [4,
 5, 4]  completed Tasks respectively
-------------------------------------------------------------
Check-5 : Analyzing Task Execution times

Mean Values of Map and Reduce Exection times are : 113192.7 323908.0
Standard Deviation of Map and reduce  Execution times are 89495.8571623 0.0
There is a deviation of 79.0650432071 % of values from mean for Map task and 0.0 % of values from mean for r
educe task
```

Fig. 11.11 Example of anomaly detection by analyzing run times in provenance profile

detecting anomalous behavior in the cluster. The next section describes a novel approach to capture provenance of data stored in NoSQL data stores.

11.4   Provenance for Big Data Stores

The massive data generated from the different IoT sources are usually stored in highly scalable databases like NoSQL data stores. In order to have an end-to-end provenance captured, there needs to be provenance captured in NoSQL stores and also in analytic frameworks. This section explains the type of provenance required for NoSQL stores and approaches to capture provenance in two different contexts:

- Data stored in NoSQL store, analyzed using MapReduce Framework
- Data stored in NoSQL store, analyzed using SQL interface

11.4.1   Data Provenance Requirement in NoSQL Stores

To vouch for the credibility of data in the NoSQL stores, there is a need for three levels of provenance capture: tuple and schema provenances for data stored and data provenance for output of analytics done.

In NoSQL stores, the data on operations that cause the tuple to reach its current state can be categorized as *how provenance*. The *how provenance* answers the query on how the tuple attained its current value. Complex operations like join and aggregate are not present in NoSQL queries. So in the context of data stored in NoSQL store, *why provenance* is not relevant. However when analytics are done to produce meaningful insights, the *why provenance* becomes critical to explain the result. When analytics are done on the data stores, the provenance of output constitutes the details of the input tuples that contributed to selection of the output and history of how each of the input tuples reached its current state.

NoSQL databases are designed with fault-resistant logs to enable replication of changes to ensure transparent scalability. The logs are fixed size tables (capped collection) that capture changes happening in the data store. The information from logs can be augmented and reused to deduce *how provenance* of data stored. *Why provenance* is captured for analytics done on the data in the NoSQL data stores. Two strategies of analytics are explored here.

1. Using inbuilt MapReduce
2. Using SQL interface

In the next section, MongoDB is used as an example to demonstrate the practical approach for capture of "how provenance" and "why provenance."

11.4.2 Capture of "How Provenance"

MongoDB supports basic CRUD (create, read, update, and delete) operations only. It provides an inbuilt MapReduce option to run complex analytic queries. The *how provenance* was tracked by setting up a tailable cursor in Python on the *operation log (oplog)* of MongoDB. *Oplog* is a special capped collection that keeps a rolling record of all operations that modify the data in the database. As provenance capture incurs storage overhead, the logger provides provision to select the tuples/documents that need to be tracked for provenance by using *resource expression.* Logger monitors the *Oplog* for any changes happening to the tuples for which provenance tracking is requested for. Whenever a log entry is made about tuple/collection that is being tracked, the cursor reads the data and deduces provenance details and records the provenance in an "append only" provenance collection. The information thus deduced from the log constitutes the *how provenance* and gives information on how a data item stored in the data store reached its current state. The following example demonstrates the use of provenance captured.

In the MongoDB database called "hospital," there exists a collection called "patients." To track the provenance for a particular patient, say "P123," resource expression is specified as <hospital/patients/P123>. The current state of the patient record is shown in Fig. 11.12. "How provenance" captured is shown in Fig. 11.13.

Both data and schema provenance are available on querying and are demonstrated by an example. Data provenance shows how the data reached its current state, i.e., the details of document creation and details of when each field value was added/updated. Schema provenance shows the addition and deletion of new fields in the document. For example, in the "hospital" database sample, a new field called "Allergy" has been added by user "Dr Jacob" on 29 April 2015 which was not there initially.

234

A.M. Chacko et al.

Fig. 11.12 Current state
of patient record P123

```
{
  "_id" : "P123",
  "Name" : "John",
  "Doctor" : "Dr.jacob",
  "Disease" : "Asthma",
  "Medication" :[ "Doxil4","Laxin" ],
  "Allergy" : "Sneezing "
}
```

```
{
  "_id" : "hospital.patient.P123",
  "Provenance" : [
  {        "Op_Type" : "i"
           "Operation" : "{    'Name': 'John', 'Disease' : 'Asthma',
                               'Medication': ['Doxil4' , 'Aadrone' ],
                               'Doctor' : ' Dr. James '
                          }",
           "Time" : ISODate("2015-04-29T12:56:49Z"),
           "user" : "Dr. James",
  },
  {        "Op_Type" : "u"
           "Operation" : "{'$set': {'Medication':['Laxin]},
                                    {'Doctor': 'Dr. Jacob'}}",
           "Time" : ISODate("2015-04-29T1:57:08Z"),
           "user" : "Dr. Jacob",
  },
  {        "Op_Type" : "u"
           "Operation" : " {'$set': {'Allergy': 'Sneezing'},
                                    {'Medication:[Doxil4, Laxin]'}}",
           "Time" : ISODate("2015-04-29T32:57:16Z"),
           "user" : "Dr. Jacob",
  }
           ]
}
```

Fig. 11.13 "How provenance" for P123

11.4.3 Capture of "Why Provenance"

"Why Provenance" is significant to explain results of analysis done on data stored
in NoSQL stores. This section explores the capture of *why provenance* in two scenarios of analytics:

1. When MapReduce is used to conduct analytics on data stored in the NoSQL
   stores
2. When SQL interface is used to analyze the data in the NoSQL stores.

11.4.3.1 "Why Provenance" for Analytics Using MapReduce

Why provenance was captured for the MapReduce shipped with MongoDB. A wrapper-based approach similar to the approach used in the previous section was used to make MapReduce provenance aware. The provenance collected characterizes as *why provenance* as it gives reason/witness for why an output was obtained.

MongoDB MapReduce runs on one input collection at a time. The mapper reads the output of the document reader and emits them as key value pairs (k_i, v_i). Along with the input for the reducer, the mapper writes the provenance-related information (p_i, k_i) to a temporary file, *file1*, where p_i is a provenance id that uniquely identifies the document which consists of key k_i and value v_i. The reducer applies the reducer logic and processes $(k_i, [v_1, v_2 \dots v_n])$ and generates the output key value pair (k_i, V). The document writer writes the key value pair (k_i, V) generated by the reducer to the output collection and temporary file *file2*.Once the MapReduce task is complete, the provenance logger reads *file1* and *file2* and extracts the ids $\{p_1, p_2, \dots p_n\}$ of the documents with key k_i from *file1* and appends the set $\{p_1, p_2, \dots p_n\}$ to the pair (k_i, V) in the output collection specified with MapReduce. Thus the set $\{p_1, p_2, \dots p_n\}$ is the provenance of the pair (k_i, V). From this, one can identify and trace back the documents inside the collection that contributed to that particular output value.

To illustrate *why provenance*, a simple example is considered. The collection of patient's medication bills at different times in hospital database is illustrated in Fig. 11.14.

The total bill for each patient can be calculated by running a MapReduce job. The output of the job is shown in Fig. 11.15.

Patient id	Bill Date	Prescribed Doctor	Items	Price(₹)
P127	2012-12-13 22:00:00	Dr.Jacob	{"Medicine":"Aidol7","qty":10,"price":2.5} {"Test":"MRI","qty":1,"price":1250}	1275
P133	2012-09-04 00:00:00	Dr.Ajeeb	{"Medicine":"Laxin","qty":5,"price":10} {"Medicine":"Mentol","qty":5,"price":2.5} {"Test":"Blood Test","qty":1,"price":50}	111.5
P123	2012-10-03 14:00:00	Dr.Ajeeb	{"Medicine":"Ameco7","qty":5,"price":20} {"Medicine":"Mentol","qty":5,"price":2.5} {"Test":"ECG","qty":1,"price":125}	234.5
P127	2012-12-13 22:00:00	Dr.Jacob	{"Medicine":"Aidol7","qty":10,"price":2.5}	25
P127	2012-12-13 22:00:00	Dr.Ajeeb	{"Medicine":"Demol Tab","qty":20,"price":2.5} {"Test":"ECG","qty":1,"price":250}	300
P123	2012-12-13 22:00:00	Dr.Jacob	{"Medicine":"Abeol","qty":10,"price":25}	250
P123	2012-10-04 00:00:00	Dr.Jacob	{"Medicine":"Laxin","qty":5,"price":2.5} {"Test":"ECG","qty":1,"price":125}	137.5
P133	2012-12-04 04:00:00	Dr.Ashly	{"Medicine":"Laxin","qty":5,"price":2.5} {"Medicine":"Aloxenol","qty":25,"price":25}	625
P333	2013-01-04 04:00:00	Dr.Hema	{"Medicine":"Laxin","qty":5,"price":2.5} {"Medicine":"Aloxenol","qty":25,"price":25} {"Test":"ECG","price":125}	150

Fig. 11.14 Snapshot of patient's medical bill collection

Fig. 11.15 Snapshot of
output MapReduce to
consolidate total bill

Key	Value
P127	1600
P333	150
P123	622
P133	736.5

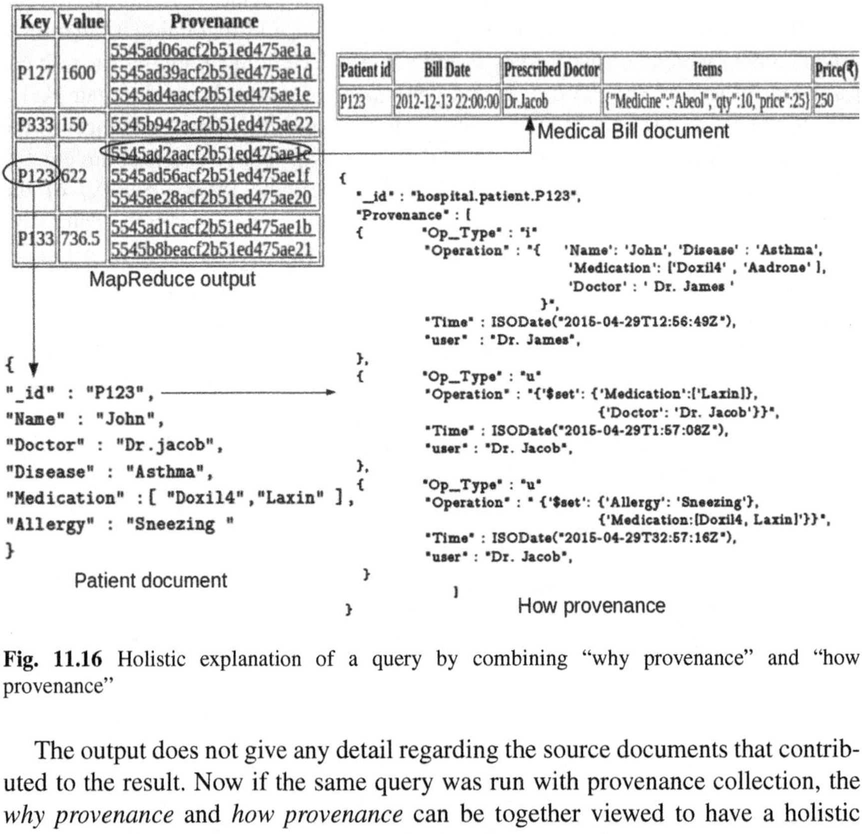

Fig. 11.16 Holistic explanation of a query by combining "why provenance" and "how provenance"

The output does not give any detail regarding the source documents that contributed to the result. Now if the same query was run with provenance collection, the *why provenance* and *how provenance* can be together viewed to have a holistic explanation of the result as shown in Fig. 11.16.

11.4.3.2 Provenance of NoSQL Stores Queried through SQL Interface

The SQL/MED, or Management of External Data, extension to the SQL standard defined by ISO/IEC 9075–9:2008 (originally defined for SQL:2003) [17] provides extensions to SQL to define foreign data wrappers (FDW) and data link types to allow SQL to manage external data. Popular commercial relational databases like

PostgreSQL and IBM DB2 adopted these standards so as to work with data stored in external data stores by providing provisions to define FDWs.

FDW defines external data views called "foreign tables" to access external data through foreign data wrappers. Thus, in this approach data always resides in the remote data store, and query manipulations are done on the "view" defined by the foreign table. Provenance of query results run through FDW is important for debugging result, in case of unexpected results.

A novel idea for provenance representation is used in provenance model called PERM (Provenance Extension of the Relational Model) [4], developed by IIT (Illinois Institute of Technology) database group. The provenance model defined by PERM [4] attaches provenance information to query results by extending the original query result with the details of tuples that contributed toward the query result. PERM displays provenance by means of query rewrite mechanism which transforms a normal query Q into provenance query $Q+$ that computes provenance of Q. PERM module rewrites the query so as to include provenance specific details. This rewritten query is a relational query and hence gets the advantage of all inbuilt optimizations.

When analytics are done in NoSQL stores using SQL interface, the results are usually presented as views. So PERM model was extended to capture provenance of data accessed through foreign data wrappers. The idea is demonstrated by building a proof of concept to analyze data in MongoDB by building a MongoDB FDW and accessed through modified PERM interface. An extension of PERM model was built in stable PostgreSQL version 9.3 and tested by writing a FDW for MongoDB to capture "why provenance" of SQL query run on MongoDB through PERM. The result of simple query versus provenance query on a *SQL Select* statement is shown in Fig. 11.17.

SELECT BRAND,INSTOCK FROM SELLER_1 JOIN COUNTS ON
ID=ITEMID WHERE INSTOCK<4;

brand	instock
lenovo	2
asus	1

SELECT PROVENANCE BRAND,INSTOCK FROMO SELLER_1 JOIN COUNTS ON
ID=ITEMID WHERE INSTOCK<4;

Brand	Instock	prov_public _seller_1_id	prov_public _seller_1_br and	prov_public _seller_1_pri ce	prov_public _counts_ite mid	prov_public _counts_inst ock
Lenovo	2	113	Lenovo	25000	113	2
asus	1	117	asus	5000	117	1

Fig. 11.17 Normal select query result vs provenance query result

11.5 Summary and Conclusion

The power of Big Data generated through IoT can be leveraged only if the data captured can be analyzed and reliable results can be obtained. In this chapter, various schemes for capturing provenance of Big Data analytic tools like MapReduce and NoSQL data stores are discussed. It was demonstrated that provenance captured in MapReduce framework was not only useful for debugging but also for improving certain classes of job reruns and detecting anomalies in the framework. Improving performance of workflows using provenance collected as part of the workflows is a significant use of provenance, as it can save computational power and time for execution. Extending the work to efficiently perform selective refresh on MapReduce workflow is an interesting problem. The proposed approach of capturing transformational provenance using logs and the use of transformational provenance in identifying anomalies in job execution are promising and can be further improved by extending the collection of logs used in analysis. The "how provenance" and "why provenance" captured help in providing explanation for data stored and analytics done on the data stored in NoSQL stores, respectively. "How provenance" and "Why provenance" together provide a holistic picture to explain the results of decisions based on analytics on data stored in NoSQL stores.

This chapter restricted the focus to analysis of Big Data. In the context of IoT, the challenges in capturing provenance of data produced by sensors are very critical, and the area opens up many research problems which need serious research attention. Refer to [18–22].

References

1. Simmhan YL, Pale B, Gannon D (2005) A survey of data provenance in e-science. SIGMOD Rec 34(3):31–36. https://doi.org/10.1145/1084805.1084812
2. Tan W (2004) Research problems in data provenance. IEEE Data Eng Bull 27(4):45–52
3. Agrawal P, Benjelloun O, Sarma A D, Hayworth C, Nabar S, Sugihara T, Widom J (2006) Trio: a system for data, uncertainty, and lineage. In: Proceedings of the 32nd international conference on very large data bases (VLDB '06), VLDB Endowment, pp 1151–1154
4. Glavic B, Alonso G (2009) The PERM provenance management system in action. In: Proceedings of the 2009 ACM SIGMOD International conference on management of data (SIGMOD '09), ACM, New York, USA, pp 1055–1058. https://doi.org/10.1145/1559845.1559980
5. Muniswamy-Reddy K, Holland D, Braun U, Seltzer M (2006) Provenance-aware storage systems. In: ATEC '06 Proceedings of the annual conference on USENIX '06 annual technical conference, Boston, 2006, pp 4–4
6. Tariq D, Ali M, Gehani A (2012) Towards automated collection of application-level data provenance. In: Proceedings of the 4th USENIX conference on theory and practice of provenance (2012), USENIX Association, Berkeley, CA, USA, June 14–5, 2012, pp 16–16
7. Muniswamy-Reddy K K, Macko P, Seltzer M (2010) Provenance for the cloud, FAST, 15–14
8. Sletzer MI, Macko P, Chiarini MA (2011) Collecting provenance via the Xen hypervisor, TaPP
9. Ikeda R, Park H, Widom J (2011) Provenance for generalized map and reduce workflows, CIDR, 273–283

10. Akoush S, Sohan R, Hopper A (2013) HadoopProv: towards provenance as a first class citizen in MapReduce. In: Proceeding TaPP '13 Proceedings of the 5th USENIX workshop on the theory and practice of provenance, 2013, Article No. 11

11. Amsterdamer Y, Davidson SB, Deutch D, Milo T, Stoyanovich J, Tannen V (2011) Putting lipstick on pig: enabling database-style workflow provenance. In: Proceedings VLDB Endow. 5, 4 (December 2011), 346–357. http://dx.doi.org/10.14778/2095686.2095693

12. Middleware, Wikipedia – the free Encyclopedia. https://en.wikipedia.org/wiki/Middleware. Accessed 6 Mar 2017

13. Belhajjme K, Missier P, Goble C, Cannataro M (2009) Data provenance in scientific workflows, medical information science reference, 2009

14. Apache, Apache Weblog. https://httpd.apache.org/docs/1.3/logs.html. Accessed Nov 2016

15. Bhatotia P, Wieder A et al (2011) Incoop: MapReduce for incremental computation. In: Proceedings of the 2nd ACM symposium on cloud computing (SOCC '11). ACM, New York, NY, USA, Article 7, p 14. https://doi.org/10.1145/2038916.2038923

16. Schad J, Quianeé-Ruiz JA, Dittrich J (2013) Elephant, do not forget everything! Efficient processing of growing datasets. IEEE Sixth international conference on cloud computing, Santa Clara, CA, 2013, pp 252–259. doi:https://doi.org/10.1109/CLOUD.2013.67

17. SQL/MED, Wikipedia – the free encyclopedia. https://en.wikipedia.org/wiki/SQL/MED. Accessed 6 Mar 2017

18. Cuzzocrea A (2014) Privacy and security of big data: current challenges and future research perspectives. In: Proceedings of ACM PSBD 2014, pp 45–47

19. Cuzzocrea A, Bertino E (2011) Privacy preserving OLAP over distributed XML data: a theoretically-sound secure-multiparty-computation approach. J Comput Syst Sci 77(6):965–987

20. Cuzzocrea A, Russo V (2009) Privacy preserving OLAP and OLAP security. Encyclopedia of data warehousing and mining, pp 1575–1581

21. Cuzzocrea A (2015) Provenance research issues and challenges in the big data era. In: Proceedings of IEEE COMPSAC workshops 2015, pp 684–686

22. Cuzzocrea A, Fortino G, Rana OA (2013) Managing data and processes in cloud-enabled large-scale sensor networks: state-of-the-art and future research directions. In: Proceedings of IEEE CCGRID 2013, pp 583–588

Chapter 12
Networking Topologies and Communication Technologies for the IoT Era

P. Beaulah Soundarabai and Pethuru Raj Chelliah

Abstract A kind of deeper and decisive connectivity is the most indispensable requirement for the projected and promised IoT era. To start with, every common and casual thing in our midst gets systematically digitized. There are several peculiar advantages being accrued out of the digitization process as well as any digitized entities/smart objects/sentient materials. The digitization technologies, if appropriately leveraged, can make ordinary objects in our daily environments into extraordinary articles. Digitized elements are self-, surroundings-, and situation-aware individually as well as collectively. Not only the physical assets but also all kinds of mechanical, electrical, electronics, and IT devices in our places are accordingly instrumented and interconnected. They are interconnected to purposefully and precisely communicate, collaborate, corroborate, and correlate to be innately cognitive in their operations, offerings, and outputs. Further on, everyday electronics, instruments, machines, equipment, wares, utensils, robots, and other fixed, portable, wearable, hearable, implantable, mobile, and nomadic devices in our personal, professional, and social environments are seamlessly integrated. This integration is made feasible with the help of cloud-hosted (traditional IT servers and private, public, and hybrid clouds) cyber applications, services, and data sources in order to be empowered adequately to join in the mainstream computing. Even fog or edge computing is beginning to blossom so that localized and user-centric devices are capable of forming ad hoc clouds of devices. The main objective of fog computing is to set a stimulating foundation for producing next-generation, real-time, insights-filled, context-aware, event-driven, and people-centric applications. Thus, clearly we are heading toward the tightly interconnected world. This chapter is specially crafted for conveying all about the emerging network topologies and communication technologies; key limitations of these technologies have also been discussed. In addition, the chapter provides details on how the inherent issues can be tackled so that

P. Beaulah Soundarabai
Department of Computer Science, Christ University, Bangalore, India
e-mail: beaulah.s@christuniversity.in

P.R. Chelliah (✉)
Reliance Jio Cloud, Bangalore, India
e-mail: peterindia@gmail.com

© Springer International Publishing AG 2017   241
Z. Mahmood (ed.), *Connected Environments for the Internet of Things*,
Computer Communications and Networks,
https://doi.org/10.1007/978-3-319-70102-8_12

the expressed liabilities, vulnerabilities, threats, drawbacks, and loopholes can be surmounted toward secure, safe, and smart IoT era.

12.1   Introduction

The technologically inspired capability of instrumenting and interconnecting computationally powerful as well as resource-constrained devices (physical, mechanical, electrical, and electronics) with one another in the vicinity as well as with cloud-hosted software applications and data sources over any network is to enable the devices to exhibit a kind of shrewdness and sagacity in their operations and outputs. Not only everyday instruments, machines, appliances, wares, utensils, equipment, etc. but also common and casual articles such as cots, chairs, cups, tables, pipes, doors, sofas, windows, etc. in our personal, professional, and social environments are being technically tuned and turned to exhibit hitherto unforeseen smart behavior and to join in the mainstream computing. Further on, the environments wherein those embedded yet empowered devices are being deployed in large numbers ultimately become smart in their contributions for the occupants and owners of the environment. These transitions are being enabled through the systematic leverage of hugely powerful edge technologies such as disposable and diminutive sensors, actuators, chips, controllers, codes, stickers, pads, tags, labels, specks, smart dust, etc. That is, the aura and era of the Internet of things (IoT) have started to beckon and dawn upon us powerfully with the overwhelming use of promising, proven, and potential technologies. Our living, working, social, edutainment, and entertainment places are being systematically decked and demonstrated to be lively and lovely. The methodical adoption and adaptation of scores of digitization and distribution technologies are to bring a series of disruptions and transformations in our lives. The much-anticipated digital living, economy, and the world are bound to see the light at the end of the long tunnel. The capabilities such as connectivity, networking, communication, integration, and orchestration of digital elements, devices, and IT systems are imperative to seamlessly share their unique capabilities and capacities.

In this chapter, we are extensively covering the connectivity technologies, topologies and tools, and their contributions for setting up and sustaining smarter environments (smarter homes, hospitals, hotels, etc.) and ultimately the smarter planet.

12.1.1   Describing the Context

A growing array of open standards is being formulated, framed, and polished by domain experts, industry consortiums, and standard bodies to make the IoT idea more visible, viable, and valuable. National governments across the globe are setting up special expert groups in order to come out with pragmatic policies and procedures to take forward the solemn and sublime ideals of IoT and to realize the strategic significance of the IoT paradigm in conceiving, concretizing, and providing a bevy of context-aware and citizen-centric services to ensure and enhance peoples' living. Research students, scholars, and scientists are working collaboratively toward identifying the implementation challenges and overcoming them via different means and ways especially standards-sticking technological solutions. This chapter is specially crafted to throw light on the emerging integration tools and techniques in order to integrate and orchestrate digitized and connected entities and elements, some typical integration scenarios being as follows:

- Sensor and actuator networks
- Device-to-device (D2D) integration
- Cloud-to-cloud (C2C) integration
- Device and sensor-to-cloud (D2C) integration [1]

Figure 12.1 gives a glimpse of how disparate devices are getting connected with one another indirectly.

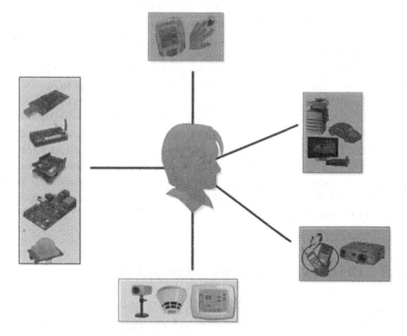

Fig. 12.1 Connected sensors and actuators

Table 12.1 Comparison of wireless technologies and their usefulness in IoT

Technologies/factors	Bluetooth low	802.15.4	Wifi
Cost	Excellent	Very good	Fairly good
Security	Fairly good	Fairly good	Excellent
Power consumption	Excellent	Excellent	Very poor
Ecosystem	Excellent	Very poor	Excellent
Reliability	Excellent	Fairly good	Fairly good
Ease of Use	Excellent	Fairly good	Excellent
Range	Fairly good	Good	Excellent

12.1.2 IoT Communication Protocol Requirements

One definition of IoT refers to connecting devices to the Internet that were not previously connected. A factory owner may connect high-powered lights. A triathlete may connect a battery-powered heart-rate monitor. A home or building automation provider may connect a wireless sensor with no line power source. But the important thing here is that in all the above cases, the "thing" must communicate through the Internet to be considered an "IoT" node. Since it must use the Internet, it must also adhere to the Internet Engineering Task Force's (IETF) Internet protocol suite. However, the Internet has historically connected resource-rich devices with lots of power, memory, and connection options. As such, its protocols have been considered too heavy to apply wholesale for applications in the emerging IoT.

There are other aspects of the IoT which also drive modifications to IETF's work. In particular, networks of IoT end nodes will be lossy, and the devices attached to them will be very low power, saddled with constrained resources, and expected to live for years. The requirements for both the network and its end devices might look like the Table 12.1. This new model needs new, lightweight protocols that do not require a lot of resources. Considering these unique needs, gaining a deeper knowledge of IoT connectivity and data transmission protocols is paramount. This chapter is specifically crafted for that.

12.1.3 The Growing Importance of the IoT Paradigm

The ensuing era of IoT is to play a very stellar role in shaping up our everyday environments. The IoT concept is an engrossing and essential disruption for everyone in this extremely connected world. In this section, we discuss the prime and paramount shifts sweeping the entire human society. It is an important point to note that there are a number of noteworthy technology-induced transitions happening in the IT field.

12.1.4   The Meteoric Rise of Device Ecosystem

With innumerable devices, sensors, controllers, and actuators getting fervently deployed in distributed and decentralized fashion in important locations such as offices, manufacturing floors, retail stores, food joints, shopping plazas, nuclear installations, forest and border areas, critical junctions, malls, entertainment centers, etc., the amount of data getting generated and collected goes up tremendously. The machine-generated data is far larger than man-generated data.

The device ecosystem is embracing a bevy of miniaturization technologies to be slim and sleek yet smart in their operations, outlooks, and outputs. That is, multifaceted devices are hitting the market in plenty. For example, highly miniaturized yet mesmerizing smartphones are being produced in millions these days. Smartphones are not only connecting people with people but also turning out to be capable of operating machines locally as well as remotely [2].

Digitization and distribution are gaining a lot of ground in the present days; thereby all kinds of tangible items in our home and social and office environments are getting transfigured to be computational, communicative, sensitive, perceptive, capable of knowledge discovery and dissemination, decision enabling, and accomplishing. That is, ordinary articles become extraordinary. Casually found objects in our working, walking, and wandering places become digitized. Thus, IT-enabled things are cognitive enough to seamlessly and spontaneously join in the mainstream computing process. In short, every tangible thing gets emboldened to be smart, every electronics becomes smarter, and every human being is set to become the smartest in his or her actions, reactions, and decision making with the pervasive, unceasing, and unobtrusive assistance of service-oriented and smartness-ingrained devices, game consoles, media players, consumer electronics, and business as well as IT services and communication networks.

Extreme and deeper connectivity is another well-known phenomenon in order to establish and sustain ad hoc connectivity among dissimilar and distributed devices to share their unique capabilities. Further on, it is all about the purposeful integration with remote off-premise, on-demand, and online applications. These days, devices are accordingly instrumented in the factory itself to collect or generate data from their environments and users to be transmitted to centralized control systems. That is, lately, devices are empowered by embedding a number of newer modules internally. In addition, devices are enabled to connect with outside world.

12.1.5   The Emergence of Sensor and Actuator Networks

Sensing is tending to be ubiquitous. Sensors are being touted as the eyes and ears of next-generation software applications. A number of technologies especially miniaturization, networking, communication, etc. are contributing immensely to the unprecedented success of the sensing paradigm. Sensors are becoming exceptionally tiny to be easily disposable, disappearing, and yet elegantly deft. Therefore, sensors, which are typically low-cost, power, and memory systems, are gradually and graciously penetrative, pervasive, and persuasive. Sensors are becoming smart in the sense that they are able to conserve and preserve their battery energy in order to prolong their lives. Smart sensors are capable of buffering and transmitting the data captured or generated. Sensors are increasingly complying with the mesh topology toward increased maneuverability and reliability. Sensors are mainly for environmental and asset monitoring. All kinds of physical, mechanical, electrical, electronics, and IT systems are being fitted with a variety of sensors for monitoring, measuring, and managing various aspects, conditions, and situations of the systems. For example, all kinds of vehicles and their body parts are being fitted with smart sensors in order to proactively and preemptively attend their needs in time so that any kind of collapse and failure can be prevented. Smartphones are being embedded with numerous sensors. Even large-scale IT data centers and server farms are being sensor-enabled in order to capture their operational values [3].

Thus, sensors are very vital for our everyday environments especially rough and tough ones. Sensors are being networked toward taking data from sensors to remote control systems. There are data fusion algorithms in plenty in order to dynamically capture and aggregate various sensor values to come out with composite indicators. Further on, there are ways and mechanisms being prescribed in order to eliminate all kinds of sensor data impurities, deviations, deficiencies, and disturbances so that the primary needs of data trustworthiness and timeliness are being fulfilled. Increasingly sensor data are subjected to a litany of investigations in order to squeeze out valuable intelligence for taking informed decisions in time. There is a growing array of sensor-centric data transmission protocols. Further on, sensor data modeling is an interesting phenomenon.

There are industry-strength data formats for unique and unambiguous representation, exchange, and persistence and interpretation. The list of sensor-centric software services is steadily growing. Sensor gateways, middleware, brokers, adaptors, connectors, drivers, and controllers are being leveraged in order to collect and transmit sensor data. There are frameworks and platforms to speed up the process of sensor-cloud integration so that sensor data can be accumulated in one centralized place to enable cloud-based data analytics. Sensor data and the insights extracted out of it are tactically and strategically sound for various service providers. Thought-provoking industry and personal and social use cases are being published with the continued growth and adoption of the sensor technology. Actuation is generally based on sensing, and hence actuators and sensors go hand in hand. Actuators are the ones that accomplish the execution based on the sensor findings.

Sensors and actuators are therefore the essential ingredients for any environment to be smart. Actuators are designed in such a way to receive sensor values and act strictly based on that. Thus, networking of sensors and actuators turns out to be an important affair for setting and sustaining smarter environments [4]. Clouds are the most sought-after IT infrastructures for hosting sensor-specific platforms and applications. With sensor data analytics being crucial for formulating sophisticated and people-centric applications, sensor data analytics platforms are increasingly deployed in clouds.

The pragmatic use cases out of sensor networks are emerging and evolving. A wireless sensor network (WSN) is a network formed by a large number of sensor nodes where each node is equipped with a sensor to detect different physical phenomena such as light, heat, pressure, presence, gas, etc. WSNs are regarded as a revolutionary information gathering method to build next-generation people-centric IoT applications. There are several research papers depicting the growing and glowing sensor applications in the peer-reviewed sensor journals, e.g., [5, 6].

Body sensor networks (BSNs) are also very popular challenges related to IoT. BSNs are to improve the quality of life and for providing ambient assisted living (AAL) facility. BSNs ensure improved healthcare of disabled, debilitated, and diseased people. Also, they improve our daily routines such as playing sports. The distributed and changeable character of BSNs introduces new concerns and challenges to solve. As per experts, the research in the area of BSNs must cover low-level hardware design to higher-level communication and data fusion algorithms, up to top-level applications.

12.1.6   Sensor-to-Cloud Integration

Sensor and actuator data need to be taken to nearby or faraway clouds for storage and analytics. There are multiple cloud options ranging from off-premise and on-premise to edge clouds. Public clouds are typically for historical, comprehensive, and batch processing, whereas interactive, stream, and real-time processing in a secure fashion are better accomplished by edge/fog clouds wherein proximate or local processing gets done comfortably. Edge or fog clouds are being formed dynamically by clubbing and clustering together several resource-intensive devices in the particular environment. Connected devices are bound to produce futuristic fog clouds as there is a lot of interest in real-time analytics for gathering tactical and timely insights. Increasingly IoT application enablement platforms (AEPs) situated at cloud environments in association with IoT data analytics platforms are able to receive ground-level data and work on it to carve out pragmatic intelligence.

There are several unique advantages being associated with clouds these days. Clouds are being positioned and prescribed as the best-in-class IT infrastructure for sensor data storage and analytics. Cloud infrastructures inherently support IT resource elasticity, application/workload scalability, etc. through IT consolidation, centralization, federation, sharing, automation, and virtualization techniques and tools. Geographically established clouds are getting integrated through standards and brokers; thereby distributed resource and service orchestration get facilitated with just a single click. Data virtualization and information visualization platforms are seamlessly integrated with data analytics platforms to speed up the transition from data to actionable insights that gets disseminated to machines as well as men in time to proceed with the accurate actuation and execution with clarity and confidence.

In summary, everyday objects are being equipped with embedding sensors to gain the communication capability. This will create a range of potentially powerful and promising services in many different domains. Fire, flame, and fall detection procedures are automated through the employment of several sorts of sensors. Similarly, there are multiple scenarios being identified and articulated well for sensor and actuator networking. Thus the fact that sensors are talking to local as well as remote sensors, actuators, and applications collectively as well as individually, is going to be a real game-changer for the forthcoming IoT world.

12.2   Deciphering the IoT Connectivity Methods

In the last few years, the Internet of things (IoT) idea has been drawing a huge attention from academic professors and industry practitioners. The worldwide enterprises and organizations are striving hard and stretching further to use this strategic idea efficiently and elegantly so that they can derive the required strength to keep up their brand value and the position in the coming decades. Figure 12.2 vividly illustrates how ground-level physical assets get networked with one another as well as integrated with off-premise/on-premise/edge infrastructures in order to deposit data to be crunched instantaneously to squeeze out usable and reusable intelligence. There are three prominent layers in any IoT system/environment setup. The first layer is all about collecting the environmental as well as digitized assets' state information. Once the timely and trustworthy data gets collected, they need to be transmitted to data processing, storage, mining, and analysis systems toward knowledge discovery and dissemination.

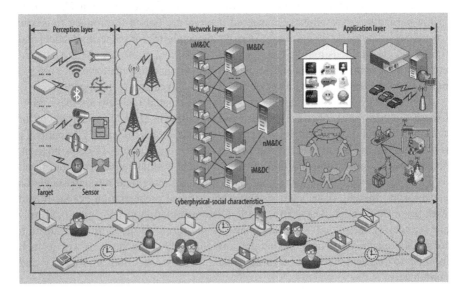

Fig. 12.2 Layers of IoT

According to Machina Research, the low-power wide area (LPWA) network will outperform 2G, 3G, and 4G by providing a higher rate of IoT connectivity. It also predicts that there would be around 50 billion connected things by the year 2020. LPWA networks also support M2M applications which are usually deployed in remote areas and require longer battery life as they might be kept unattended for a longer duration. So, these characteristics of LPWA technology provide an apt solution for many IoT applications [7].

The backbone of IoT is the connectivity of devices. It networks with people, things, and software applications and transfers data between them through the Internet communication infrastructure, which is public and open. And through that, a variety of everyday activities are monitored, controlled remotely, and studied for further intelligence. If there is no interconnection, there will not be any communication between smart objects and devices. Therefore it is very important to understand the IoT network topology.

12.3   Network Topologies

There are plenty of purpose-specific and agnostic devices which are of different varieties. Thus many factors will affect the working and performance of IoT if the right topology for optimal networking is not chosen. A network topology is a method through which the objects of the IoT are arranged in the network. The majorly used IoT network protocols are point-to-point (P2P), star, and mesh. These are briefly discussed in the following sections.

12.3.1   Point-to-Point (P2P)

P2P topology devices communicate with each other directly without the intervention of cloud services. These P2P networks have a great potential for scalability, distributed system for data sharing, and robustness as peers are connected to other devices independently. In alternative P2P protocols [5] [6], there are hash functions used to choose the devices to be connected with them randomly. Adaptive P2P protocols [8] are also available to have a self-organized topology which allows the peer to directly choose and connect with them so as to get the desired data from them. This model is resistant to the attacks and active peers get the connection, and malicious nodes are avoided through the choice-based selection of peers. Peers in the network are warned with the identity of malicious nodes so that the malicious nodes are completely avoided for communication. Each node can choose a limit x as the number of peers with which it wants to connect; this is useful to save the bandwidth.

12.3.2 Star Topology

In this type of topology, each object is connected to the data center through its dedicated cloud services. Most of the internet services work in this type of topology. The centralized approach makes it easier to control and manage as data is received, processed, and analyzed in a single data center. The entire devices in the network can be hacked by hacking a single server. It is not much scalable; as the number of devices increases, the collection and processing of data also increase which makes it difficult to maintain the cloud service architecture due to the centralized approach. There is also a high latency as the devices communicate with each other through the same network.

12.3.3 Mesh

In this model, each device is connected to all other devices in the network, and each can send and receive data among them. This is the mostly used topology for IoT, as all the devices are connected to all other devices in the network and through this data transfer among the devices are enabled completely without much delay. Each module works independently as a centralized module. Its major limitation is that it is tough to implement as each object should know the address of the other devices; adding a new device into an existing topology would complicate the hardware implementation. If wireless communication is used such as nrf24L01RF, the implementation would be easier than the wired communication. These radio frequency models are widely used in healthcare wearable devices as they do not require line of sight for data transfer.

Figure 12.3 illustrates the relevance of application protocols such as REST, CoAP, etc. in establishing IoT systems. There are data communication protocols such as ZigBee, WiFi, Bluetooth, etc. for establishing connectivity between devices as shown in the figure. Figure 12.4 extends the personal and local area networks to the remote software applications via the public Internet. The various technologies contributing for such kinds of people-centric applications are described pictorially. Table 12.1 clearly delineates the various factors of IoT protocols.

IoT is the driving force for a wide variety of manufacturing firms, and it scales from a single confined device up to enormous devices with embedded techniques; using cloud infrastructure, they get connected in the real time.

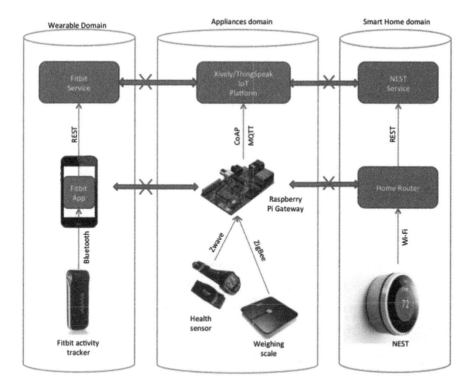

Fig. 12.3 Application protocols of IoT

12.4   Wireless Technologies

12.4.1   Low-Power Wide Area Network (LPWAN)

Low-power wide area network is the latest wireless technology that uses low bit rate (bandwidth) long distant communication by consuming low battery power. So it is also known as low-power network (LPN). Its main aims are to achieve the following features so as to address the economy and the power concerns than the mobile network standards:

- Long communication range (10 KM to 50 KM)
- Low bandwidth
- Low cost

Network technologies could not provide a long range with low cost and bandwidth wherein LPWAN is meant for most of the IoT and M2M business solutions which majorly use sensor applications. Traditional network technologies are of a wired network. Due to the introduction of 802.11 standards,the huge impact has been made on the market because of wireless communication.

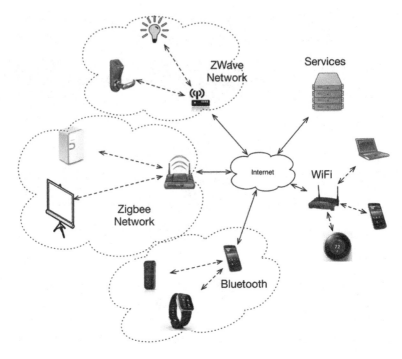

Fig. 12.4 IoT networking

Table 12.2 shows the comparison of various wireless technologies for the very important factors of range and the bandwidth ranging from low to high. It is very clear that LPWAN is the one and only wireless technology which offers a long range of data transfer with low bandwidth. It uses very few base stations and gateways to cover a long range of up to 50 km. It also has very good network coverage in rural regions where there is more open space. It is expected that the most of the 50 billion connected objects in the year 2020 will use LPWAN for the transmission of data. Applications that use smoke detectors, parking management, healthcare bands, GPS services, etc. use LPWAN to connect their sensors which are cost effective at the same time they are also rapid.

The protocols of IoT are categorized into many levels such as infrastructure, communication, network, security, etc. We will see infrastructure protocols and communication data protocols in detail.

Table 12.2 Comparison of wireless technologies for the range and bandwidth

Range	Bandwidth	Wireless technologies
Short range	Low	Bluetooth 802.15.3
		RFID NFC
		WBAN 802.15.3
	Medium	802.11a
		802.11b
		802.11 g
	High	802.11c
		802.11 ad
		802.11 g
Medium range	Low	WPAN 802.15.3
	Medium	ZigBee 802.15.4
		2G, 3G
	High	4G, 5G
Long range	Low	LPWAN
	Medium	VSAT
	High	–

12.5 Infrastructure Protocols

12.5.1 Context Centric Networking

This protocol is from the project CCNX that developed an architecture for the data sharing by avoiding the limitations of scalability and security. This protocol can be deployed on an existing network with the help of middleware software; this has tremendous power on content networking. CCN is an open protocol and so it can be altered as required. Its only goal is to make a dynamic and secured and massively scalable network to a varied set of devices to communicate and share data with them.

This protocol is exclusively for such environments with high-speed data communication where the source and destination are heterogeneous in nature. The traditional source-destination TCP/IP model does not provide the best solution. In CCN [9], the content publishers create named payload packets with content object messages. Signatures are used with the packets to secure the content with the combination of name, publisher's id, and the payload. The consumers or clients issue an *interesting message* as a request with the name of the desired content. This request traverses all over the network and kept in a table called Pending Interest Table (PIT) [10]. When a content object matches with the interest, then the content object is sent to the client on a reverse path by following the information on the PIT. Along the way, this content object can be cached, and the matched one with the interest message may be then used. This content is self-identifiable as the security binding is of interest [11], publisher key and the payload it can be decrypted at any point in time. This provides a complete security of data in the network.

12.5.2   LoRaWAN

Long-range (**LoRa**) WAN is an exclusive LPWAN design, which is meant for the wireless objects that work with battery power right from a small region to global level networks. It addresses the key design issues of IoT such as mobility, unidirectional and bidirectional connectivity, and communication along with localization services. It provides a high level of independence to the developers and to the business. LoRaWAN has the star of star topology in its network architecture that has a transparent bridge called gateways, between the network servers and the smart objects. All these objects are enabled with broadcast, multicast, and unicast communication, and the required one can be chosen dynamically according to the mass distribution of data to efficiently handle the communication time and the bandwidth.

Different data rates and frequency channels are used for the communication between the gateways and smart objects. Based on the communication range and the duration of the message, the data rate is selected. It is because of these different data rates and the wide-spectrum technology; the communications do not interfere with one another by creating the virtual channels and thus increase the gateway's capacity. The adaptive data rate is used for managing each end device's data rate and frequency output. The security of the data communication of Internet of things is essential as it is the universal problem that involves lots and lots of confidential personal data of the individual and the society. This is achieved by encryption layers such as:

- Unique network key (EUI64) for the security on the network level
- Unique application key (EUI64) for the security on end to end in the application level
- Device-specific key (EUI128)

Longer range, high robustness, multipath resistance, Doppler resistance, and less power consumption are the key characteristics of LoRa. LoRa transceivers can operate between 137 MHz to 1020 MHz, and so they are used in licensed bands. They are also often deployed in ISM bands (Europe, 868 MHz and 433 MHz; the United States, 915 MHz and 433 MHz). The LoRa physical layer is enabled to be used with any MAC layer, but LoRaWAN is the MAC which is majorly used as it operates in the star topology.

Apart from the size of the payload, the communication parameters such as spreading factor (SF), bandwidth, carrier frequency (CF), and coding rate(CR) have a significant impact on the airtime of LoRa transmission. A packet of 20 bytes can have the airtime **ranging** from 9 milliseconds to 2.2 s based on the choice of these parameters [12]. We shall also discuss the emerging low-power technologies.

12.5.3 Narrowband IoT

Narrowband is the initiative from 3rd Generation Partnership Project (3GPP) that writes standards for the cellular network for the devices which require very low data rate in the mobile communication and are powered by batteries. It is an LPWAN standard designed for mobile IoT. NB-IoT technology will connect the smart things such as simple wearable in the coverage area as they require very low battery power and low data rate. It majorly focuses on low-cost, low battery power, and a large number of things connected in an indoor coverage area. It can be deployed to inband spectrum which is allocated to long-term evolution (LTE) or stand-alone spectrum.

12.5.4 NB-IoT Vs LoRa

NB-IoT and LoRa technologies are unique in comparison with each other as they serve different commercial and technical requirements and are exclusively for different applications such as the technologies like WiFi and Bluetooth. LoRa works with unlicensed spectrum below 1 GHz which procures no cost for the applications using it, whereas NB-IoT uses licensed bands which are less than 1 GHz. The bands from 500 MHz to 1 GHz are optimum for the long-range communications. LoRa and LoRaWAN are asynchronous protocol and used for simple implementation and cost effectiveness but cannot offer a better quality of service (QoS). NB-IoT is a time-slotted protocol which is very much optimal for the quality of service but cannot provide a durable battery lifetime comparing LoRa. The higher-level applications which really require the assurance of QoS opt for NB-IoT, and the lower-end business solutions prefer LoRa. NB-IoT is the best option for applications that require very frequent communications, low latency rate, and a large volume of data transfers. The applications which look for durable battery life and lower cost and do not need frequent communication opt for LoRa.

12.6 Technologies for Applications

At any point in time, there will not be only one technology that will rule the world of IoT. The deployment strategies, application nature, and requirements, technical differences, device specifications etc. will decide the technology as its best fit. As the number of devices getting connected to IoT grows day by day, the underlying networking technologies are also expected to scale up to the growing needs where the expected number of smart things is not in millions but in tens of billions. For instance, if we consider the electric meters, these devices require high data flow and low latency with frequent communication. As they are connected to the electric power source, they do not require low battery power with a long life of the battery.

The power grids of electric meters have to be monitored continuously to take decisions on interruptions, power consumptions, load, etc. NB-IoT would be better for this application as it is static, has frequent communication, and has high data rates and it is easy to give a better coverage through NB-IoT rather. LoRaWAN might not be a solution for this as this is mainly for low latency which is not required for electric meters at all.

Consider smart building application, which focuses on monitoring the temperature, moisture, humidity, water flow, electric leakages, security, etc. and in turn alerts the administrator of the building with alarms or messages immediately to safeguard the building. Such applications will have many numbers of sensors which are of low cost and with high battery life. These sensors do not require frequent communication, and so LoRa might be a better solution for this kind of applications.

12.6.1 Random Phase Multiple Access (RPMA)

Random phase multiple access technologies are a combination of technologies that uses low-power wide area channel access method exclusively designed for wireless machine-to-machine communication. It has been designed by ingénue [12]. It uses 2.4 GHz spectrum which is free of cost and can cover up to 300 square miles which takes nearly 30 cellular towers to cover the same area. In the static position, its speed is 642 kbps for uplink and 156 kbps for downlink which is 10 times speedier than the dial-up connection. On the move, its speed drops down to 2 kbps, and this speed is more than enough for almost all the IoT mobile objects.

The special feature of RPMA is that it has backward compatibility with network longevity for decades. RPMA provides reliable network coverage and reliable message transmission. In the open space like desserts and large swathes of lands, it has the coverage of 450 square miles, and in the land, with tall buildings and trees, its coverage drops to 300 square miles as the radio waves require more access points. It has optimization in all layers of the protocol for low-power consumption; long battery life is assured by adaptive data rates. In the case of a cellular network, the battery power drains out quickly due to the overheads of the protocols used, but RPMA has the minimized protocol overhead which leads to durable battery life. All these abovesaid advantages would be useless if there is no unprecedented coverage. It can penetrate through concrete inside buildings and underground to reach the devices by giving a broad range of coverage.

12.6.2 Time Synchronized Mesh Protocol (TSMP)

This is a protocol developed by Dust Networks as a communication protocol for self-organizing wireless networks of independent devices. These devices synchronize with each other from time to time, and they communicate with each other in their time slot as in the case of round robin or time division multiplexing [13]. They transmit and receive signals over a common path by synchronized switching, and each signal is available in the common signal path for a fraction of the time period. So this protocol requires high-speed transmission. This protocol is designed for a reliable data delivery even in a noisy environment. Channel hopping is used to avoid the packet interference by sending the TSMP packets with different radio channels.

DigiMesh is another protocol of the same type developed by Digi International. They adopt routing protocols such as Dynamic Source Routing (DSR) and Adhoc On-Demand Distant Vector Routing (AODV). TSMA tries to achieve the following:

- Reliability – with low battery power with a higher rate of packet delivery for all its sensor nodes. [14]
- Scalability – this protocol is scalable to thousands of nodes in the mesh topology in the same radio frequency (RF).
- Security – TSMP authenticates all the packets so as to provide integrity and security for all its data packets.
- Environment and climate – TSMP nodes can operate between the temperature of −40 degree Celsius to 85 degree Celsius and also with varied radio frequency noise levels with a layer 4 of quality of service (QoS).

12.6.3 Nano-Internet Protocol (NanoIP)

Nano-Internet protocol creates a miniature of the internet-like network for its embedded devices majorly sensor devices [15]. It avoids the overhead of TCP/IP by keeping the local addressing for its wireless network. This protocol is used for the subcategory of IoT, known as Internet of Nano-things which is the interconnection of nano-things with the existing internet communication. But it requires different network architecture. Exclusive architectures are proposed for intra-body networks for healthcare monitoring-related applications and for interconnected office where each and every internal component of objects in the office is provided with transceivers that allow them to be connected all the time in the network. The user can track of his entire office not only his employees but all his office gadgets from anywhere easily. The components such as nano-routers, nano-nodes, and nano-microinterface devices and gateways are required for this nanoIP protocol.

Different channel-accessing models are required for nano-networks depending on the data and how they are encoded. Carrier sensing-based MAC protocols [16] will not work with this pulse-based communication as there is no carrier signal available for sensing. Very complex protocols cannot be used for the simple nanodevices. Synchronization of these nanodevices is also a very open research issue. The short pulses transmitted by the nanodevices might face collisions among the other nodes as they all try to access the same communication channel.

These protocols use help to connect the host name to IP address within the network and also help to see the list of URLs that are being broadcast by the peers in the network using bluetooth low-energy beacon (BLEB). There are protocols such as Universal Plug and Play that uses open connectivity. These protocols permit the peer devices to view each other device's presence on the network and establish the network services for data sharing.

12.6.4   Multicast Domain Name System (mDNS)

The small networks which do not have a local name server use this multicast DNS that resolves hostname with IP address. In this protocol, when a client wants to resolve a host name, it sends a probe query message looking for the host having the same name. The particular host machine will now multicast a message with its IP address, and all the nodes in the same subnet can use this message to update their cache memories. Table 12.3 describes the various fields of query message present in the template of mDNS.

Table 12.3 Query message format of mDNS

Field	Meaning	Length of the field (in bits)
QNAME	Name of the node to which the query is addressed to	String size of the name
QTYPE	The type of the query, i.e. the type of resource record which should be returned in responses. All the records of the answer, name servers, additional records are together called is resource records	16
UNICAST-RESPONSE	Boolean flag indicating whether a unicast response is desired. This is majorly used to avoid the broadcast in the network. If this field is set, then the reply should go as a direct unicast message to the node which has sent the query through which unnecessary broadcast to the whole network is avoided	1 or 0
QCLASS	Class code. The code of the resource record being requested by the client	15

12.7   Communication Data Protocols

12.7.1   Message Queuing Telemetry Transport (MQTT)

This message queuing telemetry transport protocol is exclusively designed for machine-to-machine connection so as to have a lightweight data transfer between the devices. It uses low bandwidth but has high latency, and it is an unreliable network. It was developed by IBM in 1999. This protocol is suitable for mobile devices where the battery power and bandwidth utilization are very crucial. It uses TCP/IP port 1883 and TCP/IP port 8883 for using it over Secured Socket Layers (SSL). MQTT does not provide security as it is a lightweight protocol, but the security can be achieved by adding a layer of an application that encrypts the data in that level. MQTT-SN is another variation of MQTT which exclusively used the machine-to-machine and mobile applications that involve sensors. [17].

12.7.2   Constrained Application Protocol (CoAP)

This is a special web-based data transfer protocol for the usage among the constrained nodes such as very low battery power, bandwidth, and lossy networks. These nodes generally have a simple microcontroller with a low RAM and ROM. IPV6 on low-power personal area network usually has a high level of packet loss and error rates with a very less throughput. This CoAP is for such nodes and networks so as to utilize the battery power smartly and achieving automation. It supports multicasting and has very low overhead, and so it is very simple for constrained applications and environments such as M2M applications and IoT applications.

The key characteristics of CoAP are as follows:

- Web-based protocol for M2M and constrained applications
- Supports unicast and multicast at the same time
- Uses asynchronous message passing and achieves simplicity
- Supports URIs
- Uses simple caching techniques
- Minimizes the complexity of HTTP by using RESTful protocol
- Low overhead for the header and has low parsing complexity
- Supports content type and discovery of resources (CoAP services)

12.7.3 Extensible Messaging and Presence Protocol (XMPP)

XMPP is for open technologies that support instant messaging, presence, multiuser chat, video calls, voice calls, routing of XML data and lightly weighted middleware with the content association. This protocol is a discovery against the closed instant messaging [14]. Key Characteristics of XMPP are:

- Simple: XMPP protocols are very simple, open, and free which are easily implementable and understandable. There are multiple implementations freely available for clients, servers, libraries, server, and client components.
- Standard: It follows Internet Engineering Task Force standard (IETF) to make the XML streaming protocols. Its specifications are available as RFC 3920, RFC 3921, RFC 6120, RFC 6162, and RFC 7622.
- Popular: there are more than 10,000 XMPP servers and millions of users for the XMPP's instant messaging across the world. Google Talk is one among the instant messaging application. It enables the users to build and deploy real-time applications using its varied services.
- Secured: End-to-end encryption is used to secure all its communication, and the server can be removed from the public network at any point of time.
- Distributed architecture: The decentralized architecture of XMPP can be adapted by any user to run their own XMPP server making the organizations and individuals to experience the fun in communication.
- Flexible: XMPP also provides network management, content organization, gaming, chatting, audio and video sharing, web services, remote system collaboration, and monitoring with cloud computing.
- Scalable: Through the power of XML, any application and functionality can be built on top of XMPP protocols making it scalable vertically.

XMPP-IoT is another version of XMPP where it is dedicated to people-to-people, people-to-machine, machine-to-people, and M2M communications effectively. Software implementation for the toolkits, client, server, and client and server components is available in major programming languages.

12.7.4 Data-Distribution Service for Real-Time Systems (DDS)

It is a middleware protocol which revolves around the data connectivity and distribution. By integrating the system components, it provides data connectivity with low latency and high scalable and reliable architecture for Internet of things.

It abstracts the application from the core operating system. This protocol acts as the middleware between the application software and operating system and makes the system components to interact with each other without concentrating on how to pass a message between the system and application. It allows various programming languages to write the application program and to share data across the operating system and processor architectures. The connectivity, data discovery, scalability, QoS, and security are taken care by the middleware. Features of DDS include:

- **Data centric** – DDS provides quality of service-based data sharing by enabling the applications to publish and subscribe to topics that are identified with their topic names. Subscription specifies the content filters and time and filters only the sublevel data which are published on the particular topic but not the complete content of topic thus reduces the data size being transferred in the communication network. It also forces all the messages to include the metadata such as contextual information that the DDS need to understand when it receives the data. Thus DDS knows the type of text and controls the order of sharing the data.
- **Data space transparency** – DDS keeps the data storage transparently by keeping the local and global data in the application with the single directory view. So every data looks like it is stored in the local storage, and requesting for this data is also in the same way as of accessing the local data. If the data is in the remote nodes, then DDS takes care of sending the request to appropriate node.
- **The quality of service (QoS)** – Data reliability and security for the real-time data are provided by what each node needs. DDS efficiently decides what part of the whole topic data is required by the node and sends only that part of data. It also tracks whether the data reaches the destination, and if it does not reach, the middleware implements the reliability algorithm and retransmits the data to the destination till it receives it. When the systems change their locations, DDS makes the changes in the system registers, and the sending and receiving to such location-changed systems is taken care of effectively. It sends the update messages as a multicast to many remote nodes in a single instance. As data undergoes lots of changes from time to time, DDS updates the different version numbers and automatically translates the data as and when updated. It also encrypts the data on the fly.
- **Dynamic discovery** – As the nodes keep changing their location, DDS takes care of tracking them, and the client and server do not need to know their physical IP addresses. The dynamic discovery of DDS helps to achieve this, and it also discovers the publishing data and also works with the different machine architectures. The addition of any communication participant on any type of operating system platform or hardware platform is achievable by the tremendous power of DDS.
- **Scalable architecture** – DDS architecture is capable of adding from a small device to an enormous architecture of cloud systems. It also scales to thousands and millions of nodes and delivers data in a very high-speed network and also manages the data objects reliably. It has a high availability and security to all its data in a single communication channel.

12.8   Communication Protocols

Various communication protocols are listed below:

- **Ethernet** – Ethernet is used in local area networks, metropolitan area networks, and wide area networks. It follows the IEEE 802.3 standard and supports higher bit rates and longer distance communication. It was the first one to replace the wired LAN-like token ring and ARCNET. It has a good backward compatibility.
- **IEEE 802.15.4** is a standard that defines the operations for low-rate wireless personal area network (LR-WPAN) in its physical layer and media access layer. By keeping these protocols as the basis, ZigBee, ISA100.11a, WirelessHART, and MiWi have been proposed as the extended standard. The upper layers have been developed in these new standards. IEEE 802.15.4 can be used with 6LoWPAN and Internet protocols for building wireless embedded Internet.
- **NFC** – IoT networks which require a very close communication can use this Near-Field Communication (NFC). When we use our identity card over a card reader for entry into offices, it uses NFC for such applications. It is based on ISO/IEC 18092:2004 standard and uses a center frequency of 13.56 MHz with the data rate of up to 420 kbps. The range can vary from few meters which are shorter range compared to the wireless sensor networks. When two NFC-enabled devices are brought nearer to each other, they can establish a network communication automatically without any prior configuration or setup. The devices can exchange data such as small text messages, audio, and small image files. Some features of NFC include ease of implementation and use, automatic and instant connectivity, no requirement for prior configuration, and smart key access for security.
- **ANT& ANT+** – ANT and ANT+ are wireless sensor network technology that has a protocol stack for wireless communications with a semiconductor radios operating in the 2.4 GHz to communicate using the standard protocols for coexistence, data representation, security, and reliability by including error detection.
- **Bluetooth** – Bluetooth works in 2.4 GHz ISM band personal area network with frequency hopping. It can range up to 100 m with the data exchange rate maximum of 3 Mbps. Wireless headphones and speakers use Bluetooth, and simple audio, video, and text messages can be exchanged through Bluetooth.
- **Bluetooth Low Energy (BLE)** – BLE is derived from Bluetooth, which is used for low battery power devices and with less data usage. Whenever there is no data exchange requires, BLE continues to be in sleep mode. BLE is majorly used in wearable healthcare tracking and monitoring devices and for fitness-related applications.
- **ZigBee** – The ZigBee protocol uses the 802.15.4 standard, and it is a mesh LAN protocol with 2.4 GHz frequency range with 250 kbps. It is exclusively designed for building and home automation applications such as switching on and off of lights and thermostats. It can connect up to 1024 nodes in the network within 200-m range. [18]

- **EnOcean** – EnOcean is an energy-harvesting wireless technology which works at a low frequency. Its transmit range is up to 30 m indoors and 300 m outdoors. It is for applications with extremely low-power requirement such as smart buildings, wireless control of lights and fans, etc. These energy-harvesting technologies use power generation elements to convert energy from various sources to electric energy from natural sources like solar cells, electro-thermal elements, light, wind, vibration, and hydro-energy. There is a lot of research happening in the energy harvest technology which can easily solve the quick power loss factor in the wireless sensor nodes which are used in IoT ecosystem.
- **WiFi and WiMAX** – These protocols are based on the standard IEEE 802.16 and are intended for wireless metropolitan area network (MAN). Its transmission range can go up to 50 km for fixed stations, and for mobile devices it is between 5 km and 15 km. WiMax works with the frequency between 2.5 GHz to 5.8 GHz, and its data transfer rate is up to 40 Mbps.
- **Narrowband IoT (NB-IoT)** – Narrowband IoT is designed for low-power devices and can be used for M2M for low-power devices. It follows LPWAN radio technology standard and used to connect a wide range of devices that use cellular telecommunication bands. It is based on a DSSS modulation. It focuses on low-cost, low battery power aims at connecting a large number of devices with the indoor applications.

12.8.1 5G Technology

The 2G technology was designed for voice and 5G for voice and data; 4G is for broadband internetwork applications; 5G is aimed at fusing the capabilities of computing techniques with the data everywhere, and so trillions and zillions of things in the connected world such as wearable devices to home automation nanodevices exchange data without worrying about the computing power and speed as the 5G network can do all these processes as and when required. 5G will not only be faster but also smarter; all the devices with sensors which are location aware, and context-aware objects will sense the data and work together with each other automatically without the intervention of human being. The 5 g technology uses network functions virtualization and software-defined network to achieve all its goals. The features of 5G that support IoT are as follows:

- The massive number of heterogeneous devices to be connected which are more than 200% of the number of devices in the existing networks
- Enables high data transfer (100 times more than the traditional networks)
- Low latency between the sender and receiver devices
- Consistent quality of services (QoS) and quality of experiences (QoE)
- Achieving the abovesaid goals with the reduction of cost

12.8.2 Software-Defined Networking (SDN)

The spread of IoT has created new paradigms among the networking and networking protocols in the current and future networks as IoT welcomes heterogeneous devices and heterogeneous networking approaches and protocols. The entire IoT environment has a broad networking of several networks, devices and objects, and nano-objects with heterogeneity. The integration of IoT with software-defined networking is to coordinate with the different types of payload that emerge from IoT elements. The structure and the modular level of IoT controller are determined through the SDN controller, and it has to interact with the higher-level controllers and to respond to the IoT activities.

SDN is the protocol through which the network control is modularized from and separated from the lower-level networking devices and is embedded in a software tool known as SDN controller. The networking services thus get abstracted from the lower-level components, and the higher network is independent of these modules. Application layer takes care of the user applications, and the components of SDN stay in the control layer and interaction with the infrastructure layer which contains all the networking components and with the application layer components.

The core of the SDN is its SDN controller which controls the whole network. The SDN controller looks to be a logical switch for the network components. This brings the complete independence to the networking devices to concentrate on their own application functionality alone without the intervention of networking overheads. The network administrators can change the network settings at any time with the help of SDN software. SDN uses *OpenFlow* protocol for all such activities. The core advantages of SDN are briefly presented below:

- **Centralized control of heterogeneous network devices:** The network that uses SDN protocol for communication can get the centralized control with the help of SDN controller irrespective of the type and or manufacture of the device.
- **Complete automation:** SDN framework enables the complete automation of networking functionalities and thus eliminates the dependencies and operational cost and error rates.
- **High-level security: Configuring each network device is not at all required in** SDN framework, and this feature eliminates all the possible security threats and other reliable issues that might be faced during the implementation otherwise.
- **Flexibility**: SDN protocol provides flexibility to user applications and runtime changes to the configuration and thus flexibility and improves the user experiences.

12.8.3 Network Functions Virtualization (NFV)

NFV is a virtualization technology that provides network services without the need customization of hardware appliances for each of them. It designs the communication network, its various functionalities, and the procedure of operational principles. SDN used NFV for the virtualization and the management skills of SDN together with NFC give the advantage of both the paradigms.

As NFC is an evolving approach, lots of research issues such as addressing of migration of a virtual machine and their services, higher availability and reliable services of NFC have to be designed effectively.

12.8.4 Specialized IoT Networks

We have seen mobile networks. There are unique networks getting formed and firmed for wearable, implantable, portables, nomadic, and wireless devices. There are body area networks, car area networks, personal area networks, etc. with the addition of special-purpose devices, sensors, actuators, controllers, stickers, codes, etc. Drones, robots, home, building, industry automation systems, etc. mandate for highly advanced protocols, as articulated below:

- Wearable devices (shoes, watch, glasses, belt, etc.) can be used to detect biometric information. Figure 12.5 depicts the majorly used wearable devices used for biometric data communication.
- Smart devices collect the information and communicate with the control center and/or medical server using the Internet. The diagram below clearly depicts the devices, how they communicate with one another, how the data gets collected and transferred to data storage and processing systems in order to crunch the aggregated data to squeeze out actionable insights.

12.9 Sample IoT Networking Architecture

Figure 12.6 clearly accentuates and articulates how different and distributed devices can find, bind, and leverage each other's unique device-centric services in order to fulfill the goals of producing people-centric, real-time, adaptive, and context-aware applications. The various protocols come handy in linking various devices, data sources, and software systems in order to fulfill the varying requirements of individuals, innovators, and institutions.

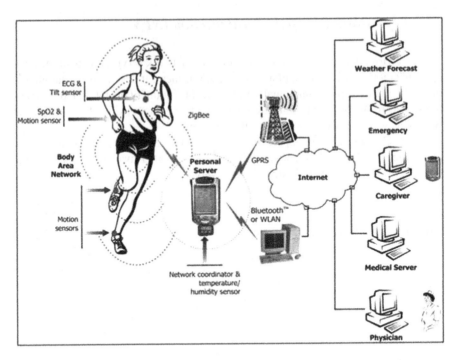

Fig. 12.5 Wearable IoT networks

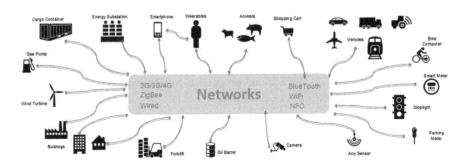

Fig. 12.6 Data communication protocols for the diverse things of the Internet

12.10   Conclusion

The emerging and evolving network topologies and communication technologies are foretelling the speedy arrival of the anticipated IoT era. As there is a widespread recognition that the IoT technologies and tools are bound to bring in the desired digital transformation, there are a variety of concerted and collaborative research activities in order to identify the brewing limitations and surmount them through path-breaking technologically sound solutions. Connectivity is one such issue, and there are several enabling connectivity protocols being formulated and firmed. As connectivity is the core requirement for the projected IoT era, we are to dig deeper and dwell at length about various data transmission protocols.

In this chapter, we have incorporated the relevant details about the connectivity mechanisms and communication protocols. There are several initiatives in the communication space to simplify, streamline, and speed up the process of setting IoT applications, services, and environments. This chapter has supplied the pros and cons of each of those protocols in order to empower our readers to take the correct decisions. As most of the IoT devices are embedded and resource-constrained, we have given the preference for lightweight and energy-efficient protocols in our chapter. There are specific protocols coming up fast in order to target specific industry verticals and applications.

References

1. Chaouchi H (2013) The internet of things: connecting objects. Wiley, Hoboken
2. Zhu L, Zhang Z, Xu C (2017) Secure and privacy-preserving data communication in internet of things. Springer, Singapore
3. Holler J, Tsiatsis V, Mulligan C, Avesand S, Karnouskos S, Boyle D (2014) From machine-to-machine to the internet of things: introduction to a new age of intelligence. Academic, Oxford
4. Zhao B, Kubiatowicz J, Joseph A, Tapestry AD (2001) An infrastructure for fault-tolerant wide-area location and routing. Technical Report UCB/CSD-01-1141, Computer Science Division, U. C. Berkeley, April 2001
5. Liang W, Cheng L, Tang M (2016) Identity recognition using biological electroencephalogram sensors. http://www.hindawi.com/journals/js/. Hindawi Limited, Accessed 12 Feb 2017
6. Lin L, Yue X (2017) Sensors, http://www.mdpi.com/journal/sensors. Accessed 20 Feb 2017
7. Condie TE, Kamvar SD, Garcia-Molina H (2004) Adaptive peer-to-peer topologies, Stanford University, Stanford, CA 94306, 2004
8. Stoica I, Morris R, Karger D, Kaashoek MF, Chord HB, (2001) A scalable peer-to-peer lookup service for Internet applications. Technical Report TR-819, MIT, March 2001
9. Perino D, Varvello M (2011) A reality check for content-centric networking, bell labs, alcatel-lucent, Villarceaux, France, Bell Labs, Alcatel-Lucent, Holmdel, USA, 2011
10. Carofiglio G, Gallo M, Muscariello L, Perino D (2011) Modeling data transfer in content-centric networking, Bell Labs, Alcatel-Lucent, France, Orange Labs, France Telecom, France, 2011
11. Named data networking (2016) http://www.named-data.net/. Accessed 20 Dec 2016
12. RPMA Technology. (2017) www.ingenu.com. Accessed 5 Jan 2017
13. Kristofer S. Pister J, Doherty L (2008) TSMP: Time Synchronized Mesh Protocol, Proceedings of the IASTED International Symposium on Distributed Sensor Networks (DSN08), Orlando, Florida, USA, 2008
14. Bor M, Roedig U, Voigt T, Alonso JM, (2016) Do LoRa Low-power wide-area networks scale?, MSWiM '16, ACM, 13–17 November 2016
15. Akyildiz IF, Jornet JM (2010) The internet of nano-things georgia institute of technology, IEEE wireless communications, December 2010
16. XMPP Internet of Things (2016) http://www.xmpp-iot.org/. Accessed 7 Dec 2016

17. Singh M, Rajan MA, Shivraj VL, Balamuralidhar P (2015) Secure MQTT for Internet of Things (IoT), Fifth international conference on communication systems and network technologies, Gwalior, 2015, pp 746–751
18. Kuzlu M, Pipattanasomporn M, Rahman S (2015) Review of communication technologies for smart homes/building applications, IEEE innovative smart grid technologies – Asia (ISGT ASIA), 2015

Chapter 13
Data Distribution Service-Based Architecture Design for the Internet of Things Systems

Bedir Tekinerdogan, Ömer Köksal, and Turgay Çelik

Abstract The Internet of Things (IoT) is the internetworking of people and physical devices often called "things" that enable the collection and exchange of data. The number of connections between people and things, as well as the volume of data that is generated by the "things," is dramatically increasing. In this context, various kinds of data are generated by multiple heterogeneous devices, which operate in different ways and used by different applications with different aims. To realize the distributed execution of IoT systems over multiple resources, different requirements and quality factors must be satisfied. Traditionally, to reduce the effort for developing distributed systems, middleware architectures have been introduced that provide common services such as name and directory services, discovery, data exchange, synchronization, and transaction services, etc. To address the needs and integration of IoT systems, the adoption of middleware seems to be a feasible solution. The Data Distribution Service (DDS) is a middleware that is directly related to data-intensive systems and explicitly considers the quality of service. It is a standard data-centric publish-subscribe programming model and specification for distributed systems that has been applied for the development of high-performance distributed systems such as in the defense, finance, automotive, and simulation domains. In this chapter, we explore and propose the adoption of DDS as a middleware platform for IoT systems. For this, we first describe the requirements for IoT systems and present the IoT reference architecture. Subsequently, we provide a DDS-based architecture for IoT systems based on the Views and Beyond Approach.

B. Tekinerdogan (✉) • Ö. Köksal
Information Technology Group, Wageningen University, Wageningen, The Netherlands
e-mail: bedir.tekinerdogan@wur.nl

T. Çelik
OPSGENIE, Ankara, Turkey

© Springer International Publishing AG 2017
Z. Mahmood (ed.), *Connected Environments for the Internet of Things*,
Computer Communications and Networks,
https://doi.org/10.1007/978-3-319-70102-8_13

13.1   Introduction

The Internet of Things (IoT) is the internetworking of people and physical devices that enable the collection and exchange of data [25]. The number of connections between people and things as well as the volume of data that is generated is dramatically increasing. In this situation, various kinds of data are generated by multiple kinds of devices, which operate and are processed in different ways, and used by different applications. To realize the distributed execution of IoT systems over multiple resources, different specific requirements and quality factors must be satisfied.

Traditionally, to reduce the effort for developing distributed systems, middleware architectures have been introduced that provide common services such as name and directory services, discovery, data exchange, synchronization, transaction services, etc. To address the needs and integration of IoT systems, the adoption of middleware seems to be a feasible solution. A middleware that is directly related to data-intensive systems in which quality of service is important is the Data Distribution Service (DDS) [1]. The DDS is a standard data-centric publish-subscribe programming model and specification for distributed systems that has been applied for the development of high-performance distributed systems such as in the defense, finance, automotive, and simulation domains.

In this chapter, we explore and propose the adoption of DDS as a middleware platform for IoT systems. For this, we first describe the requirements for IoT systems and present the IoT reference architecture. Subsequently, we provide a DDS-based architecture for IoT systems based on the Views and Beyond Approach. We illustrate our approach for the architecture design of IoT-based smart city engineering.

The remainder of the chapter is organized as follows. In Sect. 13.2, we provide the background on software architecture modeling which is necessary for understanding the architecture views in subsequent sections. In Sect. 13.3, we describe the IoT architecture using selected viewpoints. Section 13.4 presents the architecture models specific for DDS. Based on the architecture models from Sects. 13.3 and 13.4, we present the DDS-based IoT architecture in Sect. 13.5. Section 13.6 concludes the chapter.

13.2   Software Architecture Modeling

Architectural drivers define the concerns of the stakeholders which shape the architecture [2]. A stakeholder is defined as an individual, team, or organization with interests in or concerns about a system. Each of the stakeholders' concerns impacts the early design decisions that the architect makes. A common practice is to model and document different architectural views for describing the architecture according to the stakeholders' concerns. An architectural view is a representation of a set of system elements and relations associated with them to support a particular concern. Having multiple views helps to separate the concerns and as such support the modeling, understanding, communication, and analysis of the software architecture for different stakeholders. Architectural views conform to viewpoints that represent the conventions for constructing and using a view. Obviously, the notion of viewpoint now plays an important role in modeling and documenting architectures [3]. So far, most architectural viewpoints seem to have been primarily used either to support the communication among stakeholders or at best to provide a blueprint for the detailed design.

In this chapter, we use the Views and Beyond framework in which predefined viewpoints are organized into three categories including module styles, component-and-connector styles, and allocation styles [1]. Module styles are used to show how the system is structured as a set of implementation units. Component and connector styles are used to show how the system is structured as a set of runtime elements. Allocation styles are used to show how the software elements are mapped to non-software elements in its environment. We adopt two viewpoints for our purposes including layered viewpoint and deployment viewpoint.

The layered viewpoint reflects the division of software modules called layers. In a layered architecture, the system is depicted as a set of layers which are stacked on top of each other. Hereby, a layer can only access the next lower layer, and callbacks from lower layers to higher layers are not allowed. In the following sections, we note that both IoT and DDS systems include a layered architecture. In addition to the layered viewpoint, we also apply the deployment viewpoint, which is used to show how the software elements are allocated to hardware of a computing platform. It is useful for analyzing and tuning certain quality attributes of the system such as performance, reliability, and security.

13.3   The Internet of Things Architecture

Architectural modeling techniques help to divide and conquer complex applications such as IoT systems to enable successful realization. In this section, we provide a generic conceptual model comprising a feature model and the layered view for IoT systems.

13.3.1   Conceptual Model

Figure 13.1. provides a conceptual model including the relations among the basic IoT concepts. The model has been adopted from the AIOTI (Alliance of IoT Innovation) Domain Model (AIOTI WG03 2015) [4]. The domain model represents the basic concepts and relationships in the domain at the highest level. In the model, User interacts with a physical entity of the physical world, a thing. The User can be a human person or a software agent that has a goal, for the completion of which the interaction with the physical environment must be performed through the mediation

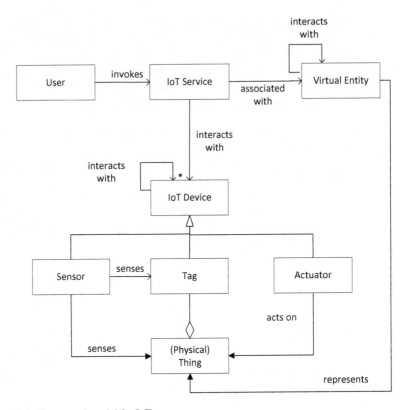

Fig. 13.1 Conceptual model for IoT

of the IoT. A thing is a discrete, identifiable part of the physical environment that can be of interest to the User for the completion of his goal. Things can be any physical entity such as humans, cars, animals, or computers.

The interaction between a User and the Thing is mediated by an IoT Service which is associated with a Virtual Entity, a digital representation of the physical entity. A Thing can be represented in the digital world by a Virtual Entity. Different kinds of digital representations of Things can be used such as objects, 3D models, avatars, objects, or even a social network account. Some Virtual Entities can also interact with other Virtual Entities to fulfill their goal.

An important aspect of the IoT is that changes in the properties of a Thing and its corresponding Virtual Entity need to be synchronized. This is usually realized by an IoT device that is embedding into, attached to, or simply placed in close vicinity of the Thing. In principle, we can identify three devices including sensors, tags, and actuators. Sensors are used to measure the state of things they monitor. Essentially, sensors take a mechanical, optical, magnetic, or thermal signal and convert this into voltage and current. This provided data can then be processed and used to define the required action. Tags are devices to support the identification process typically using specialized sensors called readers. The identification process can be different including optical as in the case of bar codes and QR code, or RF-based. Actuators are employed to change or affect the things.

13.3.2   Feature Model

In this section, we provide a feature-driven overview of IoT and its session layer protocols [21–24, 26]. A feature diagram is a tree with the root and descendent nodes. The root represents a concept, and nodes are the features. Feature diagrams might show mandatory features as well as variant features which can be represented as optional or alternative features. A feature configuration is a set of features which describes a member of the represented concept. A feature constraint restricts the possible selections of features to define configurations. The legend (abstract syntax) used for the feature diagrams is given in Fig. 13.2.

Figure 13.3 shows a feature diagram representing the layers of the IoT architecture. This diagram is similar to the layer diagram of the IoT given in the next section.

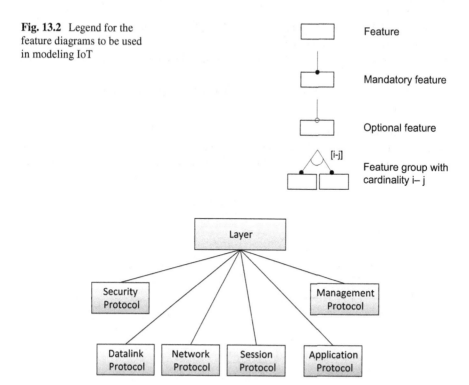

Fig. 13.2 Legend for the feature diagrams to be used in modeling IoT

Feature

Mandatory feature

Optional feature

[i-j]

Feature group with cardinality i– j

Fig. 13.3 Top level feature diagram of IoT

The session layer is responsible for setting up and taking down of the association between the IoT connection points. The session layer provides services-related issues of the session such as initiation, maintenance, and disconnection. As such, frequency and duration of various types of sessions are related to the session layer. Selection of the session layer protocol depends on many factors such as data size, the number of devices to be connected, latency, etc. Depending on the application requirements, different session layer protocols might be used in session layer of the IoT application. Focusing on the session protocols, we have derived the feature diagram given in Fig. 13.4.

The mandatory features in the feature diagram are protocol type, source target, transport type, and architecture. Although, transport type belongs to the network layer, it is shown as a mandatory feature in Fig. 13.5 since it is closely related to the protocol characteristics. Some widely used session layer protocol types are given below:

- Message Queuing Telemetry Transport (MQTT): One of the most popular protocols to collect device data and communicate with servers [5].
- Extensible Messaging and Presence Protocol (XMPP): A protocol based on exchanges of XML messages in real time that is defined to connect devices to servers [6].
- Advanced Message Queuing Protocol(AMQP): A queuing system designed to connect servers to each other [7].
- Data Distribution Service (DDS): A fast data bus for integrating devices and systems [8].
- The Constrained Application Protocol (CoAP): A specialized web-based protocol to be used in constrained nodes and constrained networks [9].

There are three types of source-target relations available in session layer protocols: Device-to-Device (D2D), Device-to-Server (D2S), and Server-to-Server (S2S) as shown in Fig. 13.4. In some literature sources, these features are named as

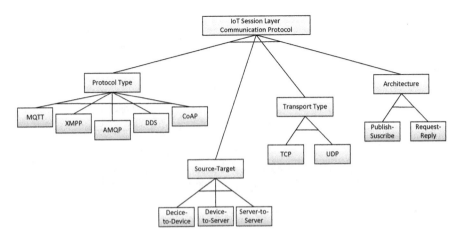

Fig. 13.4 Feature diagram for the session layer protocols of IoT

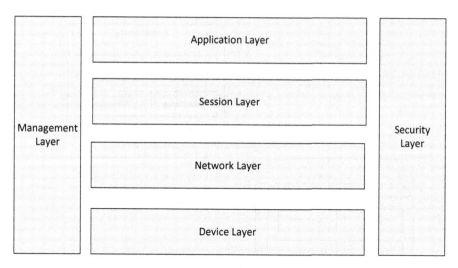

Fig. 13.5 Layered view of IoT architecture

machine-to-machine (M2M), machine-to-cloud (M2C), and cloud-to-cloud (C2C), respectively. DDS and CoAP are used for M2M communication, whereas MQTT and XMPP are used for M2C, and AMQP is used for S2S communication. Session layer protocols are closely related to the transport type. Session layer protocols use either UDP or TCP for the transport. DDS and CoAP support both UDP and TCP.

The focus of this chapter is the application of the DDS protocol.

13.3.3   Layered View

Various reference architectures have been suggested by many researchers for the IoT which is usually represented as a layered architecture with a various set of layers. Hereby, a layer simply represents a grouping of modules that offers a cohesive set of services. Based on the literature review, we provide the reference architecture as shown in Fig. 13.5.

The reference architecture consists of four layers including device/datalink layer, network layer, session layer, and application layer. The device layer includes the capabilities for the things in the network. The network layer provides functionality for networking connectivity and transport capabilities. The IoT layer consists of functionality for generic support capabilities (such as data processing or data storage) and specific support capabilities for the particular applications. The application layer contains the IoT application.

The security layer is a sidecar layer relating to the other four layers and provides the security functionality. Finally, the management layer supports capabilities such as device management, local network topology management, and traffic and congestion management.

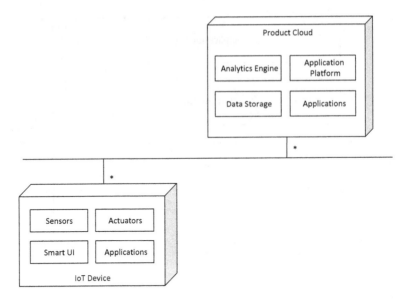

Fig. 13.6 Deployment view of IoT architecture

13.3.4 Deployment View

Figure 13.6 shows the deployment view of IoT-based systems. In essence, we can identify two distinct nodes: the IoT node and the Product Cloud node. The IoT node includes modules for sensors, actuators, smart UI, and applications. Within the IoT network, multiple IoT nodes can exist which is shown with the asterisk symbol (*). The cloud node includes functionality for data storage, application platform, the analytics engine, and the cloud applications. Again, we could have more than one cloud node.

13.4 Data Distribution Service

Data Distribution Service (DDS) for real-time system [1] is standardized by Object Management Group (OMG) [10] in 2004, and the latest release is submitted in 2015 [11]. DDS is a data-centric middleware for high-performance machine-to-machine communications. In this section, we describe the basic background information for Data Distribution Service (DDS). Detailed information about DDS can be found in different studies in the literature (e.g., [1, 12–16]).

13.4.1   Conceptual Model

Figure 13.7 presents the conceptual model for DDS middleware. In this figure, the concept domain is a logical concept which represents the set of applications that can communicate with each other. Several domains can be defined within the same DDS system to indicate a different set of applications communications with each other. One or more domain participants might exist in each domain. Domain participants represent the local membership of the application to the assigned domain. Publishers are responsible for data production and updates. Publishers include one or more data writers that publish the different types of data. Similarly, subscribers are responsible for receiving published data and making it available to the participant. A subscriber includes one or more data readers to access published data in a type-safe manner. Domain participants might include one publisher and one subscriber at most. The communication between data readers and data writers is established via topics. A topic defines a unique name, data type, and a set of quality services to the published/subscribed data. Publishers write the data to the topics, and subscribers read the data in topics.

Communication between applications can only be realized only if the topic names and the defined quality of service (QoS) parameters match. DDS provides the ability to attach QoS parameters to all these entities to specify the behavior of a service such as rate of publication, rate of subscription, how long the data is valid, etc. QoS are also useful for several quality factors such as reliability, durability, and scalability which simplifies complex network programming.

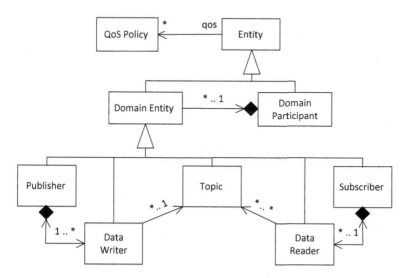

Fig. 13.7   Reference architecture for DDS-based systems

13.4.2 Feature Model

Based on a thorough domain analysis of DDS middleware systems, we have derived
a feature model that is shown in Fig. 13.8. The figure represents the feature model
for publish-subscribe systems. The DDS concepts are shown in bold. In general,
publish-subscribe middleware systems can be distinguished based on the *type* and
the *service model*. Regarding the type, we can identify data-centric, message-
centric, or object-centric approaches. In the message-centric approach, the middleware is not aware of the content of the data; it is just responsible for transmitting the
messages among participants. In data-centric approach, the middleware is aware of
the content and can impose quality of service parameter values on the data. In
object-centric approaches, the middleware is responsible for transmitting objects
among participants. As shown in the figure, DDS is a data-centric approach.

The service model of publish-subscribe middleware can be characterized based
on (1) communications model and (2) architecture model. Communication model
defines communication approach that is applied by the participants. The communication approach on its turn can be based on data distribution, shared data, queuing,
and remote procedure call. The architecture model of a middleware can be either
centralized or decentralized denoting whether the data flows through a central unit
or not. Further, the architecture model can include a *broker* that manages the data
flow. The architecture can be *unbrokered*, i.e., there is no broker defined or multi-
brokered, whereby multiple brokers manage the data flow. As shown in the figure,
the architecture model for DDS is decentralized and unbrokered.

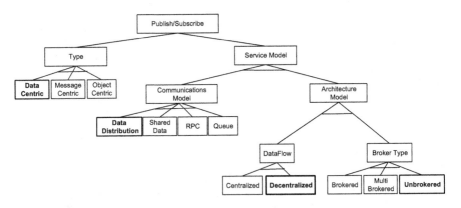

Fig. 13.8 Feature model of publish-subscribe systems (DDS components highlighted)

13.4.3   Layered View

The DDS can be modeled as a three-layer structure as shown in Fig. 13.9, and as mentioned below:

- The Data-Centric Publish Subscribe (DCPS) layer provides efficient delivery of the shared information to the related recipients. DCPS layer is in the specification and it is mandatory for the DDS implementations.
- The optional Data Local Reconstruction Layer (DLRL) enables simple integration of the services defined in DCPS layer into the application layer. The aim of this is to provide a seamless integration with object-oriented language constructs.
- Finally, an additional specification DDS Interoperability Wire Protocol is provided, which is needed for supporting the interoperability among different DDS implementations.

The last layer shown in Fig. 13.9 is related to the transport. DDS might use both UDP and TCP in the transport layer. But DDS also supports UDP and multicast UDP. In fact, one of the powerful features of the DDS is supporting multicast UDP that enables high-performance machine-to-machine communication. On the other hand, since multicast and UDP transports are not supported by many wide area networks (WANs), some additional concepts like interconnection services or routers shall be used in DDS systems to assure end-to-end QoS in WANs [17]. For further details about these specifications, we refer to OMG DDS Specifications [1].

13.4.4   Deployment View

A typical DDS-based system is deployed on a number of application *nodes*. As stated before, publish-subscribe interaction pattern has been applied in several applications and infrastructures, which share similar structure and concepts. Figure 13.10 shows the result of a domain analysis to publish-subscribe systems and

Fig. 13.9 Layered architecture of the DDS with the DDS specifications (Adapted from [11])

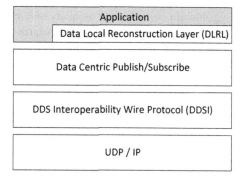

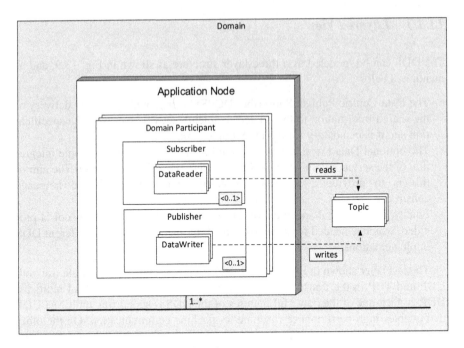

Fig. 13.10 Deployment view for DDS-based systems

represents the deployment view of DDS-based systems. Refer to Sect. 13.4.1 on DDS conceptual model, for detailed information about DDS concepts (such as publishers, subscribers, topics, etc.).

Defining the deployment view of a DDS-based system is a crucial step in design. The deployment model defined determines the allocation of domain participant instances throughout the available physical resources such as available memory and computing power. Although many different deployment alternatives can be defined readily, designing the deployment extremely effects the performance of the overall system.

Sometimes, it is possible to deploy all domain participants (publishers and subscribers) to the same node. But such a deployment design cancels the benefits of distributed computing causing single point of failure. On the other extreme, deploying domain participants has many side effects such as increasing communication overhead and inefficient use of resources. So, it is always advised to analyze the domain participants' communication structure through topics and designing the deployment model accordingly.

13.5   DDS-Based IoT Architecture

In this section, we present the architecture for DDS-based IoT systems. For this, in Sect. 13.5.1, we first present the conceptual model that shows the integration of the earlier conceptual models for DDS and IoT. Subsequently, we present the layered view in Sect. 13.5.2 and deployment view in Sect. 13.5.3.

13.5.1   Conceptual Model

Figure 13.11 shows the conceptual model for the DDS-based IoT architecture. Similar to the IoT conceptual model as shown in Fig. 13.1, the concept IoT device can be a sensor, tag, or actuator which observe, identify, or act on an IoT Thing. A thing has a virtual representation. The DDS concepts Publisher, Subscriber, DataWriter, and DataReader are in the Virtual Entity. Services, that is, topics in DDS are thus associated with these elements. Domain participants can include a number of Virtual Entities. Similar to DDS, a DDS entity can specify QoS parameters.

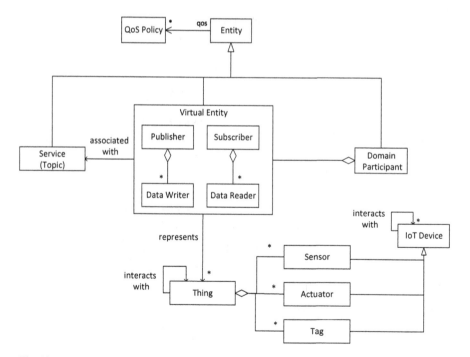

Fig. 13.11 Conceptual model for publish-subscribe-based IoT Systems

13.5.2   Layered View

Figure 13.13 shows the layered view that combines the layered view of DDS with that of IoT. The dominant decomposition is taken from the IoT reference architecture as defined earlier in Fig. 13.5. Hence the layers are similar to the IoT layers. What is specific is the session layer which now includes the concepts of DDS including DLRL, Data-Centric Publish Subscribe, and DDSI [12] (Fig. 13.12).

13.5.3   Deployment View

Figure 13.13 presents the layered view for the DDS-IoT system. In essence, it defines two different nodes, that is, the IoT node and the Product Cloud node. The IoT node now communicates using the DDS. Hence it includes an application module that realizes the DDS concepts. That is, it includes the domain participants and herewith the subscribers and publishers. The Product Cloud nodes are similar to the IoT deployment model.

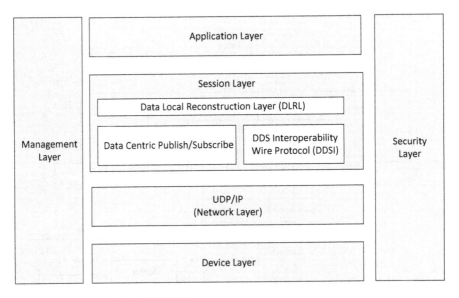

Fig. 13.12 Layered view for DDS-IOT systems

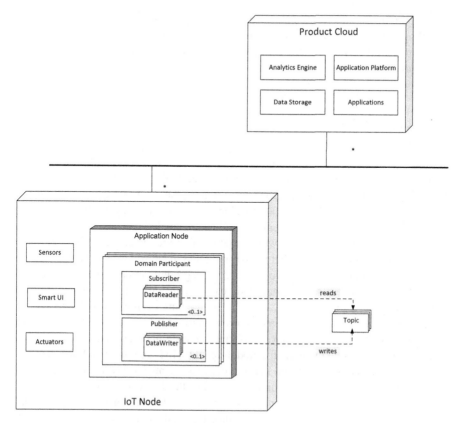

Fig. 13.13 Layered view for DDS-IoT systems

13.5.4   DDS-Based IoT Architecture in Action

We provided different perspectives for architectural modeling of DDS-based IoT systems. In this section, we discuss some use cases of these models and views.

In the conceptual model Sect. 13.5.1, we provided a metamodel for DDS-based IoT systems. This metamodel can be used to develop a modeling environment, e.g., by using Eclipse Modeling Project [18]. Such a modeling environment can be used to analyze and design complex IoT systems before realization.

The model that we provided in the layered model Sect. (13.5.2) shows high-level decomposition of an IoT system. This model can be used for deciding the high-level system components, separation of development teams, and different expertise areas that an IoT team has to have. This layered view also provides a foundation for IoT frameworks that will speed up the development of large-scale systems.

The model that we provided in the deployment model (Sect. 13.5.3) can be used for developing a modeling environment that enables modeling allocation of system components to available resources. In addition to manual component distribution, the deployment model architecture can be used as a foundation for a tool that will enable generation of feasible deployment models for DDS-based IoT systems. We developed a tool similar to the reference architecture presented in [19] for distributed simulation systems.

13.6   Conclusion

The IoT has now become an important paradigm that is invasive in different application domains. One of the important issues for the IoT is the management of communication and distribution aspects. To support the communication among the different DDS nodes, it is important to adopt a feasible middleware. In this context, the DDS is considered as a potential middleware for IoT because of its focus on event-driven communication in which quality of service is also explicitly defined. Research on both paradigms, that is, IoT and DDS, have so far been carried almost independently. In recent years, we now observe a growing interest in the application of DDS for IoT. The results of our study can be considered from this perspective. Our main focus in this chapter was on the architecture design of a DDS-based IoT system. So far no systematic approach has been provided yet to model the architecture for DDS-based IoT. We have performed a systematic approach in which we adopted architecture viewpoints for modeling DDS, IoT, and finally DDS-based IoT systems. Since both the DDS and IoT are often represented as layered structures, we have applied the layered viewpoint to represent the DDS-based IoT. Further, we have also defined the deployment view for DDS-IoT. We can state that we succeeded to integrate and represent the architecture models that can be used to model DDS-based IoT systems for various application domains. In our future work, we intend to enhance our study for adopting other architecture viewpoints. Also, we aim to adopt the viewpoints for real-world industrial IoT projects in which DDS is applied.

References

1. Clements P, Bachmann F, Bass L, Garlan D, Ivers J, Little R, Merson P, Nord R, Stafford J (2011) Documenting software architectures: views and beyond, 2nd edn. Addison-Wesley, Reading
2. Tekinerdogan B (2014) Software architecture, chapter. In: Gonzalez T, Díaz-Herrera JL (eds) Computer science handbook, 2nd edn. Volume I: Computer science and software engineering, Taylor and Francis
3. Tekinerdogan B, Sözer H (2011) Defining architectural viewpoints for quality concerns. In: Proceedings of the 5th European conference on software architecture, pp 26–34
4. AIOTI (2016) Role of AIOTI WG03 in IoT Standardisation. Available: http://www.aioti.org/2016/11/03/role-of-aioti-wg03-on-iot-standardisation
5. OASIS (2017) Message Queuing Telemetry Transport (MQTT). Available: http://mqtt.org
6. IETF (2017) Extensible Messaging and Presence Protocol (XMPP). Available: http://xmpp.org

7. OASIS (2017) Advanced Message Queuing Protocol (AMQP). Available: http://www.amqp. org
8. OMG DDS (2015) Data Distribution Service for Real Time Systems (DDS), v1.4. Available: http://www.omg.org/spec/DDS/1.4
9. IETF (2017) Constrained Application Protocol (CoAP) Specification. March 2017 [Online]. Available: http://coap.technology
10. Pardo-Castellote G, Farabaugh B, Warren R An introduction to DDS and Data-Centric Communications. [Online]. Available: http://bpmn.omg.org/news/whitepapers/
11. OMG (2015) Data Distribution Service for real time systems (DDS), v1.4. http://www.omg. org/spec/DDS/1.4
12. OMG (2014) The real-time publish-subscribe wire protocol DDS interoperability wire protocol specification (DDSI), V2.2. http://www.omg.org/spec/DDSI-RTPS/2.2/
13. MilSOFT (2014) MilSOFT DDS. http://dds.milsoft.com.tr/en/dds/dds-home.php.
14. OCI (2014) OpenDDS. www.opendds.org
15. Prismtech (2014) Vortex OpenSplice. http://www.prismtech.com/vortex/vortex-opensplice
16. Real Time Innovations (2014) RTI Connext. http://www.rti.com
17. Köksal O, Tekinerdogan B (2017) Obstacles in data distribution middleware. Future Gener Comput Syst J 68:191–200
18. Eclipse Modeling Project (2017) Available: https://eclipse.org/modeling/
19. Celik T, Tekinerdogan B (2013) S-IDE: a tool framework for optimizing deployment architecture of high level architecture based simulation systems. J Syst Softw 86(10):2520–2541
20. Twinoaks Computing – CoreDX (2014) http://www.twinoakscomputing.com/coredx
21. Palattella MR, Accettura N, Vilajosana X, Watteyne T, Grieco LA, Boggia G, Dohler M (2013) Standardized protocol stack for the internet of (important) things. IEEE Commun Surv Tutor 15(3):1389–1406
22. Sheng Z, Yang S, Yu Y, Vasilakos AAV, Mccann JA, Leung KK (2013) A survey on the IETF Protocol Suite for the IoT. IEEE Wirel Commun 20:91–98
23. Gazis V et al (2015) A survey of technologies for the IoT. Wirel Commun Mob Comput Conference (IWCMC). doi:https://doi.org/10.1109/IWCMC.2015.7289234
24. Al-Fuqaha A, Guizani M, Mohammadi M, Aledhari M, Ayyash M (2015) IoT: a survey on enabling technologies, protocols and applications. IEEE Commun Surv Tutor 2347–2376
25. McEwen A, Cassimally H (2014) Designing the internet of things. Wiley, Chichester
26. Karagiannis V, Chatzimisio P, Vazques-Gallego F, Alonso-Zarate J (2015) A survey on the application layer protocols for the IoT. Transaction on IoT and Cloud Computing, V.1

Index

© Springer International Publishing AG 2017
Z. Mahmood (ed.), *Connected Environments for the Internet of Things*,
Computer Communications and Networks,
https://doi.org/10.1007/978-3-319-70102-8

Printed in the United States
By Bookmasters